THE ISLE OF THANET

THE ISLE OF THANET

from Prehistory to the Norman Conquest

GERALD MOODY

First published 2008

The History Press
The Mill, Brimscombe Port,
Stroud, Gloucestershire, GL5 2QG
www.thehistorypress.co.uk

Reprinted 2010

© Gerald Moody, 2008

The right of Gerald Moody to be identified as the Author of this work has been asserted in accordance with the Copyrights, Designs and Patents Act 1988.

All rights reserved. No part of this book may be reprinted or reproduced or utilised in any form or by any electronic, mechanical or other means, now known or hereafter invented, including photocopying and recording, or in any information storage or retrieval system, without the permission in writing from the Publishers.

British Library Cataloguing in Publication Data.
A catalogue record for this book is available from the British Library.

ISBN 978 0 7524 4689 9

Printed in Great Britain

CONTENTS

	Acknowledgements	7
1	A history of discovery	9
2	Geological foundations	26
3	A river or the sea? The Wantsum divide	35
4	What came before? Traces of the earliest human settlement	53
5	How the east was won – Thanet in the Neolithic	62
6	Beakers and barrows	79
7	Bronzes and boats	92
8	Islanders – the Iron Age in Thanet	116
9	An Imperial outpost – the Romans in Thanet	139
10	New identities – the fifth century to the Norman Conquest	158
	A final passage from Thanet	175
	Bibliography	178
	Index	188

ACKNOWLEDGEMENTS

I would like to thank my colleagues and the Trustees at the Trust for Thanet Archaeology for their support and encouragement in the writing of this book, and in particular to Emma Boast, Paul Hart, Phillipa Fisk, Christopher Pout and Chris Tucker for reading and commenting on each of the chapters. I would also like to thank Keith Parfitt for his comments on the sections of the geological material and the formation of the Wantsum Channel. I have been greatly assisted in compiling the chapters dealing with the prehistoric archaeology by the comprehensive gazetteers of finds for these periods assembled by Paul Hart of the Trust for Thanet Archaeology for publication on the Trust's Virtual Museum website. I am grateful to Dr Colin McClean for processing the NASA SRTM (Shuttle Radar Topography Mission) data on which the topographical relief and contour maps are based. I would also like to thank Geoff Orton of the Isle of Thanet Archaeological Society who encouraged me to put forward my idea for a book on the long history of the Isle of Thanet.

I would like to express my thanks to Peter Kemmis Betty of Tempus for responding so quickly to my suggestion that Thanet's archaeology deserved greater attention and commissioning this book, and to Wendy Logue of Tempus for managing the production of the manuscript and being patient.

I would like to express my gratitude to the great archaeologists and historians who have created a vast resource for the study of Thanet. Some are known to me from the pages of their publications and archives and a work ten times the length would be far too short to fully describe their contributions. I know some of the more recent contributors personally, not least Dr David Perkins whose body of work of the Isle of Thanet joins those of great historians like John Lewis who did so much to make the past of the Isle of Thanet better known. It has not been possible to do full justice to the personalities and efforts involved which have often been heroic. I would encourage anyone who feels I have missed a piece from this complex jigsaw to make a contribution to filling the gap with their own record of their experience. The chapters of the book indicate some ways in which efforts are being made to collate the material, not least with my own efforts with the Trust for Thanet Archaeology's Virtual Museum.

This book was written at an important time in the history of archaeological study in Thanet. In 2008 the Trust for Thanet Archaeology reached its twentieth year of operation. Celebrations will take place at a new purpose-built headquarters at The Antoinette Centre on the Quex Park estate at Birchington, close to the Powell-Cotton Museum where so much of the archaeology of Thanet is preserved. We hope that the Trust for Thanet Archaeology's aim to educate all in the archaeology of Thanet can be carried out effectively and efficiently by this fortuitous association. More information on the archaeology of the Isle of Thanet can be found at www.thanetarch.co.uk.

1

A HISTORY OF DISCOVERY

The Isle of Thanet is located at the north-eastern limit of the county of Kent. Its principal towns are Ramsgate, Margate and Broadstairs and it is a place of historical significance with a unique archaeological heritage revealed over nearly three centuries of discovery (*1*).

John Lewis, vicar of the parish of Minster, was Thanet's first historian (*2*). In his book, *The History and Antiquities of the Isle of Thanet* (1736), he produced a study of the area that had been his home for 30 years. His work ranged widely, from the etymology of local place names, to the geography of the island, and it embraced the events of early history. Although much of the book is taken up by general surveys of the surviving documentation of the parishes, most of it post-Tudor, and a description of the present state of the agriculture and fisheries of the island, the earlier part of the work has considerable scope. Lewis balanced his sources well, often adding his own scholarship to achieve an acceptable balance between the authority of his sixteenth- and seventeenth-century sources, and his own learning and practical experience. He was aware of the growing interest in the survival of ancient features in the landscape and of various artefacts that indicated the presence of early settlements. His book included plans and illustrations of notable places and finds of such antiquarian interest. The chronological model that Lewis (1736, 37) was working with was relatively short and did not stretch far beyond the ancient British material he recognised:

> Of these inhabitants [The Britons of pre-Roman Kent] we have some memorials yet remaining in their coin and amulets, which have been found here both of gold, or electrum, and brass. Of two of these I've given a description, but by what prince they were coin'd, I am not Antiquary good enough to say. They are both convex, and have the rude figure of a horse on the hollow: the impression on the other side (as I was told by the late Earl of Winchelsea) was conjectured by some to be a representation of the head dress worn by the ladies of distinction. The biggest weighs seventeen shillings, the least about six shillings.

The Isle of Thanet – from Prehistory to the Norman Conquest

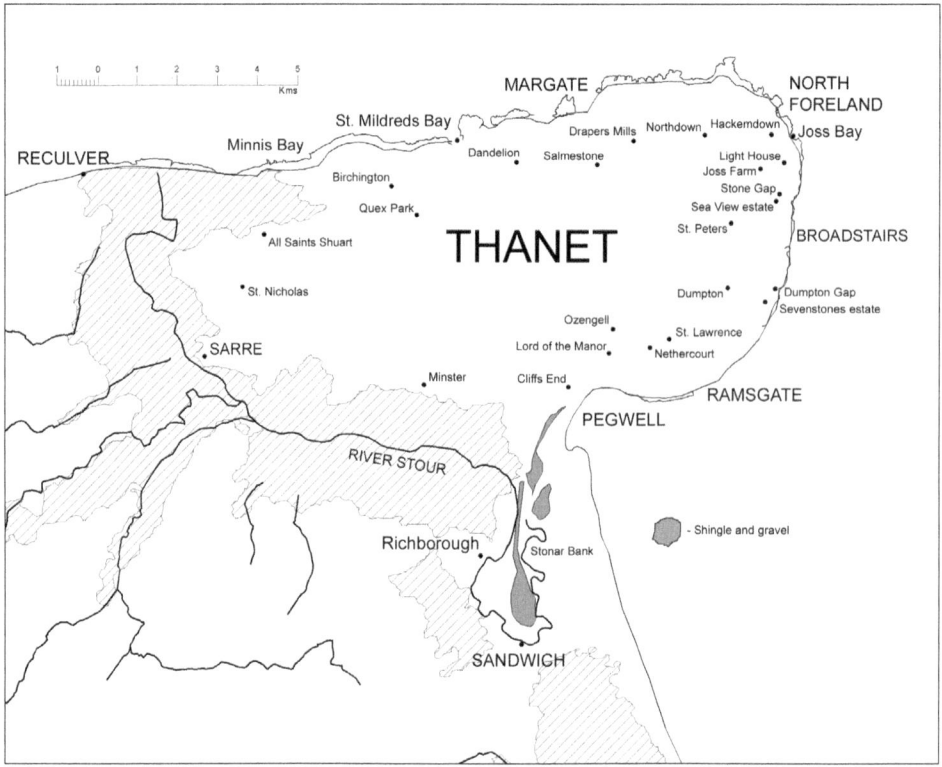

1 Map of Thanet, showing sites referred to in Chapter 1. The hatched areas show low-lying alluvial plains. © *Trust for Thanet Archaeology*

Lewis also described a number of the Roman coins that had been encountered, particularly after cliff falls in the area near Broadstairs. Perhaps his most famous passage is the description of the hoard of bronze axes that were discovered near Motherwicks, a small hamlet close to St Mildred's Bay, near Westgate. Lewis was thorough in his research, collecting and copying many works relevant to his study, the illustrations of the bronze hoard may have been taken from a drawing of the hoard by Stukeley (Ashbee 2005). The dating of these objects provided some difficulty and Lewis thought they were part of the kit of a Roman soldier (1736, 138). He made some practical comments on their function and the relative frequency with which they were found.

> … every soldier must have one or more of these chizels, this may be the reason why so many of them are found in different places … The only objection I have to it is, that the nature of the metal seems to make it impracticable to give such an edge to these tools, that they should be sharp enough to cut wood. But if, as this ingenious gentleman supposes, this was the use which the Roman soldiers made of the chizels of flint which are found among us, we need not, I think question these instruments

A history of discovery

2 Reverend John Lewis (1675-1746)

being fit for such a use. It is plain by the very sight of these instruments that they have as sharp an edge as they can have, and one would think therefore they were made to cut with.

The antiquarian world was becoming aware of the possibility that the mounds and hillocks still scattered around the countryside were ancient burial sites. Lewis (1736, 167) described one mound that was known to him:

A little way off from th[e] light-house (at North Foreland) is a small point of land, called watch house point … Just by are two large butts of banks of earth, called by the country people hackendon or heckingdown banks. The tradition is, that these banks are the graves of those English and Danes which were killed in a fight here, and that, as one bank is greater than the other, that bank is the place where the Danes are buried, who are said to have been defeated.

These banks were to become better known in later years. One passage written by Lewis (1736, 174), dealing with a local tradition, was to haunt the study of Thanet's archaeology for some time to come:

> The vanity of the Inhabitants, who, like the natives of other places, are fond of having it famous for its antiquity, has fancied the name of it to be Romansgate, from its being used as a port of landing place by the Romans. But, besides that its name is never so written in the most ancient writings that I have seen, it may well be doubted, whether in the time of the Romans frequenting this island, there was any gate or way at all into the sea. It seems plain it was first dug thro' the cliff, as the rest of the sea gates in this little Island were, for the conveniency of the fishery. I never could hear that any Roman coins etc were ever found here, as at Bradstow, where if any where in this island, the Romans seem to have had a station.

As the town of Margate developed into a seaside retreat for fashionable Londoners, a number of traveller's guides were published. Some were collations of texts of varying quality, often paraphrasing Lewis as their primary source of local history. Others were of more readable quality and preserve much interesting local information. Thomas Fisher's *Kentish Travellers Companion* of 1779 (p. 94), provides us with the first narrative of an archaeological excavation in Thanet at the Hackemdown Banks as they are now known:

> One of these banks was opened on the 23rd of May 1743, by Mr. Thomas Read, owner of the lands, in the presence of many hundreds of people. A little below the surface were found several graves, cut out of the solid chalk, and covered with flat stones; they were not more than three feet in length, into which the bones had been thrust almost bent double. Several urns made of coarse earthenware, capable of containing about two or three quarts each, had been buried with them, which crumbled into dust on being exposed to the air. Ashes and charcoal were found in them. Many of the bones were large but not gigantic, and for the most part perfectly sound.

In the late eighteenth century, the Northdown Estate on the east coast of Thanet, which included the Hackemdown Banks, was bought by Henry Lord Holland for his retirement. He built a number of curious structures and follies where he stored his large collection of ancient artefacts, and the mounds on his land did not escape his attention (Fisher 1779, 94):

> In June, 1765, the smaller tumulus was opened by order of the late Henry Lord Holland, who had then purchased the lands. The appearances were much like the former, with this exception only, that no urns were found.

Edward Hasted used many local sources to assemble his ambitious *History of the County of Kent* (1800). The section devoted to Thanet is largely a transcript of Lewis' history, except for occasional amendments and updates. The passage describing the discovery of the bronze hoard at Motherwicks abandons Lewis' Roman date and substitutes for this the newly fashionable attribution to the native British Druids. Margate was continuing to expand at this time and new discoveries had been made in the town. Although Hasted inserted a valuable new account of the discovery of Roman cremations and inhumations near the Charity School at Margate, he reproduced Lewis' Roman Ramsgate passage, which was copied from his work by several other later authors.

Under the influence of Charles Roach Smith, and the circle of the British Archaeological Association, the middle years of the nineteenth century were very productive for the careful investigation and reporting of archaeological sites on Thanet. The open marshland and downs of Thanet were bleak and isolated but among them, at Richborough, was one of the largest surviving structures of the Roman period. Charles Roach Smith studied the Roman fort at Richborough in detail. His efforts to visit every antiquarian collection and archaeological site in the country brought him into contact with William Rolfe of Sandwich, who had an extensive collection of material from the area and, through him, Roach Smith kept in close contact with any new discoveries. It was becoming clear that the isolated rural character of this extremity of east Kent preserved many significant archaeological sites.

Ramsgate was growing into a prosperous port, with connections to the Baltic trading network of the North Sea coast, and the town began to expand on to the cliffs on either side of its medieval core. Proposals were made to improve Ramsgate's harbour so that is could accommodate naval ships and, although progress was irregular, much work was carried out on the old haven in the 1830s. Captain Kennett Martin, Junior Harbour Master of the new port in the 1830s, reported many discoveries of Roman date that had been made during the construction works. From practical experience Captain Martin (1857, 83) was firmly in the 'Romansgate' camp and took issue with the continued repetition of Lewis' sceptical and anachronistic quote in recent historical works:

> It is not a pleasant occupation to analyse the discrepancies of ancient authors, inasmuch as they are not here to vindicate themselves ... but we should pervert the truth if we did not correct mistakes which proceeded from their entire ignorance of their subject ... a history of Kent, recently published has copied from Hasted or Lewis ...
>
> ... it does not appear that any Roman coins have been found here, as they have at Braidstow, where the Romans (if they had any at all) might have had a station on this island.
>
> "Might have had a station!" what? a highly civilised and intellectual people, have possession of a kingdom five hundred years, and not have a station immediately opposite, and only four miles removed from one of their noblest fortifications at Richboro', and on the opposite side of its estuary.

The evidence of empirical experience had finally come into direct conflict with the literary traditions of historical research. Archaeology began to emerge as a discipline in its own right.

The construction of a railway to Margate in 1845 revealed another site of immense importance to Thanet's history. In making a cutting through the chalk at Ozengell, on the slopes north-west of Ramsgate, remains from a large cemetery had been cast up with the spoil. William Rolfe had obtained some of the artefacts from the graves in the cutting, including a Roman lead coffin. The site was described by Thomas Wright in 1847 (p. 74):

> A pleasant walk of about a mile and a half brings the visitor from Ramsgate to the top of Ozengall downs, and is well repaid by the magnificent prospect it affords. It is still open ground, the only habitation being a house known by the name of the Lord-of-the-Manor, which it bore recently as a public-house, but it is now a private residence … the operation of cutting for the railway about two years before our visit led to the discovery that the whole summit of the hill is covered with the graves of the early Saxon settlers in the Isle of Thanet. Within the narrow space of the railway cutting about two hundred graves are supposed to have been destroyed, and their contents were thrown heedlessly and confusedly into the immense heap of chalk and soil cleared out of the excavation, with the exception of a comparatively small number of interesting articles which found their way into the hands of Mr. W.H. Rolfe, of Sandwich, one of the most zealous antiquarian investigators and collectors in this part of Kent. Mr. Rolfe's attention was immediately called to the spot, and through his exertions and intelligence only, the true extent of the discovery was made known to science.

William Rolfe obtained permission to excavate at the site and, with the assistance of Charles Roach Smith, opened a number of graves. The discoveries made during their excavations were later recorded in Roach Smith's series *Collectanea Antiqua* (*3*). The Ozengell cemetery was to be revisited on many occasions in the next century and a half.

A discovery of significance to the developing understanding of prehistory was made in 1853 while laying out gardens at Quex Park, Birchington. A hoard of as many as 600 Iron Age potin coins was packed in two tiers, apparently in a rectangular wooden box (Barrett 1893). William Rolfe had some of these coins in his collection and six were illustrated in John Evans' *Coins of the Ancient Britons*, one of the earliest systematic surveys of prehistoric coinage (Evans 1864).

A significant development in the study of archaeology in Thanet was the formation of the Kent Archaeological Society in 1857. This was largely through the efforts of the Rev. Lambert B. Larking, Vicar of Ryarsh near West Malling. The newly formed society was offered accommodation and the services of a curator at the Charles Museum at Maidstone, latterly Maidstone Museum, where an inaugural meeting was held on 14 April 1858. Many attempts were made to persuade Charles Roach Smith to take an official position in the society but he refused, although he was influential in its affairs and his advice was often sought (Jessop 1957). A system of regional secretaries was established who collected the Society's subscription of ten shillings per year and distributed the volumes of the Society's journal *Archaeologia Cantiana*. The first local secretary for the Isle of Thanet District, between 1858 and 1860, was the Rev. Saunderson Robins, Vicar of St Peters in Thanet.

Occasional finds of Anglo-Saxon material had been made in the area, but in July 1860 works on Sarre Windmill uncovered some graves with a fibula, gold coins, a bronze bowl and other items, suggesting that a rich cemetery was present (Smith 1860). The major exploration of the cemetery at Sarre was one of the first major projects undertaken under the banner of

A history of discovery

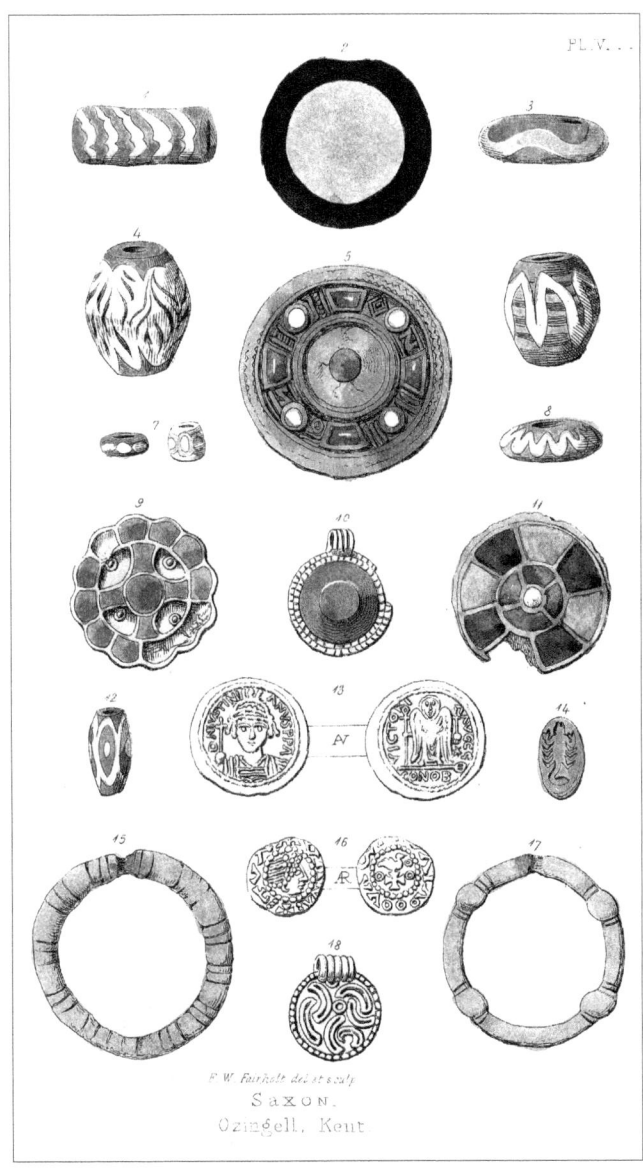

3 Artefacts found within the graves investigated at Ozengell. Illustrated in C.R. Smith's *Collectanea Antiqua* (iii) by F.W. Fairholt

the Kent Archaeological Society. This site was relatively unknown and the richness of the graves and their similarity to the discoveries at Ozengell were of great interest.

The Kent Archaeological Society opened negotiations with the Marquess of Conyngham to carry out further work on his land adjacent to the find spot, and between 17 September and 17 December 1863 John Brent excavated 187 graves near the Sarre Windmill. The variable weather conditions on Thanet will be well known to many archaeologists and were noted by Godfrey-Fausett in Brent's descriptions of his discoveries in *Archaeologia Cantiana* in 1863:

> The society owes a very great debt to Mr. Brent who has been working most kindly and laboriously in our interests. The scheme which he has so successfully carried out has been of no small fatigue, and from its engrossing nature one of no small inconvenience; to say nothing of the discomfort, the real personal risk involved in carrying out such works for three or four days in every week, during the last three unusually stormy months, and on as bleak and exposed a down as Saxon ever chose for his burying place.

In 1869 Augustus Lane-Fox (who was to take the name Pitt Rivers in later years) made a visit to Thanet in search of evidence for flint work on the chalk downs. He discovered three sites between Broadstairs, North Foreland and St Peters, where he found evidence of flint working, comparable to material he had seen in the Yorkshire Wolds. In a brickearth quarry near St Peters, he discovered a large pit from which he obtained Roman pottery, animal bone and several more struck flints. Lane-Fox was the first of many distinguished archaeologists to recognise the similarity of Thanet's archaeology to that of other chalkland areas of the country.

In the early years, the organisation of the Annual Meeting of the Kent Archaeological Society was left to a local committee. On 1-2 August 1877, the Annual Meeting was held for the first time in the Isle of Thanet. With the Earl of Darnley presiding, eight members of the committee and 110 other members gathered for the preliminary meeting in the Assembly Rooms in Ramsgate High Street. The meeting thanked the Thanet members for the hearty welcome they had extended and heard that the Council had voted in favour of the small sums of £3 and £5 for two excavations. These were carried out by George Dowker at Reculver and at Joss Farm, near the North Foreland Lighthouse in the Isle of Thanet. As might be expected, in an age when many of the men of learning in the society were clergymen, a tour of the historic churches at St Lawrence, Minster, St John's, Birchington, St Nicholas at Wade and Reculver was made over the two day meeting. Some of the older country houses, at Minster Court (formerly Minster Abbey), Nash Court, Salmestone Grange and the gatehouse towers of Dandelion, were visited and they also passed the site of the Anglo-Saxon cemetery at Sarre where John Brent had already carried out excavations on behalf of the Society. The members gathered would no doubt have been pleased to hear that sufficient arrears had been gathered by the local secretaries to publish Volume XII of *Archaeologia Cantiana*, particularly as the learned papers describing the architectural and historic significance of the buildings were published in that volume.

One of the attractions of the Annual Meetings each year was a Temporary Museum, erected in some convenient place, to display local artefacts and curiosities for the duration of the meeting. The Temporary Museum for the Thanet meeting was set up at the Waterworks Office, beneath the Church Institute in Hawley Square, Margate. Items on display included rare religious and secular books, maps, china, coin collections and a warming-pan inscribed '*God save King Charles*'. The items lent reflect the large number of archaeological discoveries that were being made as Thanet's small seaside towns expanded:

> Mr. Horace Cotton ... lent a cup used by William III at Quex, pistols exquisitely inlaid with silver, *much Roman pottery*, and a large number of *leaden counters or coins, supposed to*

be Roman, found at Quex, and many other objects of interest. Mr. Bubb of Minster, lent an old church clock of Minster, the old Parish account books, tokens issued in Thanet during the Commonwealth, old coins, an indulgence of Pope Gregory XVI, *much Roman pottery* and old china, and a variety of other interesting objects. Mr. Hillier lent *much Roman Pottery* found at Ramsgate, a well ornamented stone-polisher dated 1605 with initials A.C., and many other objects. Mr. R. Paramour lent an earthen vase, and a ball, found beneath old houses in high street when those now inhabited by Messrs. Willett and Brown were built; pieces of coloured glass bearing crowned initials T.W. or W.T. found in the wall of the tower of St. John's Church; a piece of stone carved with Norman ornaments and two heads; Mr. Sibert Saunders sent *a number of Roman vessels* of earthenware that had been dredged up near Whitstaple [sic]; Mr. Bentley lent the old Parish chest of St. John's Church; Mr. Jas. Dentry lent *vases dug up at the back of Warrior Square*; Dr. Richardson lent numerous books full of rare illustrations; many rubbings of monumental brasses were lent by Mr. W.J. Mercer and other friends; drawings and plans of Reculver and St. Nicholas, by Mr. G. Dowker and Mr. Joseph Clarke; etchings by Mr. Mercer; tapestry and needlework, lent by Mr. Swinford, and many other things – models, weapons, padlocks, etc., etc., formed a 'tout ensemble' of extreme and varied interest.

Archaeologia Cantiana, 1878, xl
(my italics highlighting the archaeological material of interest)

The vessels exhibited by Mr Bubb and described by Scott Robertson (1878, 331) were:

Roman remains which were found by the late Mr. Petley near his house at Cliff's End. One large Amphora, which held six or seven gallons was six feet in circumference at its widest part, and within it were three other vessels. One was a glass bottle, another was a Samian patera, and the third was an urn containing calcined bones. They were found midway between Mr. Petley's house, and the boundary stone of Minster parish.

These passages represent the state of archaeological research at the time. An atmosphere of primitive wonder prevailed at the antiquity of objects. Everyone was collecting something and everyone, it seems, had a quantity of Roman pottery that they could turn out for show.

Dowker's investigations in the North Foreland area, funded by the Kent Archaeological Society, were the first of a long series of significant discoveries and excavations carried out until the present day. His account (Tucker 2007a) was perhaps the first to draw attention to the stunning cropmarks that are still visible on the rolling chalk slopes of the promontory.

Along the high ridge on which the lighthouse is built are several circular marks observable in the corn, these are in one particular line along the highest point of the hill, and they are about one hundred yards apart. These circular patches are marked by a more luxuriant growth of corn in a circle, as if the roots penetrated a trench below

> – Some years back in altering or building the wall of the present lighthouse one of these circles was cut through and a skeleton was found …

This note is the first record of the excavation of a round barrow cropmark on Thanet.

The discovery of archaeological sites and artefacts in Thanet has often resulted from economic development involving major construction projects. The discoveries associated with the rebuilding of Ramsgate Harbour in the 1830s and the excavations at Ozengell in the 1850s, were driven by works associated with the establishment of major improvements to transport infrastructure. Other finds were made as a result of the expansion of the two main towns. In 1878 Robert Hicks, a Ramsgate surgeon, published an article summarising the finds that had been made in the West Cliff area of Ramsgate since the 1830s. A comment he made on the fortunes of discovery will resonate with all field archaeologists (Hicks 1878, 16):

> I will now describe in more detail, and as shortly as I can, the different finds, only remarking that it seems always necessary to build a house in order to discover them; for whenever we have made an attempt by trenching, in a likely spot, we always draw the covers blank.

Throughout the later nineteenth century, arrangements were made by local antiquarians, usually professionals of another discipline altogether, to monitor development works. The records of archaeological discovery throughout this period are derived from their notes and letters published with growing frequency in newspapers and journals. The diversity and historical significance of these finds, and the frequency with which they were coming to light, was a motivating factor in the development of organised responses and proactive monitoring. The appointment by the Kent Archaeological Society of George Payne as curator at Maidstone Museum established a semi-professional monitoring system and his records of researches and discoveries contain many valuable accounts of finds in Thanet. Significant discoveries included the many Roman burials discovered in the development of the Sea View estate (now known as the Chessboard estate after the names of the roads) near Stone Bay and west of North Foreland (Payne 1895, 1). Other spectacular finds were the large Late Bronze Age hoard discovered at Ebbsfleet farm and a Bronze Age burial with four bronze bracelets found near Ramsgate, reported to Payne by W. Hills of Ramsgate. Following the discovery of a number of burials in Birchington. George Payne (1895, 1) noted:

> The information we have hitherto received concerning discoveries on the border of the county in this locality has been meagre and imperfect. I have therefore taken steps to ensure systematic watchfulness when land is again disturbed for building purposes at Birchington.

'Systematic watchfulness' on Thanet was ably assisted by several active groups of amateur archaeologists and members of the Kent Archaeological Society, notably Cumberland

Woodruff, editor of *Archaeologia Cantiana* at the turn of the nineteenth century, who lived at Westcliff Terrace. He was able to assist in reporting the discovery of a rich Roman 'amphora burial' found at Southwood, Ramsgate (Woodruff 1902).

Major construction around the seaside towns in Thanet involved the excavation of quarries into the deep loess filling Thanet's dry valleys, for clay to make bricks. Many finds were made in these quarries and in 1904, Roman cremations and a hoard of palstave axes in a vessel were discovered in brickearth quarries near Birchington. An account of these discoveries was published by Major P.H.G. Powell-Cotton of Quex Park, Birchington in 1924 (Powell *et al* 1924).

In 1897 Howard Hurd was appointed Surveyor and Water Engineer to the Urban District Council of Broadstairs and St Peters, in charge of the water supply and other services (*4*). His work on the new estates being constructed in the Broadstairs area brought him into contact with many archaeological discoveries. He was a keen archaeologist and many of the local construction workers were aware of his interest and approached him with finds. Hurd also published comprehensive reports of his discoveries, well illustrated with photographs and plans. His work is the first accurate, scientific archaeological recording that was carried out on Thanet and stands the test of time. It was possible to overlay the plans of recent excavations at Dumpton Gap exactly over Hurd's plans of excavations carried out in 1907 (Boast & Gardner 2006).

In February 1910, during the construction of a private roadway up to Valletta House, Broadstairs (later known as Bradstow School), an Anglo-Saxon cemetery was discovered. Further excavations were carried out in 1911 with the permission of the owner Miss Bartrum:

> ... During the summer of 1911 it was noticed by Miss Bartrum's gardener that the grass did not grow satisfactorily in certain parts of the playing field, and that these spots appeared to form a large circle ... After examining the site, he came to the conclusion that it ought to be explored, and arrangements were accordingly made, which eventually resulted in the interesting discovery of what is believed to be the first recorded instance of Bronze Age man in Kent. As is well known Bronze Age implements and objects have been discovered from time to time in various parts of the County, but not the unearthing of skeletons such as occurred on this occasion.
>
> Hurd 1913, 18

Howard Hurd had investigated a number of round barrows at Dumpton Gap and Broadstairs, but this may have been the first time a Bronze Age burial was discovered, examined scientifically and the results of the analysis of skeletal material published (Hurd 1913, 25; Parsons 1913). As a result of the excavations at Valletta House, the Broadstairs and St Peters Archaeological Society was founded in 1911. Miss Bartrum, the owner of Valletta House, was on the first executive committee along with Howard Hurd.

In 1910, Dr Arthur Rowe, a general practitioner and surgeon born in Margate, retired at the age of 51 to concentrate on other interests (*5*). He produced significant work on the microfossils and formation of chalk strata, and had an interest in local history and

The Isle of Thanet – from Prehistory to the Norman Conquest

4 Howard Hurd (1865-1950)

archaeology. In 1924, Dr Rowe carried out archaeological excavations on an Iron Age settlement and a Roman building discovered during the construction of Tivoli Park Avenue on the valley side, west of Margate. A lively exchange of postcards records Rowe's correspondence with Howard Hurd, who gave advice on the excavation. Rowe discovered a number of burials eroding from the cliffs at Westgate in 1925 and excavated several, noting that they looked as if they had been buried in haste. In 1926, while working on a report on his excavations, Rowe died from an untreated tooth infection and his work on the Tivoli Villa remains largely unpublished.

Discoveries continued to be made in Thanet and in 1924 Roman cremations discovered in the new Minster cemetery were published (Whiting 1924). More Roman cremations and other finds were made when the esplanade area on Ramsgate's West Cliff was developed by the Borough Council (Couchman 1924). These were an interesting complement to the excavations that were being carried out at the Roman fort at Richborough on the other side of the marshes. In March 1929, workmen digging foundations for a new biological laboratory at St Lawrence College, Ramsgate unearthed a hand-made pottery urn with three large cast-bronze pins inside. The finds were collected by Mr C.E. Baldwin, the Senior Science Master, and published some years later by Christopher Hawkes (Hawkes 1947). The Kent Sites and Monuments Register records that

5 Dr Arthur Rowe
(1858-1926)

several skeletons and cremation vessels found in Birchington were donated to Margate Museum by Kathleen Hawkes, the wife of a builder who had helped to construct the many bungalows and houses in this expanding seaside town. In 1932, shortly before his retirement, Howard Hurd examined a single Anglo-Saxon burial discovered in Ramsgate.

Interest in archaeology was not restricted to the learned men of Thanet. In April 1938, 14 year-old James Beck discovered eight pits cut into chalk on the foreshore at Minnis Bay, near his home in Birchington. The beach had been scoured by a great north-easterly gale in February, sweeping away the sand that covered the area. With the assistance of Major Powell-Cotton's daughter Antoinette, 'Jimmy' Beck excavated and recorded the eight pits, publishing an account of his work in December 1938 in the *Cantuarian*, the magazine of Kings School Canterbury where he was a pupil. The finds from this first group of pits were predominantly Late Iron Age and Roman pottery, and springs observed emanating from three of the pits suggested that these were wells cut from a ground level now lost to the erosion of the nearby cliffs. These features were remarkable in Thanet's archaeological record for their preservation of organic material; wood, sticks, straw and bone were recorded in three of the pits along with two quern fragments and a millstone 0.95m in diameter. In August 1938, James Beck discovered another group of features further west. His investigation of these features, with his friend R. Grace, produced a Late Bronze Age 'founders hoard' containing personal ornaments and decorative material, weapons and implements. Pottery was found in association with the hoard, and nearby pits and postholes contained human remains, animal bone, flints and preserved timber including wattle hurdles and posts. Under the guidance of C.F.C. Hawkes, F.H. Worsfold carried out an excavation of the features (Worsfold 1943).

The report on this site reached a new level of sophistication for the recording of Thanet's archaeology. The account contained a detailed plan and sections of the site, along with a pottery report and the results of the analysis of the animal bone and botanical and insect remains that had been preserved in the unique conditions. The material was brought quickly to publication and many of the finds still reside in the Powell-Cotton (Quex) Museum at Birchington.

During the Second World War, the Ministry of Works continued to fulfil their obligation to protect ancient monuments, and excavations were carried out by W.F. Grimes prior to improvements to Manston airfield. Part of a round barrow and a Roman iron-working area were recorded (Grimes 1960). In the post-war period, the expansion of many of the housing estates on Thanet's coastal fringe led to more discoveries. In 1947, a Roman well shaft was excavated by J.P.T. Burchell, near Birchington, and W.P.D. Stebbing discovered a Neolithic burial on a large housing estate at Nethercourt in 1949. Improvements to the sea defences at Minnis Bay produced many finds in the 1950s. The discoveries were recorded by Antoinette Powell-Cotton and many of the finds are in the museum at Quex Park. A large pit, close to Burchell's well shaft, was investigated by J.B. Calkin when it was exposed by a mechanical grab working the cliff face, and Iron Age burials were found in 1960 in the same area (Trust for Thanet Archaeology archives).

A Stone House School excavation group was formed in 1953 to further investigate a site discovered by Howard Hurd at Lanthorne Road, near Stone House School at Stone Gap, Broadstairs. In a small area of the playing field they discovered several features and finds ranging from a Palaeolithic handaxe to Roman roof tile. In 1959, Early Iron Age burials were discovered while a house was being built near Cliffsend.

The pace of discovery increased in the 1960s with the discovery of more burials on the Sea View estate, a Roman cremation cemetery on Boxlees Hill and work at Drapers Mills School, by Mr J. Coy and the Thanet Excavation Group. In 1966 graves from the Ozengell Saxon cemetery were disturbed by gas-pipe laying and in 1967 a bell Beaker was discovered at Cliffsend (Macpherson-Grant 1968).

The Kent Archaeological Research Groups Council was formed in 1964, with the aim of coordinating the efforts of the county's archaeological societies to 'ensure minimum overlapping of effort, full coverage of the County for emergency work, rapid dissemination of results, and perhaps a centralised research policy' (Penn 1965, 2). Following a meeting of county archaeological groups at Canterbury on 10 October 1964, the Council was formed with the participation of 14 groups. Membership was open to all organised groups 'actively engaged in any form of field archaeology' (Penn 1965). Pressure was mounting throughout the 1960s for more active intervention in the destruction of archaeological sites through development. Alongside the formal local societies, parallel archaeological 'groups' were formed with a more practical agenda.

Groups were encouraged to produce Regional Archaeological Surveys, systematic assessments of the archaeological sites in their area, with a corresponding card index and large-scale map plots (Ocock 1969a and b). The Reculver Excavation Group, formed in 1957, carried out emergency recording on a number of sites including the discovery of a hoard of Roman coins at Ramsgate in 1969 (Cullen 1970). In the same year, excavations began of the large St Peters Anglo-Saxon cemetery, in advance of the construction of a council refuse destructor. The excavations were led by A.C. Hogarth, Head of Archaeology at Chatham House School, Ramsgate, assisted by his pupils and advised by other distinguished archaeologists including Sonia Chadwick-Hawkes.

The early 1970s were the beginning of the age of rescue archaeology, literally in the form of the epic excavations undertaken on sites at Dover, and institutionally with the formation of the RESCUE organisation to coordinate the archaeological investigation of major sites threatened by development (Jones 1984). This movement stimulated a new urgency to the investigation and reporting of archaeological sites. It is possible that the renewed focus on archaeology obscured the fact that steady and effective monitoring and excavation in the front line of archaeology was already well developed in Kent, under the umbrella of the Council for Kentish Archaeology (CKA), formerly the Kent Archaeological Rescue Group. In 1971 the Kent Archaeological Rescue Unit (KARU) was formed as a full-time professional rescue unit.

Also in 1971 a major rescue operation was launched to monitor the excavation of a gas pipeline across Thanet. This was the first of many such long narrow transects that have been carried out all over Thanet. Further work in the Stone Gap area, on the site of the Stone House School playing fields and other sites nearby, were undertaken by a new Stone House Archaeology Group in that same year (Minter and Herbert 1973). Excavations had been carried out on the development of the Seven Stones estate at Dumpton by the Thanet Excavation Group throughout the 1960s, and other discoveries had been made during the construction work. In 1971, excavations were carried out by Tim Champion, then of the Oxford University Institute of Archaeology. Renewed interest in Archaeology in the 1970s prompted the Broadstairs and St Peters Archaeological Society to publish a small volume reproducing some of the important excavations carried out in the early twentieth century and some more recent excavations by small groups and individuals within the same area (Minter and Herbert 1973). The volume was well received by the reviewer (Williams *et al* 1974, 21) in the *Kent Archaeological Review*.

> This booklet ... certainly deserves to be brought to the attention of everyone interested in the history of the area ... If only more of our towns and villages in Kent and, indeed throughout Britain, could produce such accounts of local archaeology, far more local interest would be aroused.

The development of a new multi-storey car park and shops near the centre of Margate began in 1974, revealing pits and ditches; a local member, Mr John Villette, alerted KARU and rescue excavations were begun. In July of the same year excavations were carried out by KARU on a ploughed-out round barrow ditch, burials and pits, during the development of the Millmead estate (Philp *et al* 1975). Excavations in this area continued to be carried out by KARU into the early 1980s.

In 1976 the Isle of Thanet Archaeological Unit was formed and its inaugural excavation was carried out on part of the complex of ring ditches at Lord of the Manor close to Ozengell at Ramsgate (*6*). The Unit received some financial support under the Manpower Services Commission's Community Programme, a national scheme to provide training to the unemployed. Funding was provided for the establishment of organisations to carry out cultural heritage projects and for appropriate professional staff to manage and direct the training. Projects were often sponsored by local authorities because of their value in enhancing the appreciation of cultural and historic resources in local communities. The MSC projects also provided funding for a reasonably large trainee workforce to carry out the projects. While these schemes provided much of the impetus for collating, and testing by practical projects, the cultural resources of an area, they depended on substantial funding from central government.

In 1977, a major excavation commenced on part of the unexcavated area of the Anglo-Saxon cemetery at Ozengell and by 1982, 228 graves had been excavated (Birch *et al* 1987). Between 1978 and 1979 full-time excavations were carried out by the Thanet Archaeological Unit on the lost parish church of All Saints, Shuart. Labour was provided by the Manpower Services Commission, directed by Dr Frank Jenkins and assisted by Mr David Perkins (Jenkins 1981). Between 1982 and 1984, the Unit monitored the excavation of a gas pipeline across Thanet, closely following the route of the pipe laid in 1971 (Perkins 1983).

In conjunction with Thanet District Council, the Thanet Archaeological Unit worked to create an Archaeological Implications Report listing all the archaeological sites in the area. The report was intended to form the basis of consultation with the planning department and local landowners to ensure that sites were given protection in advance of development. The Unit began to collate a Sites and Monuments Record, using data from many sources and in 1987 produced a summary booklet, *The Gateway Island* (Birch *et al* 1987).

The Manpower Services Commission funding was withdrawn in 1988 and many groups who had depended on the scheme were faced with a funding crisis. The Trust for Thanet Archaeology was formed in 1988, from the Isle of Thanet Archaeological Unit, with the support and limited grant funding from Thanet District Council, to respond to the need for a professional archaeologist to advise on planning issues, to carry out commercially funded archaeological work and to promote education in the archaeology of the Isle of Thanet. The first Director of the Trust for Thanet Archaeology was David Perkins. In 1990, the introduction of Planning Policy Guidance note 16 (PPG 16) established a framework for archaeology to be included within the planning and development process, giving local authorities powers to specify that archaeological work should be carried out in mitigation of development. The Isle of Thanet Archaeological Society was formed at the same time.

Research excavation in Thanet continued to be sponsored by the Kent Archaeological Society. In the early 1990s a Roman villa was recognised by aerial photography at Minster in Thanet. With the kind permission of the landowner, Mr Jack Clifton, the Abbey Farm site was chosen as an annual training excavation for the Kent Archaeological Society from 1996 to 2004, under the direction of David Perkins and Keith Parfitt.

A history of discovery

6 Lord of the Manor site 1 under excavation by Thanet Archaeological Unit 1976.
© *Trust for Thanet Archaeology*

In the early 1990s, the Trust for Thanet Archaeology undertook several large projects, including evaluations in advance of the improvements to the A253, the main road to Thanet, and large-scale excavations at South Dumpton Down, Broadstairs. A landmark in the study of the prehistory of Thanet was the award in 1999 of a PhD to David Perkins for his research on the island as a focus for trade with the continent in the Bronze Age (Perkins 1999b).

Over the last 15 years, there has been an explosion of archaeological work carried out in Thanet by both the Trust for Thanet Archaeology and other archaeological organisations too numerous to describe in summary. Two notable projects of recent years are the full excavation of the route of the improved A253 by Canterbury Archaeological Trust and the Trust for Thanet Archaeology, and the Margate and Broadstairs Urban Waste Water Treatment Scheme by Wessex Archaeology. Both have provided unprecedented samples of the landscape of Thanet that must be added to the story that emerged from smaller projects over 250 years of excavations. Projects are now longer and more complex and require skills unavailable to previous generations of archaeologists, such as operating the complex bureaucracy of the planning process and understanding the engineering requirements of development. The development of a coherent research framework and the synthesis of the work that has already been carried out have sometimes proved difficult tasks. On his retirement in 2003, David Perkins was replaced as Director of the Trust for Thanet Archaeology by Miss Emma Boast. The Trust for Thanet Archaeology continues in its aim to keep an up-to-date and coherent narrative of all the archaeological discoveries on Thanet and has digitised much of the available data in recent years, so that it can be used more effectively. The following pages have made extensive use of this facility.

2

GEOLOGICAL FOUNDATIONS

The mass of the Isle of Thanet is composed of Cretaceous Upper chalk, a continuation of the chalk of the North Downs of Kent (7). Overlying the eroded upper surface of the chalk are layers of hard Eocene sands, formed as seabed deposits in the ocean that settled on the chalk between 55.8 and 33.9 million years ago (Osborne White 1928). Tectonic folding of the chalk formed one of Thanet's major topographic features, a long straight ridge, or monocline, that runs east to west along the southern side. The same process created the Weald-Artois chalk ridge from the North Downs to the north-east coast of France. The northern face of the ridge falls away in a gentle slope but the southern is steeper, forming the northern edge of a downfold, or syncline, running parallel to the ridge. The southern limit of the syncline in the chalk is located on a north-east to south-west line parallel with the Thames estuary. North of this line Eocene deposits were preserved from later truncation in the hollow of the fold. The Eocene deposits west of Thanet have been eroded obliquely along the Thames estuary. The eastern section of the syncline was truncated by a mega flood event, caused when a glacial lake breached the Weald-Artois ridge, carving out the English Channel 200,000 years ago (Gupta *et al* 2007).

The ice advances of the Pleistocene cold periods did not reach the Kent area but the periglacial conditions that were prevalent in the last (Devensian) cold period were instrumental in shaping the distinctive downland landscape of Thanet. Permafrost conditions made the surface of the chalk impermeable, allowing water flowing over the chalk to erode the surface mechanically (8). The slopes to the north and south of the chalk ridge and the fringes of the eastern plateau of Thanet are scored with asymmetrical dry valleys, a product of water erosion under periglacial conditions; all the valley cutting is thought have to taken place in a single phase at least 74,000 years ago (Murton *et al* 2003).

Sheetwash from the melting glaciers scoured the deposits of Eocene material from the surface of the chalk, but patches that were trapped in the syncline and other hollows escaped erosion (Osborne White 1928). The earliest deposits of the series, termed the Thanet Beds, only remain along the steeper southern dip slope of the central ridge between Pegwell and Sarre and under more recently deposited alluvium. An east to west series of low hillocks – Weatherlees, Boxlees, Docker and Coxon's – are exposures of the

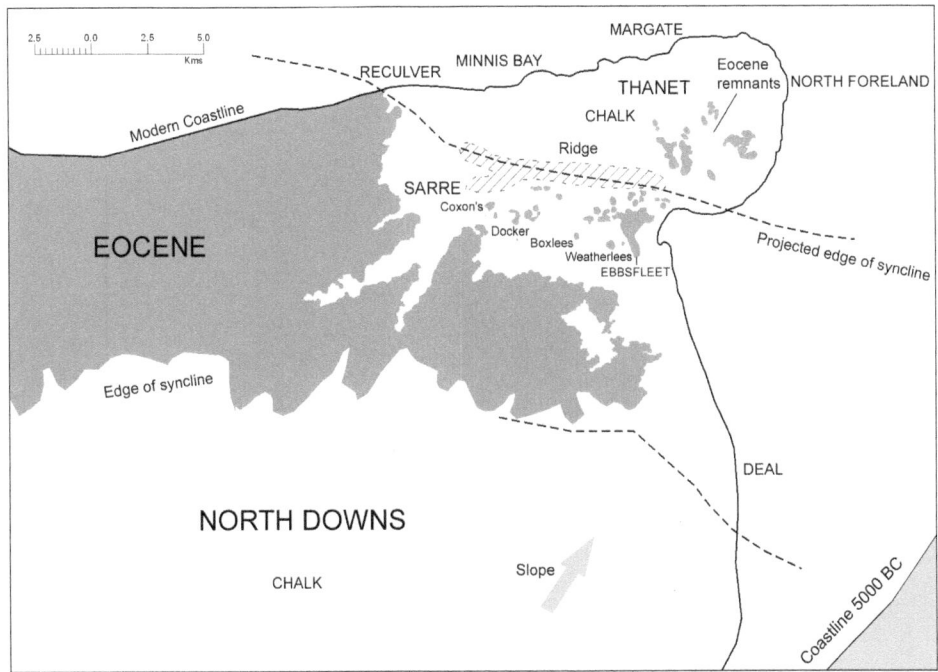

7 Regional geological deposits. © Trust for Thanet Archaeology

upper Thanet Beds series rising out of alluvium deposited at a later period: a spit of Thanet Beds sands extends south between Cliffsend and Minster forming the Ebbsfleet peninsula.

Solifluction deposits of Coombe rock, a churned mass of chalk and clay fragments washed along by meltwater over the permafrost layer, filled the sides and bottoms of the valleys. Wind-blown sands and silt (termed cover sands and loess), formed while tundra conditioned prevailed, were later deposited over the valleys. The earliest deposits in the base of a valley cutting at Pegwell Bay have given OSL dates of between 88,000 and 74,000 years BP ('Before Present', where 'present' is taken to be 1950). The first loess deposits on Thanet correlate with a major period of loess deposition in Europe around 70,000 years ago. Between deposition of more wind-blown cover sands between 24,000 and 21,000 years ago, permafrost continued to act on the chalk, shattering the upper surfaces (Murton *et al* 2003, 240).

In a warmer period around 21,000 years ago (Greenland Interstadial 2c) large areas of patterned ground were formed as the land surface went through cycles of freezing and thawing. Fine clay and silts percolated into fractures in the chalk to a depth of as much as 2m, producing linear stripes and polygons in the surface of the chalk. These areas of patterned ground are a prominent feature in aerial photographs of Thanet and are frequently observed in archaeological fieldwork; they are predominantly visible on the flatter slopes on the sides of the dry valleys (*9*). The last permafrost conditions to affect Thanet occurred between 21,000 and 18,000 years ago and the final thawing of the

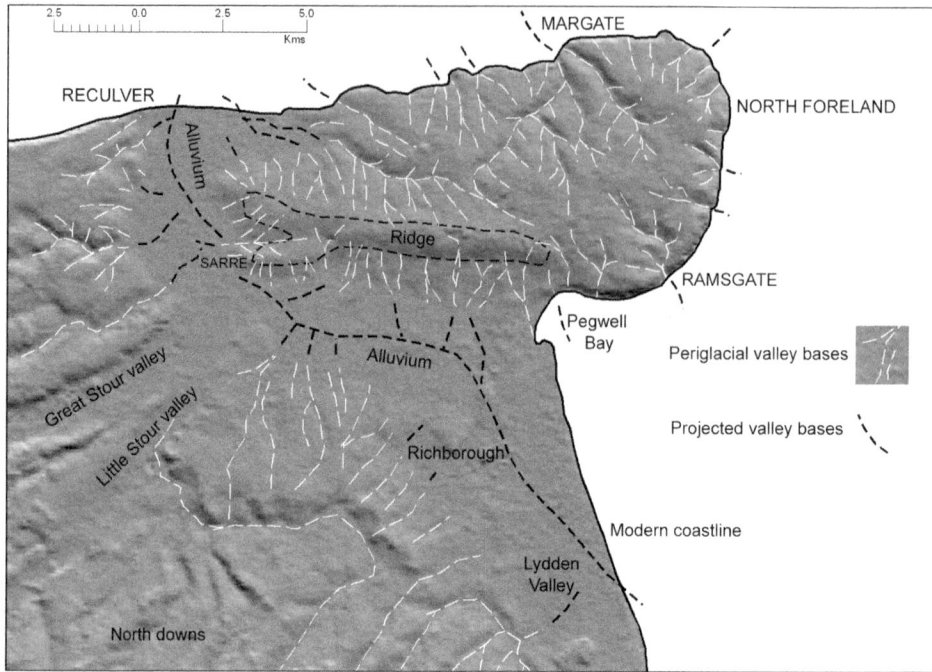

8 Periglacial features of the eastern North Downs and the Isle of Thanet, based on SRTM elevation data. © *Trust for Thanet Archaeology*

permafrost may have taken place as early as 19,500 and no later than 14,700 years ago. Further deposits of wind-blown sand and loess were deposited in separate episodes around 15,500 and 12,000 years ago (Murton et al 2003, 242).

At the beginning of the current (Holocene) interglacial warm period around 10,000 years ago, the chalk outcrop that would become the Isle of Thanet, lay west of the terminal of the English Channel that served as the outflow of the valleys of the Thames and the Rhine west to the Atlantic. The area that is now the North Sea was an extensive landmass which has been named named Doggerland by the archaeologists who have studied it (Coles 1998). This area of post-glacial forests was settled by Mesolithic people for around 2000 years before the release of water from the retreating ice sheets, between 8000 and 7000 years ago, caused a rapid sea-level rise throughout the world (eustatic), with a catastrophic effect on human settlement in the Doggerland area. The rise in this period has been measured at around 20m within the Thames estuary and east Kent marshes (Devoy 1979; Long 1992). The relief from the weight of the ice caused a slight rise in ground level (isostatic), in some areas altering the relationship between the elevation of the land and the sea. Sea levels of around -12 to -10m below Ordnance Datum achieved between 6000 and 5000 years ago were sufficient to rapidly submerge the low-lying Doggerland and eventually link the North Sea to the English Channel. Continued sea level rises isolated the area between the Thames and the English Channel into a promontory, beginning to shape the region of Kent as it exists today.

*9 Periglacial markings observed during excavations at the former West Cliff House, Ramsgate.
© Trust for Thanet Archaeology*

Reconstructing the landscape of Thanet in the early Holocene is a complex process but it is possible to trace some of the surviving topography. The coastline reconstructed for the end of the period of very rapid sea-level rise around 5000 BC follows a northeast orientated ellipse between the limits of the trench of the English Channel and the Thames estuary, at an elevation of around 8m below Ordnance Datum (Coles 1998) (*10*). The periglacial valleys north of the central ridge can be seen to form independent drainage networks separated from each other by ridges. The longest surviving networks have a form typical of water erosion with small lateral valleys intersecting with long sinuous central valleys like the branches of a tree. These 'dendritic' valley networks would have continued over the huge areas of land that were above the sea and have since been submerged forming long, radiating networks of gullies, falling to the coast between the Thames and the Channel. On the northern and north-eastern sides of Thanet 20 to 33km of land has been lost since 5000 BC and between 5 and 10km of land has been lost in the curve between Ramsgate and Deal. The eastern and southern coasts had steeper profiles, being located against the edge of the English Channel. The topography of this lost land would have been similar to that of the chalk on the North Downs today. The elevation was too low for the covering of Eocene material to remain, but each valley had its solifluction deposits and coverings of loess and sand, and would have been continuous with the remnant networks that survive on Thanet today.

The Isle of Thanet – from Prehistory to the Norman Conquest

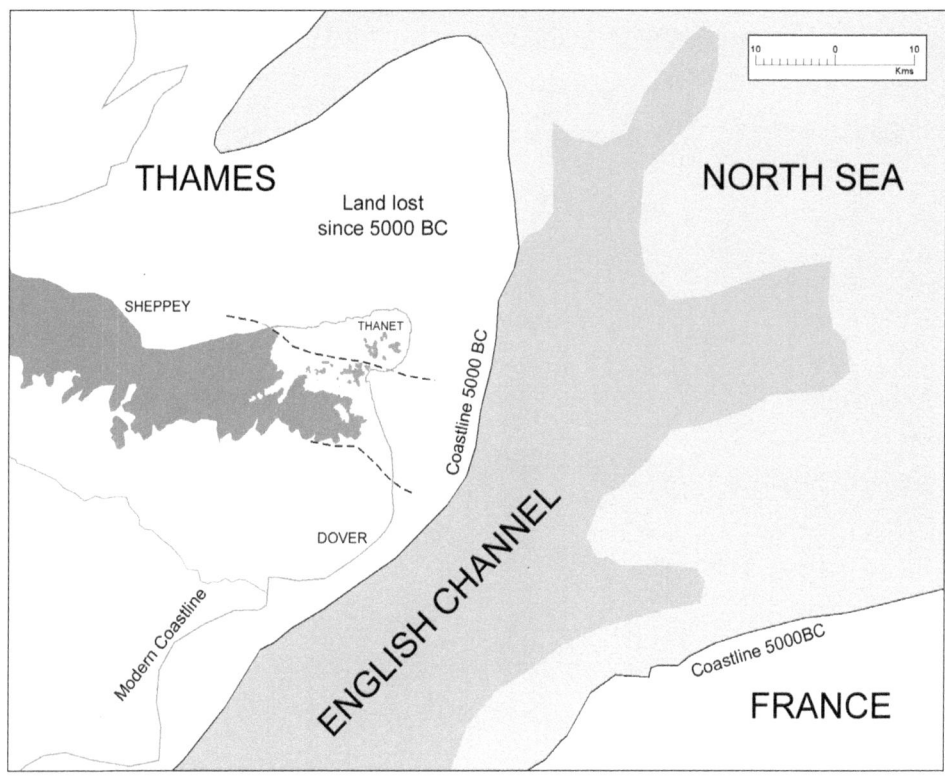

10 The coastline of East Kent in 5000 BC, partly based on Coles, B.J. 1998

The local patterns of springs and surface drainage were probably similar to those of the present day (Corcoran 2003). The valley of the Great Stour drains the north-east facing slopes of the North Downs, intersecting the Eocene deposits preserved in the syncline at Canterbury. The Stour discharged into the Thames valley at a point now kilometres offshore on the north-east coast of Kent. The pattern of drainage suggests that in the early Holocene the Stour may have curved to the north following a periglacial valley through the Eocene sand deposits. The second water course of some size is the Nailbourne which rises at Lyminge, with a second source near Ash. This flows down the north-east facing slope and enters a valley cut through the Eocene deposits at Littlebourne where these streams become the Little Stour. Small spring-fed water courses such as the Sarre Penn and North Stream drain the north-east orientated chalk valleys from Chislet to Reculver and another series of small springs follow the valleys between Stourmouth and Richborough. South of the central chalk ridge, a spine valley drained the springs and streams that rose from the chalk in the north and south banks and possibly the run-off from the surrounding valleys. Spring-fed streams were present in some of the truncated valleys in Thanet until recently and some are still active along the southern slope of the central chalk ridge (*11*).

Geological foundations

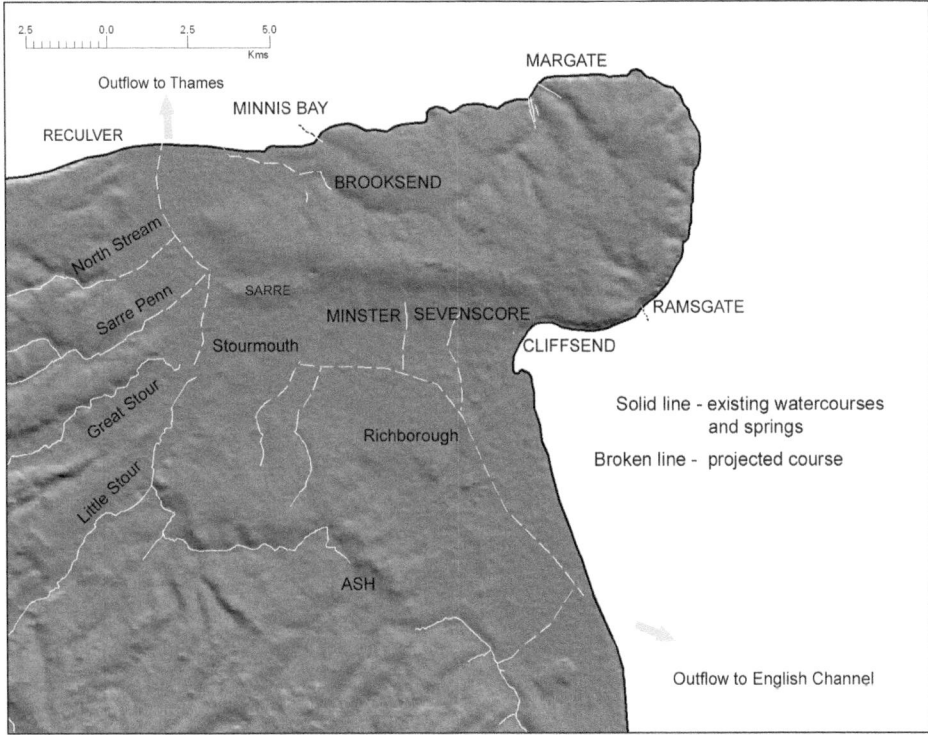

11 Water courses and springs in the Isle of Thanet area, based on SRTM data.
© *Trust for Thanet Archaeology*

As the sea continued to rise, interspersed with limited regressions, the edges of the chalk promontory extending into the North Sea between the Thames estuary and the English Channel began to erode. The action of the sea on the chalk cliffs produces particular effects, most notably the formation of vertical cliffs and sea stacks that can be of considerable height.

The sea would have entered the valley mouths and rapidly eroded the soft loess deposits creating inlets, bays and sea stacks in the chalk. The indurated sands of the Eocene deposits in the syncline were more resistant but gradually a broad bay formed at the southern mouth of the syncline where the advancing sea eroded the low sandy cliffs. Where the periglacial valleys opened in these cliffs the sea would have found its way through the channels into the hinterland.

Coastal erosion is an active process — the stability of any coastline depends on the topography at sea level and over a generation or two familiar landmarks would be entirely lost and new ones created (*12*). Although it would have been a considerable factor in the lives of the inhabitants of the Kent coast for millennia, we have only the reactions of relatively recent witnesses to help explore the effects on the community. The effect of coastal erosion on the coast of Thanet has been a subject of great interest to many local writers. In 1736 John Lewis remarked that:

The Isle of Thanet – from Prehistory to the Norman Conquest

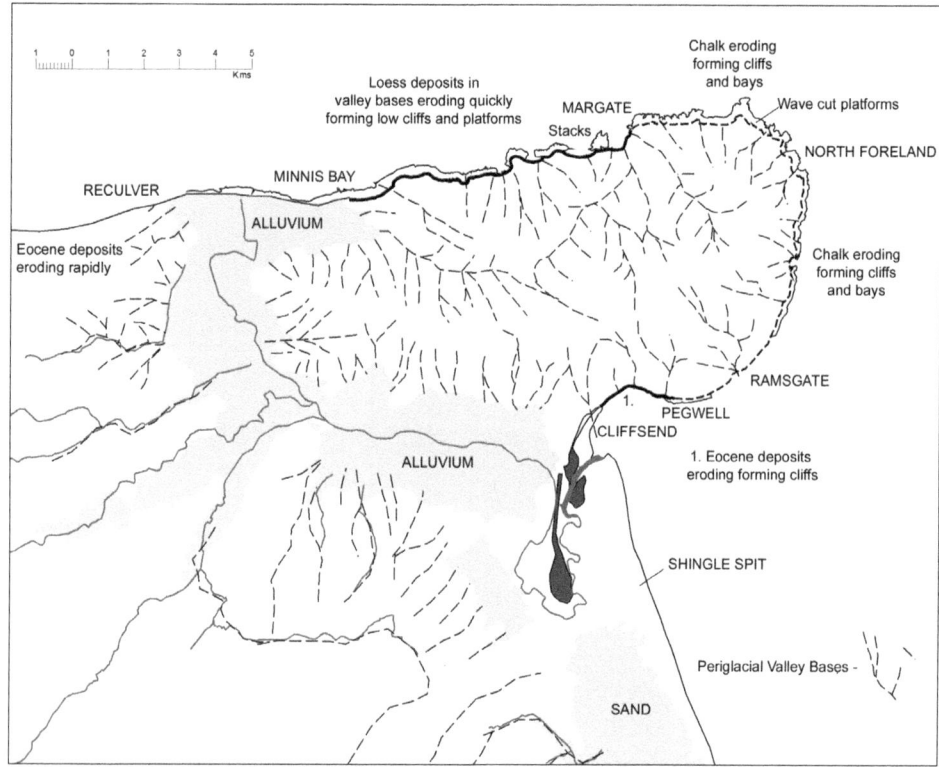

12 Coastal erosion processes on Thanet's coastline. © Trust for Thanet Archaeology

This island seems antiently [sic] to have been as large or larger than it is now … it's very plain, that formerly the land on the north and east sides of it, from the west-gate [Westgate] to cliff-end [Cliffsend], went much further out into the ocean than it does now … At this day we see at low-water, rocks, as the inhabitants call them, or footings of the chalky cliffs, on which antiently [sic] was land, above half a mile from the present shore or cliffs.

The erosion of the chalk around the north and eastern parts of the Isle of Thanet has also attracted much interest from geologists. The process of erosion is not regular nor its cause obvious. Some interesting evidence about the rate and effects of the process is contained in the unlikely source of George Fairholme's treatise on geological proofs of the Biblical flood (Fairholme 1837). Although it was written as a defence of a short geological chronology to demonstrate the truth of the force of the flood as presented in scripture, Fairholme's thesis was founded on direct observation of the erosion of the chalk cliffs, on the islands of Sheppey, Wight and particularly Thanet. Fairholme recognised that the rate of erosion could be measured and the ancient limits of the coast reconstructed. Exploring the dry valleys and observing that many terminated in sea-eroded chalk cliffs, Fairholme concluded that by projecting the original curvature of the ridges to a datum, an estimate could be made of the time that had elapsed since the erosion began. When he wrote his treatise in 1837 he estimated the erosion to have reached the rate of around one inch per year, but observed that the process was not regular (1837, 233):

> During six years, that I have studied the cliffs of Thanet, so slow, though ceaseless has been the loss, that I could not, for some time, bring myself to think it was even so much as one inch over the whole face of a cliff. But in the winter of 1835-6, during which there chanced to be a combination of severe gales, and of high spring tides, so great was the loss, and so numerous the falls, that I was taught to calculate, on the longer periods, as the only just method of striking a true average.

In 1857 Captain K.B. Martin made similar observations on the erosion of the East Cliffs of Ramsgate:

> During the last forty years, the waste of the East Cliff lodge estate full averages two feet annually; the garden wall is now falling over the precipice. During the Admiral Lord Keith's residence there, and the Princess of Wales' visit (Queen Caroline) the troops paraded between that wall, and the edge of the cliff, and marched past by companies ...

These observations demonstrate the rapid and surprising effects that the sudden erosion of the chalk cliffs could have and that significant changes could take place within the lifetime of one person.

A modern study of the coastal platforms around Thanet has demonstrated that the cliffs are not formed by the solution of the chalk by the sea, but by a process of corrasion involving storm waves of sufficient power to drive sand and flints against the face of the cliffs, mechanically eroding them (So 1965). This accounts for the sporadic but substantial cliff falls described by Lewis, Fairholme and Captain Martin. The erosion of cliff faces by storm waves generated at prevailing mean sea level created platforms of uneroded chalk at the base of the cliffs, the platform's elevation reflecting the sea level. The platforms visible along Thanet's chalk coastline today are the result of relatively modern sea levels. The outer limits of the platforms are marked by steep edges or low-tide cliffs. These are subject to less force and erode at a slower pace than the main cliff faces, so the width of the platforms gradually extends. The limiting effects of a wide platform on the energy of the waves ensures that a reciprocal, but uneven, relationship is maintained between the erosion of onshore cliffs and the low-tide cliffs on the seaward side of the platforms. This process has been going on since the major sea-level rises of the post-glacial period and fossil platforms exist, reflecting early stable tidal forces at lower elevations. Slight gradients present in the bays and variations in the level of the platforms around Thanet reflect differences in the angle of the approaching waves, which is related to the topography of the coastline. Occasionally the sea encountered faults in the chalk, and caves have formed or, where harder chalk was

13 A sea stack at Botany Bay, Margate. © Trust for Thanet Archaeology

present, sea stacks reach out into the water. These coastal features would have been familiar sights to past generations (*13*).

The attrition of the coastal fringe of Thanet by the sea has destroyed many of the sites of earlier human settlement and even those of relatively recent times. It will probably be impossible to know how much has been lost over several thousands of years to what John Lewis in 1736 called 'the rage of the sea, and falling down of the land'.

3

A RIVER OR THE SEA? THE WANTSUM DIVIDE

The historic geography of a channel that once separated Thanet from the mainland of Kent has been the subject of a great deal of scholarly debate. The chronology of the channel is poorly understood and it is not clear when the channel was formed and what the extent of the water was at key points in its history. The development of the channel in relation to changing sea levels and the influence of the periglacial topography in its development has not been considered in detail. The tidal ranges and flows through the channel at various periods would have had a bearing on what craft would have been able to navigate the channel, and what traffic there was from domestic and continental sea routes.

There are few contemporary records that describe the Wantsum channel, as it is now named, at its fullest extent; what evidence we do have comes mainly from the historic period. The earliest reference to the Isle of Thanet is contained in the second-century AD geography of Ptolemy (Claudius Ptolemaeus) with the implication that the channel was large enough to isolate Thanet in the Roman period. The Roman name *Rutupiae* for the port at Richborough at the southern entrance to the channel is attested in various forms in Latin texts of the Roman period when it was the principal port of entry to Britain. It is generally agreed that the Roman name for the port derived from a native British word having the meaning of 'mud flats' or 'a muddy creek'. Ptolemy did not mention Richborough in the list of ports in his geography but placed it in a list of the towns of the people of Kent. At the north entrance the ancient name for Reculver is recorded as *Regulbi* and *Regulbio* in the text of the fourth-century *Notitia Dignitatum*, derived from British words for a 'great beak', a metaphor for a prominent headland perhaps surrounded by inlets to form the beak shape. This accords well with the location of Reculver on a headland between sea-eroded periglacial valleys (Rivet and Smith 1979, 448 & 446).

The first recorded instance of the name Wantsum (*Uantsumu*) being given to the channel in the Anglo-Saxon period is found in the pages of Bede's *Ecclesiastical History*, written in the early eighth century (Sellar 1907). The passage contains a brief description:

On the east of Kent is the large Isle of Thanet, containing, according to the English way of reckoning, six hundred families, and divided from the other land by the river Wantsum, which is about three furlongs across and fordable only in two places, for both ends of it run into the sea.

Bede also named the north mouth of the Wantsum near Reculver, which he called the *Genlade* (altered in later periods to *Yenlade*). This word has the general meaning of 'an unloading or outlet', but this might refer to the traffic in the river as much as to the flow of water, which is likely to have had a dominant flow from the north mouth to the eastern entrance (Lewis 1736; Grainge 2007). Bede calls the Wantsum a river but his description of it as three furlongs (around 600m) wide suggests that some tidal effects operated on the extent of the water. Bede was concerned with ecclesiastical rather than geographical matters and his description was sufficient for the purpose of setting out the context of the arrival of Christianity in Kent. We do not know what source Bede used for his description, nor which point in the channel the measurement represented. Bede does imply that the Wantsum was a barrier to crossing over to the Isle of Thanet but not that it was of any great width as it could be forded in two places, probably by boat (Sellar 1907).

Apart from a brief mention in the *Anglo-Saxon Chronicle* of Harold and Godwin travelling from Sandwich to the north mouth and on to London in 1052 (Thorpe 1861), there are no further texts that describe the passage through the Wantsum channel in detail before the later medieval period. The absence of records has been regarded as an indication that the route was so common as to require no explanation; the Wantsum was considered an extension of the Thames and it is possible that the city of London had some jurisdiction over the towns of Sandwich or Stonar in the southern entrance (Scott-Robertson 1878).

From the eleventh-century embankments were built along the edges of the Wantsum to protect low-lying marshes at the edge from inundation. Some of the embankments were built by linking the small islands of Eocene sands in the channel. The Canterbury monastic houses of Christ Church and St Augustine were granted lands at Minster, that formerly belonged to the monastery of St Mildred, by Cnut in 1027. They probably undertook the work of 'inning' the channel to improve the agricultural land of their manors at Minster and Monkton; the embankments between Monkton and Ebbsfleet are known as the Abbott's Wall.

In a perambulation of the route of the Wantsum channel by the Lord Warden of the Cinque Ports in the late thirteenth century, the boundary of the channel, and the jurisdiction of the Liberty of Sandwich were defined by the high water mark at the spring tide. Part of the route taken from Sarre to Weatherlees followed the route of the Abbot's Wall ending at Henneberg, the northern limit of the Stonar shingle at the end of the Ebbsfleet peninsula. That the high water at spring tide only reached this point suggests that the tidal range of the Wantsum was limited outside the central channel and that the earthen embankments were sufficient to retain the normal rise and fall of the water. The width between the medieval banks that are still visible today varies between 300m and 600m, similar to the dimensions given by Bede.

A map by Thomas of Elmham (d.1420) from a manuscript of the early fifteenth century written at St Augustine's, Canterbury, shows the Isle of Thanet (with its western end at the bottom of the drawing) separated from the mainland by a continuous flow of water, a Christian pilgrim or monk is shown being carried on the back of another man to a ferry boat, presumably to take him over to Sarre in Thanet (facsimile page in Hardwick 1858). This map is schematic, intended to show the relative locations of the parish churches on the island and not necessarily provide an accurate depiction of the dimensions of the Wantsum channel. The map was copied and published in Lewis's history of Thanet (Lewis 1736) (*14*).

From the 1460s the Wantsum began to suffer considerably from the effects of the deposition of mud and silt in the channel, affecting its navigability considerably. These problems were popularly associated with the construction of Tenterden steeple in 1462 (Lewis 1736, 8), which, while unlikely to have had any real effect on the Wantsum, gave a clear reference to the local people of the date of the failure of the scouring effect of the tides (Scott-Robertson 1878).

The preamble to an Act of Parliament granted by Henry VII in 1485 (Scott-Robertson 1878, 341) described how from time out of mind a ferry at Sarre had allowed the passage from Thanet of 'all manner of persones, beastes, corne, and other things to passe and be conveyed at all seasons to an fro the same isle and country …'. The Act reported that the normal route of the ferry had become, in recent years, so raised with 'ouse, mud and sand' that the ferry could not operate for more than hour each day at the highest point of the spring tide. Permission was granted for the construction of a bridge from Sarre to Wall End, stipulating that it should be of sufficient height and span to allow the boats that could still use the river to have free passage through the structure.

In the itinerary of his travels across England between 1539 and 1545, Leland recorded that the sea still rose through the north mouth in a creek as far as Sarre on the north side of the Wantsum (Chandler 1998). John Lewis recognised that so long as the sea had flowed in at the north mouth of the river at the *Yenlade*, the tide had served to scour the whole length of the channel – the strong tidal flow had been crucial to its navigability. The free passage of the sea through the channel had been obstructed at the crucial narrow section at Sarre by the rapid deposition of the silts. One cause that has been suggested was the sinking of a Spanish ship outside Richborough within the Sandwich haven, which had gathered a great bank of sand and silt (Scott-Robertson 1878, 341).

A map of the Isle of Thanet and the Wantsum channel from 1585 shows all the water courses confined within embankments at both the northern and southern mouths. An embankment is also shown linking the eastern side of the Ebbsfleet peninsula with Weatherlees Hill and embankments curving from Richborough to Stourmouth on the southern side of the river (Lambarde 1585).

In his *History of the Isle of Thanet*, Lewis described the Wantsum channel as a large estuary, but by the time he wrote this it was considerably reduced and his description of a navigable waterway was not taken from direct experience but was a summary of the literary and historical evidence for the Wantsum channel presented in the works of his antiquarian sources: John Twyne (*c*.1505-1581), William Somner (1598-1669) and John Battely (1688-

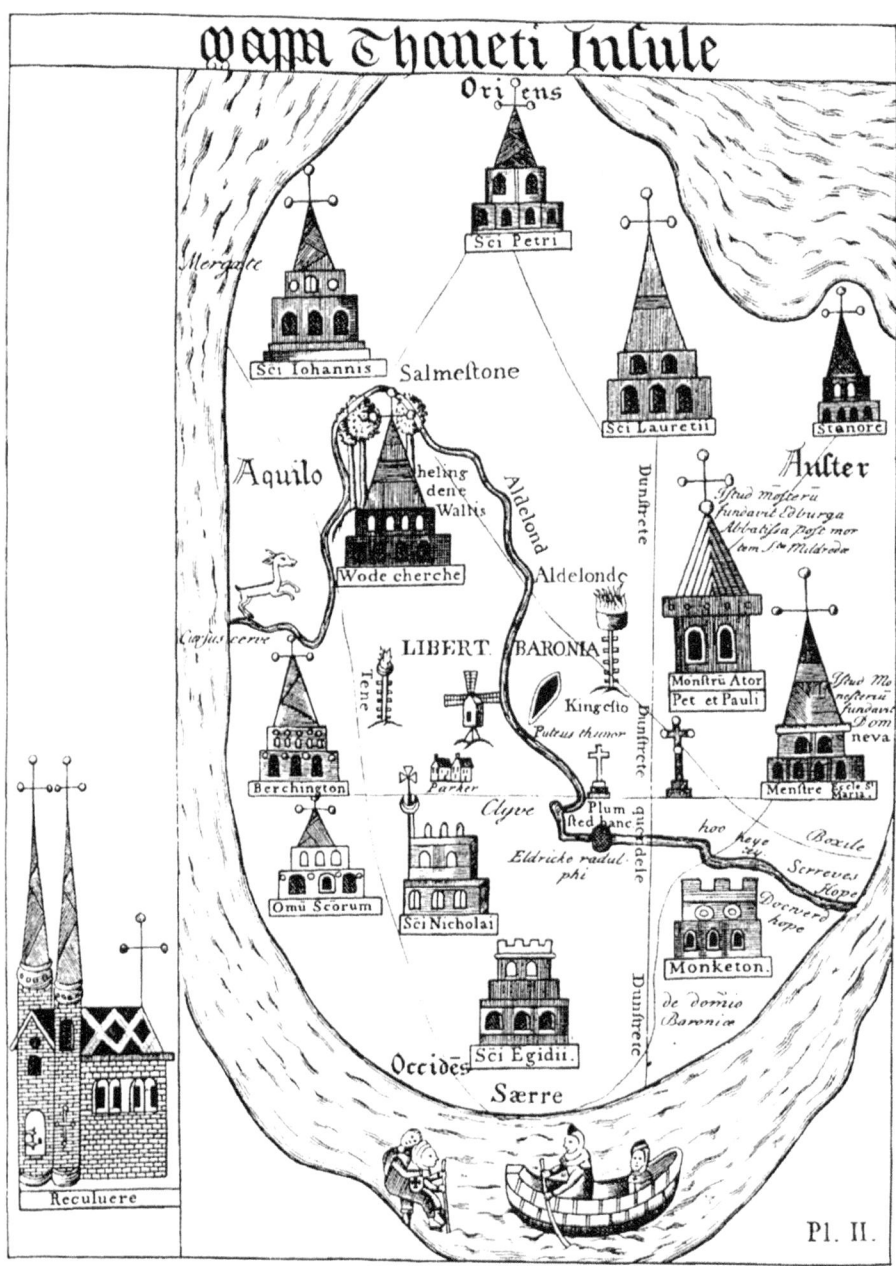

14 John Lewis' copy of a map of Thanet by Thomas of Elmham

1708). These writers had made studies of the area around Reculver, Richborough and the Wantsum including the Roman forts, finding different interpretations of how the channel had formed and why it subsequently failed. Without knowledge of the causes of rising sea levels it was suggested by these writers that at a time in the distant past, when the Dover strait was a narrow isthmus, it had acted to constrict the tides of the North Sea, forcing them into the north mouth of the Wantsum at the Thames and the southern mouth at Ebbsfleet. These explanations were based on changes in the distribution of water rather than the addition of water by the melting of polar ice. One of the causes for the failure of the estuary in the later medieval period given by the antiquarian sources was the relief of the tidal pressure from the north through the widening of the gap between the Dover straits by erosion. The retreating estuary left a 'slub of earth' over its former limits that further separated the land from the sea. An alternative explanation offered was that the historical inundations of the Low Countries in the medieval period had drawn the sea away from the Wantsum estuary by a redistribution of the flow of sea water. Lewis found neither explanation fully convincing and advises the reader that he is at liberty to choose between these explanations.

Whether the Wantsum channel was ever very wide was doubted by later writers; in 1837 George Fairholme who had studied the area wrote:

> This estuary, though probably intersected by channels of sufficient depth for navigation of that period, even at low tides, never could have been of any great depth, and must always have been either extremely shallow, or altogether dry, during ebb tides, with the exception of these channels ...

Scott-Robertson (1878, 339) also believed that the channel had not been substantial in the past:

> ... such tidal estuaries as the Wantsum [t]heir beds being to a great extent flat, not shelving until the mid channel is approached, a vast expanse of them lies dry for many hours in the day, and the distance between high water mark and low water mark is often very great.

Lewis considered a number of derivations for the Anglo-Saxon name *Wantsum* but preferred his own suggestion that it meant 'wanting - some', in the sense of lacking some water (Lewis 1736, Preface IV).

The geography of the Wantsum channel was of particular interest because of the historical events that were reputed to have taken place at a place called variously in the different versions of the *Anglo-Saxon Chronicle* 'Wypeddes floet', 'Heopwines floet' and 'Ypwines floet' (Thorpe 1861), later presumed to be Ebbsfleet in Thanet. Lewis (1736, 9) placed the location of Ebbsfleet within the Wantsum channel:

> Just at the mouth of the Richborough port is Ebbisfleet, a little Creek or Bay where the vessels used to harbour, and where was the usual landing-place in this Island from the Ocean. This being so frequented a place, we often find use made of it by both friends

and enemies to the country. Here … did Hengist and Horsa land, the commanders of the Saxon troops sent for by the unhappy prince Vortigern. Here Austin the monk came on shore. It was here Danish pirates landed, being tempted by the abbey lately built at Menstre [Minster], in which they supposed were very great riches.

Although Lewis described it as the 'usual landing-place', it appears that Ebbsfleet was considered an adjunct to the Richborough port. It is also not clear whether Lewis was writing from the authority of his local knowledge or from the descriptions of the landing place he gleaned from his sources, who were themselves primarily interested in Richborough as a Roman port. Little practical work was done to examine the geographical locations of the events in the early history of the British Isles and the sites of significance to Roman and Anglo-Saxon history.

Another key location in the Wantsum channel was the town of Stonar and the long shingle spit that extended north from it. The date and the process by which this spit formed has been the subject of another strand of debate and conjecture. In 1865 another local geologist, George Dowker, published a map of the Wantsum channel to accompany the results of excavations that he had carried out on behalf of the Kent Archaeological Society at Richborough (Dowker 1865). The channel is shown with the tidal flow from the north mouth filling a lagoon behind the Stonar spit, with two outlets at the eastern mouth, one at the tip of the Ebbsfleet peninsula and one between Stonar and Sandwich. This map implied that the Stonar Bank pre-dated the Roman period and that the Wantsum channel had two openings, one at the northern end between the shingle bank and the Ebbsfleet peninsula, as well as at the current position near Sandwich (*15*).

Dowker returned to the theme of the development of the Wantsum channel in an article published in 1897 examining the evidence for the geographical location of the landing place of St Augustine in his mission to the Anglo-Saxons of 597 (Dowker 1897). Popular tradition held that the site was on, or near, the spit extending from the southern edge of Thanet where, since at least the middle of the eighteenth century, a farm had been named Ebbsfleet (Lewis 1736; Pl II). In the article Dowker produced the earliest systematic analysis of the geography and geology of the Wantsum channel in relation to its use as a port in the Roman and Saxon periods. His critical paper highlighted the limitations of the historical literature that had attempted to identify the actual location of Ebbsfleet, the supposed landing place of so many important historical figures. He regarded the historical sources as vague and found much of the analysis to be based on a circular process of cross-quotation between the established tradition and the authority of other writers who reinforced the tradition by placing their narratives within the geography of the modern period.

Dowker could find no convincing evidence that the location of Ebbsfleet in his day had any claim to historical significance (1897, 128). Having examined all of the sources, he concluded that in all the accounts he had read of the location of Ebbsfleet, the meagre historical facts had been supplemented with the authors' own views regarding the physical changes that had taken place on the coastline. He was sceptical about the results:

A river or the sea? The Wantsum divide

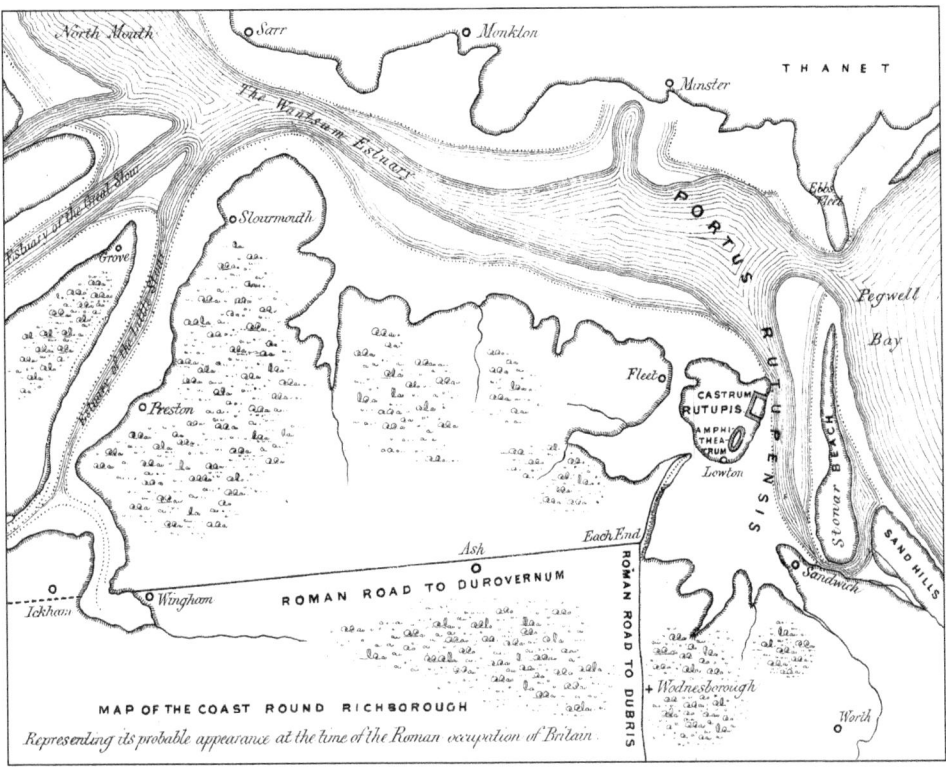

15 George Dowker's map of the coast around Richborough from *Archaeologia Cantiana* 1865

It must strike every one who reads any modern account of Ebbsfleet how all the writers draw their conclusions from the supposed configurations of the county in early times [i.e. from historical sources, Bede etc.] and as far as I am able to learn they possessed very small ability to comprehend geographical and physical forces. I need not repeat instances, for they appear in all the writers of the last, and some even of this century.

Previous attempts to show the Wantsum as a wide sea channel open from Cliffsend in Thanet as far Deal, were traced to a map that had been added to Battely's study of Richborough, *Antiquitates Rutupinae*, published in 1745; the map had been inserted after Battely's death and was even contradictory to his own text. Landscape features (such as the islands of Eocene sands in the channel) that presented well above sea level in Roman times had been ignored; the map simply left out the towns of Sandwich and Stonar presuming that they would have been below sea level in the Roman period. The shingle spits at Stonar and Sandwich Bay equally were not present on the map. This map was copied by several other later histories including Hasted's Kent history (Hasted 1800).

George Dowker was forced to the conclusion that examination of the physical aspects of the landscape was the only way to progress further with the question. Dowker had access to good-quality Ordnance Survey maps of the area on which he was able to plot the landscape and archaeological sites to demonstrate that the schematic mapping of the past had diminished or exaggerated geographical aspects of the Wantsum. Dowker also dismissed the possibility that sea levels had fallen since the Roman period; this was proved to his satisfaction by the fact that Roman building foundations were encountered in the Railway cutting at the southern end of Richborough Island not far above the present level of the Stour (Dowker 1897; Roach Smith 1850).

While carrying out a thorough survey of the area in the 1890s, Dowker was informed that excavations near the beach at Cliffsend had revealed shingle below the mud laid over Pegwell Bay. Dowker himself produced evidence of a legal action taken by the Abbot of St Augustine against the men of Sandwich for digging up material from his wall between Stonar and Cliffsend and taking it away in boats. He used this to show that the Stonar Bank shingle was continuous to Cliffsend where the Sandwich people had dug up the flints as a common right (Dowker 1878). In fact, the modern geological survey map shows shingle deposits extending in a thin band from Cliffsend, with a large spread south and east of the tip of the Ebbsfleet peninsula, cut through by the present outlet of the Stour.

Dowker believed that in the Roman period, and in the time of St Augustine (that was the subject of his article), the Wantsum channel had been a tidal estuary not greatly different in extent to the Stour in his own day except that it was open to the scour of the predominant west to east flow of the tides. The Stonar spit had already formed by the Roman period and acted as a shield from the sea creating a tidal backwater or lagoon west of the spit with the forts and town at Richborough located strategically at the entrance (Dowker 1897, 131). The extent of the highest tides was traced over the flat plane of the marshes where the shallows and mud flats would have been deposited.

> Such an estuary as I have pictured must have, in the Roman period, presented at low tide a series of mud-flats on either side of a main river, which were only covered by water at high tide, and some portions of it only at spring tides. Through these mud-flats the spring water from the chalk hills of Thanet would find their way into the main river as fleets.

The dating of the formation of the Stonar spit is significant as it has a bearing on the extent to which the southern mouth of the Wantsum was open to the sea at any point in time.

It is difficult to examine the Stonar Bank by observation at present as considerable change has taken place in the area since the survey carried out by Dowker. Shingle from Stonar Bank was extracted on a huge scale in the late nineteenth and early twentieth century. In 1895 aggregate was excavated for the concrete blocks used to build an extension to Dover Harbour. Five thousand to six thousand cubic yards of material were removed each week for the works. More ballast was extracted in the inter-war years and during the Second World War. In the post-war period Stonar shingle was exported to the Staffordshire potteries to be ground up for inclusion as a temper in the clay for making fine china. Pits were dug into Boxlees and Weatherlees hills in the Wantsum channel for building-sand in the early twentieth century and sand was extracted from a quarry on the southern side of the hill where Richborough castle is located (Osborne-

White 1928). Plans to build a port on the Stour near Ebbsfleet between 1911 and 1913 were requisitioned by the Royal Engineers Inland Water Transport Section on the outbreak of the First World War in 1914 and the site was developed as a port for the British Army. Transport barges utilised the French canal network to supply the forward battle areas of the Western Front. Shipyards, salvage yards, seaplane depots and in later years a huge new wharf to accommodate a train ferry were constructed. Extensive marshalling yards and miles of new railway tracks were laid to link to the local railway network. At the mouth of the Stour the New Wharf was cut through the meanders at the eastern end of the Stour creating a deep-water channel sufficient for the barges and train ferry. This regular, straight channel can be seen on modern mapping of the area obscuring the natural arrangements of the local landscape.

Considerable evidence was presented by George Dowker that the broad shingle outcrop of Great Stonar at the southern end of the spit was occupied during the Roman period. He cited the record on the 6in ordnance map of the discovery of 'Roman, coins, urns, swords, axes, portions of armour, and human remains' found behind the present residence at Stonar. The large-scale Ordnance Survey map of 1877 locates these finds just east of Stonar House but is not entirely clear from what authority the location of these finds were marked. The map was published before the start of extraction of shingle from the Stonar Bank for the construction of Dover Harbour. A workman involved in the mining for the Dover Harbour works had reported that he had witnessed the discovery of much pottery and some human bones 'as if a burial ground had been penetrated'. The workman also stated that, in a smaller area being worked by another company, a 'Roman Galley' had been found with timbers shaped with an adze. Workmen had tried to drag it out with a crane and it had broken up (Pierce 1939). A group monitoring the excavation during the extraction process found further Roman material within the upper deposits of the Stonar shingle (Hardman and Stebbing 1942), relating them to the finds recorded by the Ordnance Survey:

> Proof of the Roman occupation of Stonor [sic] seems clear by the recovery of various fragments of brick and tile, Neidermendig-Lava querns, a 4in. section of a white marble shaft, 3 in dia., with a drilled hole, and part of a turned Purbeck-merble bowl. It seems unlikely that these scraps were carted from the Roman site at Richborough, especially as the 6 in. Ordnance Survey marks the site of Roman remains round and about Stonar House.

More recent discoveries have confirmed that the Wantsum channel did not exceed the limits of the present level of the alluvium in the Roman period. A Romano-British cremation was discovered on Boxlees Hill, one of the Eocene outcrops in the Wantsum channel south of Minster (Coy 1965). The excavation of an area on the south-western edge of Weatherlees Hill for a railway to carry sand extracted from the hill to the Stonar port, exposed a large number of burials; unfortunately no dating evidence was recorded for them (Trust for Thanet Archaeology SMR 601).

Writing of their excavations at Stonar in the 1940s, Hardman and Stebbing revived the idea, originally presented by Dowker, that the Wantsum had formerly had two entrances at the north and south ends of the shingle (Hardman and Stebbing 1940, 1941 & 1942). In an essay on the landscape context of the Roman settlements at Richborough in relation to the Wantsum channel in 1968, Sonia Hawkes also accepted the idea of the two outlets in the south mouth:

> In the Roman period, evidently, the Wantsum was in some state intermediate between sea channel and marsh. The origin and date of the formation of Stonar beach has long been disputed, but it is generally agreed that it had come into existence before Roman times ... it is likely that there were then two entrances into the east mouth: one around the north of Stonar bank, the other around the southern end opposite Sandwich, where the Stour flows out today. The existence of a northern entrance is suggested by the fact that even today the Stour flows steadily towards Ebbsfleet only to be deflected south very sharply by the shingle bar.

Since Dowker's publication, little further work has been done to survey the actual limits of the Wantsum channel. Recent studies have continued to debate the historical sources without producing any consensus. Hawkes' summary has remained influential and there has been little attempt to reconcile the presumption of the pre-Roman formation of the Stonar shingle to the geography of the Wantsum channel in the prehistoric period in which it must have formed.

In recent years a number of studies have returned to the implication that the Wantsum was a wide sea channel. Based on his experience of the extreme erosion of the Saxon Shore fort at Reculver, Brian Philp published two maps reconstructing the eastern edge of Richborough Island in AD 43 and AD 120 where the eroded parts of the fort on the heights are projected to match the dimensions of classical fort layouts (Philp 2002). This model places the conjectured Roman harbour on a shoreline in the region of 600m from the present cliff face, west of the forts, and suggests that the extensive erosion of the islands was a post-Roman process. A map published to accompany the report on excavations at Reculver accepts the presence of only a single southern mouth to the Wantsum, showing the Ebbsfleet peninsula extended, presumably by the Stonar shingle, to a point south of the Richborough fort (Philp 2005).

The most recent restatement of the evidence for the Wantsum sea channel by Dr David Perkins has also argued in defence of the case for a wide Wantsum estuary whose waves were responsible for the post-Roman erosion of the fort at Richborough (Perkins 2007). On the basis of the rich archaeological discoveries made on the farm that bears the name Ebbsfleet in the present day, an argument was made to recognise the role of that location in Thanet's history as a seaport.

While the geography of the Wantsum in the Roman period has been debated, its development in the earliest prehistoric period has been considered only rarely. Often the assumed state of the Wantsum channel in the Roman period has been projected into earlier times, exaggerating the isolation of Thanet in prehistory. To reconstruct the features that existed in the prehistoric period, the chronological development of the marine processes that formed the Wantsum channel need to be considered. At the end of the most rapid phase of sea level rise 8000 years ago, Thanet was part of a larger chalk promontory between the Thames and the English Channel. At the outer limits of the coastline, the sea caused irregular erosion patterns as it infiltrated valley networks in the chalk, forming bays and creeks. As the sea infiltrated valley networks in the chalk at the outer edge of the promontory, it eroded the valleys into bays and creeks.

The Wantsum channel was formed as the sea penetrated two components of the periglacial drainage network that was cut through the Eocene deposits within the syncline on the northern and eastern side of the promontory. Two dendritic networks were seperated by the chalk ridge between Monkton and Sarre. Each network had a separate system of lateral valleys feeding central spine valleys, one system draining to the east and the other to the north. The northern route was used by the Stour and the springs on the north-western side of the valley to reach the Thames. In the eastern component elements of a palaeochannel, likely to be the course of the spine valley, has been traced south-west of Weatherlees Hill, north-east of Richborough and below the shingle at the southern end of Stonar, where it had been scoured to the level of chalk (British Geological Survey; Robinson & Cloet 1957; Corcoran 2003; Osborne White 1928). The pattern of the lateral drainage valleys indicates that the channel turned toward the south, reinforcing the evidence for the feature between Weatherlees and Stonar. The level of the base of the channel was 12m below Ordnance Datum and it was up to 100m wide. A water course, collecting the streams draining from the springs on the sides of the valley, may have run through the base, discharging into the English Channel somewhere east of the present Pegwell Bay. The valleys at the base of the drainage networks would have been the first to be infiltrated as the sea rose at a slower rate in the later Mesolithic period. The inlet at the base of the channel might have been at a bay in the Eocene sand much further to the south-east and the tidal effects may have been visible at least as far as Weatherlees, scouring the channels into creeks at the northern and eastern sides of the promontory (Devoy 1979).

Note that in the following series of illustrations of the proposed sequence of development of the Wantsum channel, the coastline is conjectural and not intended to represent a developed model of the topography of the region at any particular period (16).

The latest erosion interface in the Eocene deposits on the southern side can be seen to stretch in a broad irregular line between Deal and Ramsgate. The erosion of the Ebbsfleet peninsula, a finger of Thanet Beds sand extending south from the Isle of Thanet, ceased at a relatively early date, leaving an angular interface continuous from Pegwell to the area south of Cliffsend. Here the soft loess and Eocene deposits in the valley eroded at a faster rate than the chalk at Pegwell, producing a bay with a steep sand cliff. If they were produced by wave action, it is likely that the cliffs at Richborough were formed in this period, when the site was on the shore of the east creek, and were already part of the landscape when the Romans arrived (17).

The storm erosion in the bay would have been strongest before the shingle beach of Stonar Bank developed sufficiently to provide a barrier against the direct effect of the waves. The most detailed study published on the formation of the Stonar shingle spit concluded that it formed as a bay bar when an offshore bank of shingle migrated steadily west-south-west. It was then driven onshore by the dominant south-westerly winds

The Isle of Thanet – from Prehistory to the Norman Conquest

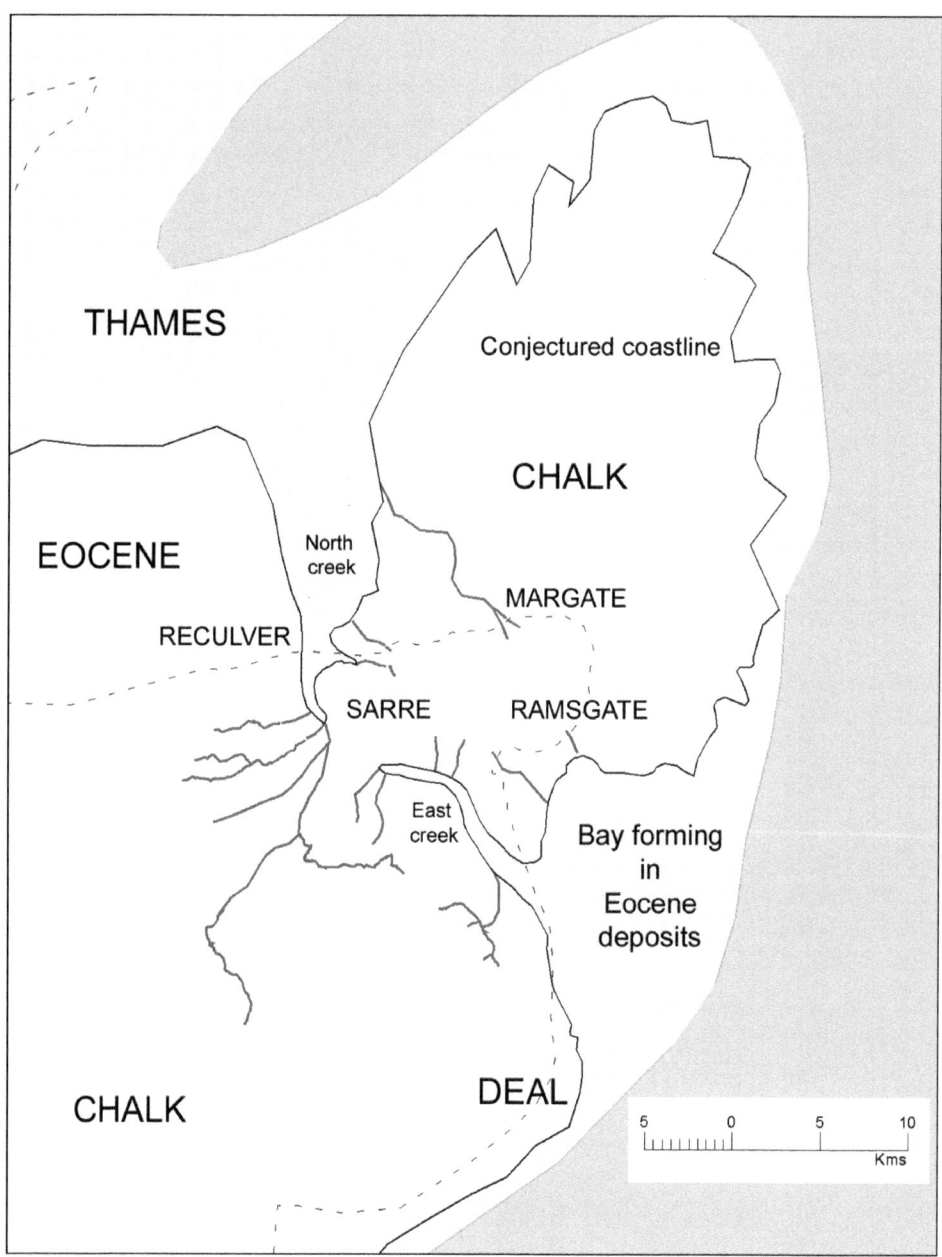

16 Conjectural reconstruction of the Thanet promontory in the Late Mesolithic Period, based on Coles, B.J. 1998

A river or the sea? The Wantsum divide

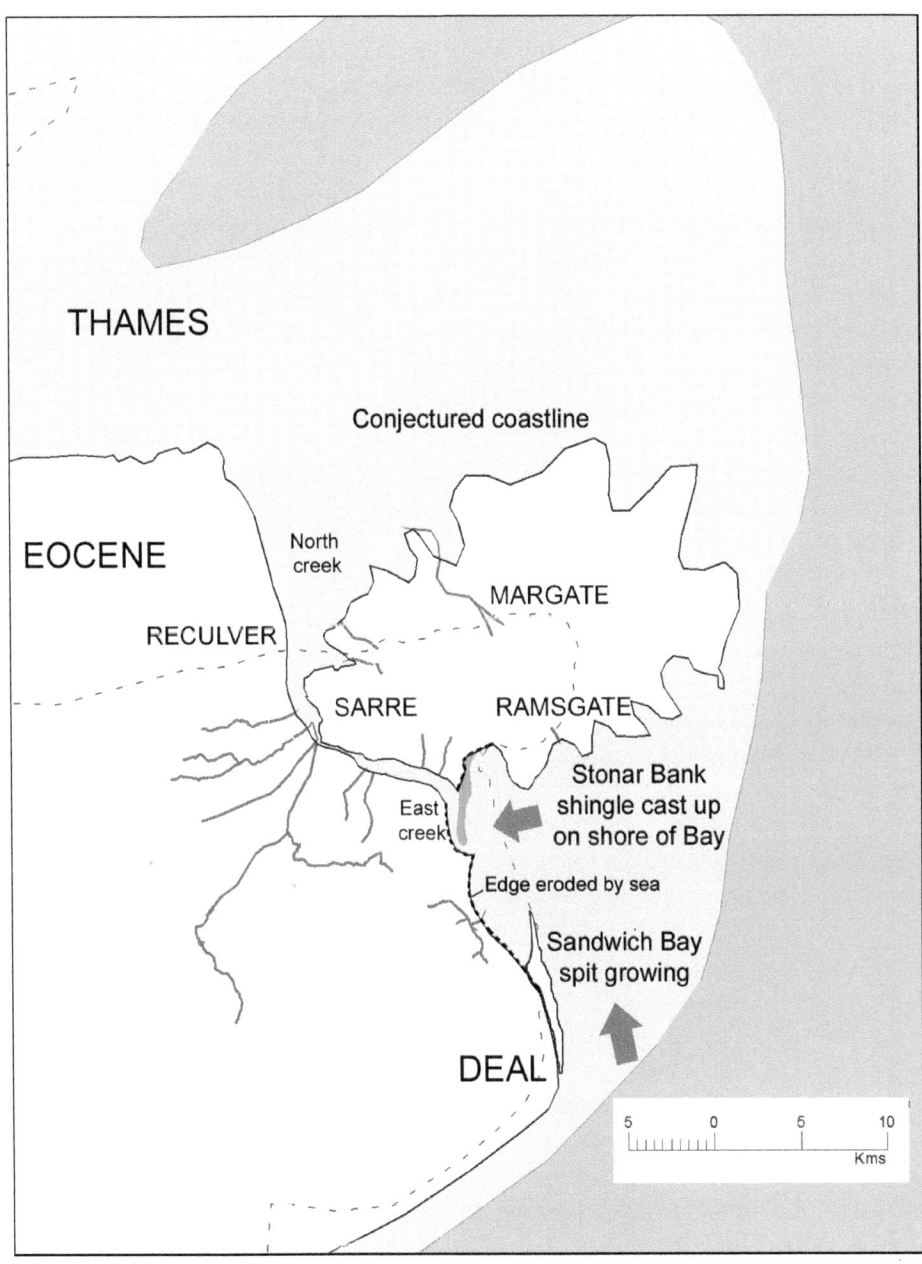

17 Conjectural reconstruction of the development of coastal features in the Early Bronze Age, based on Coles, B.J. 1998

which had greater fetch to generate powerful storm waves than the prevailing winds (Robinson and Cloet 1953). The flints in the Stonar Bank came from a variety of sources and were probably derived from an offshore bank of glacial debris. The deep channel of the spine valley filled with the earliest and most substantial shingle deposit. The remaining material built up in thinner layers from south to north as far as Cliffsend, where the shelter of the Isle of Thanet reduced the wave-building force of the wind and less shingle accumulated.

Only a speculative chronology was proposed by Robinson and Cloet's study of the Stonar Bank, suggesting that it had a pre-Roman but not a pre-Neolithic dating (Robinson and Cloet 1953). The present depth of the sea at the submerged mouth of the syncline between Ramsgate and Deal is around 4.18m below Ordnance Datum, similar to the average level of the interface between alluvium and Eocene material in the base of the cross section through the valley between Richborough and Ebbsfleet (British Geological Survey, Robinson & Cloet 1953; Admiralty Chart Data 1993). The historically significant point in both processes is the moment at which the mean sea level and the energy of south-westerly storm waves were sufficient to move the stones into their position in the mouth of the bay to form the Stonar spit. The lighter sand of the Sandwich Bay spit could be moved by normal tidal waves. The formation of the bay at the mouth of the channel by wave erosion would have taken place when the sea reached a mean level of the order of 4-5m below Ordnance Datum, estimated to be between 3000 and 1800 BC. Allowing for a slight regression at the beginning of the time range, a date in the Early Bronze Age after 2000 BC would be likely for the particular combination of sufficient sea level and storm wave energy to have cast up the shingle beaches (Devoy 1979). The Lydden valley, south-east of Sandwich, is also the product of water erosion under periglacial conditions cutting through the interface between the sloping chalk downs and the Eocene deposits in the syncline. Finds associated with an extensive buried land surface in the valley have shown that the area was dry land habitable until at least 2000 BC (Halliwell & Parfitt 1985). A radiocarbon date from a hearth at Hacklinge produced an even later date suggesting that the area was not submerged until 1380-1260 cal BC. This valley would have been inundated by the same process that was taking place at the mouth of the Wantsum channel. These sites are good indicators of the chronological progress of the inundation of the periglacial valleys.

In the modern period the tidal cycle at either end of the Wantsum channel is slightly out of phase, with the tides at Ramsgate slightly higher than at Herne Bay on the flood and the reverse on the ebb. The harmonious differences in sea level between either inlet would have encouraged tidal flows through the channel when it was fully open. In flood, the tide in the Wantsum would flow toward the north mouth; during the ebb, the flow would be toward the eastern entrance. At Spring tides, the differential between the northern mouth and the east has been shown to be greater, creating a stronger flow in both directions but with the eastward flow strongest and most sustained. At neap tides the flows would be weaker but still active (Grainge 2007). Assuming that the tidal differentials were similar in this very early period, when the two components of the channel eventually met, they were linked by a tidal system that promoted distinct flows through the channel that scoured it of debris and eroded a wider channel through the hard sands below (*18*).

The channel would have been constricted and shallowest at the intersection between the components at Sarre. The effects on the flow of water through this gap are difficult to estimate but this area was a key point in the tidal system. John Lewis noted that although the tides were broadly harmonious at either end of the channel, slight phase differences in tides were manifested as turbulence at Sarre (Lewis 1736). Alluvium from the Thames estuary would have been deposited on the sides and outflow of the southern component by the dominant flow in that direction. When the strong flows were active in the earliest period they would have exited from the deep channel near the present location of Sandwich following the existing deep periglacial channel.

The Sandwich Bay spit was created by longshore drift bringing sand south to north under the influence of the prevailing coastal currents. As it lengthened, low-lying areas to the west were filled with wind-blown sand, forming large dunes in places. The formation of the two shingle deposits at Sandwich and Stonar probably commenced simultaneously, with each driven by the wind and tidal conditions favourable to its formation process (*19*).

The Sandwich Bay spit appears to have advanced rapidly, leaving fossil beaches and a consolidated area behind it. At Dickson's Corner, close to the present-day shoreline, considerable evidence of a Roman settlement were encountered including clay and pebble floors, occupation deposits and a significant assemblage of pottery indicating an established settlement on the sand deposits (Parfitt 2000). A hoard of Roman coins and other Roman material were found in the nineteenth century between Sandown and Sandwich (Dowker 1897) and further Roman finds have been recovered recently, by test pitting and excavation, from the Sandown area east of the town (Parfitt 2006).

As the sand spit progressed north from its Roman shoreline east of Sandwich, the mouth of the Wantsum channel was pushed further north. Eventually the outlet was turned back on itself creating the lower eastern portion of the loop that it follows today (Robinson & Cloet 1957). As the wave energy driving the spit pushed the sand forward, alluvium from the channel would have settled on the inner edge consolidating the material and forcing the tidal outlet further north.

The cutting of the New Wharf for Stonar Port in the First World War established the present outflow of the Stour through Pegwell Bay, but meanders and loops are visible in early mapping. It is possible that the migration of the outflow northwards gradually reduced the energy of the tidal flow through the Wantsum to a crisis point where the flow was slack enough to deposit large amounts of debris within the channel. Other agencies, such as the Spanish ship sunk in the haven, would have compromised the system further. The northward progress of the Sandwich Bay spit eventually isolated the Stonar shingle from the sea leaving its southern ends stranded between the outlet and the spit (*20*).

It is likely that the Wantsum was never a very wide channel; the central stream was served by a number of fleets and creeks formed by the intersection of periglacial valleys and the outflow of spring-fed streams that formed the focus of settlement and trading activity. Although land reclamation was advanced in the earlier medieval period, this was not the primary cause of the failure of the stream. It is very likely that the Wantsum was at its deepest between the Roman and late Anglo-Saxon periods. Analysis of the

The Isle of Thanet – from Prehistory to the Norman Conquest

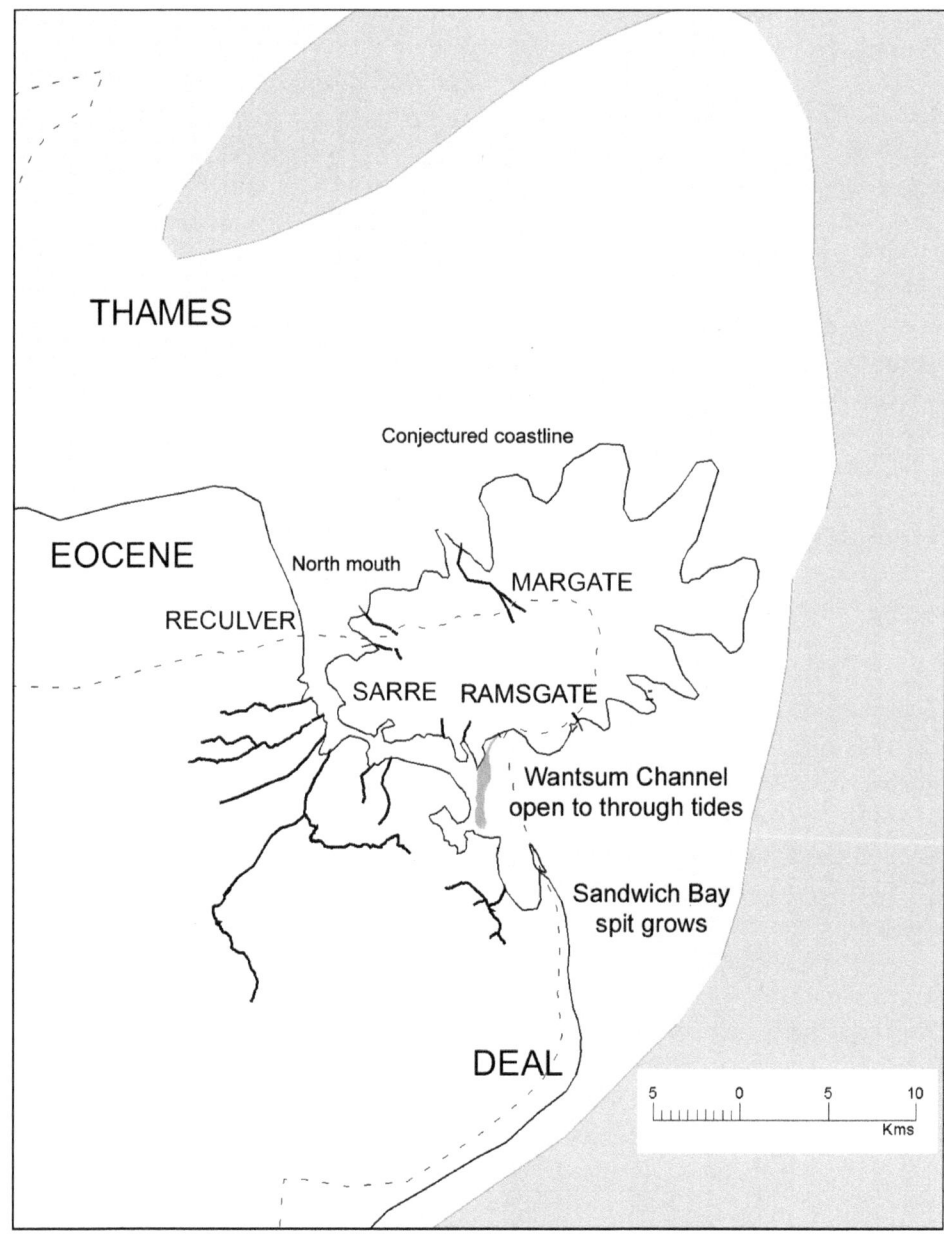

18 Conjectural reconstruction of the coastline as the Wantsum channel tidal system became established, based on Coles, B.J. 1998

A river or the sea? The Wantsum divide

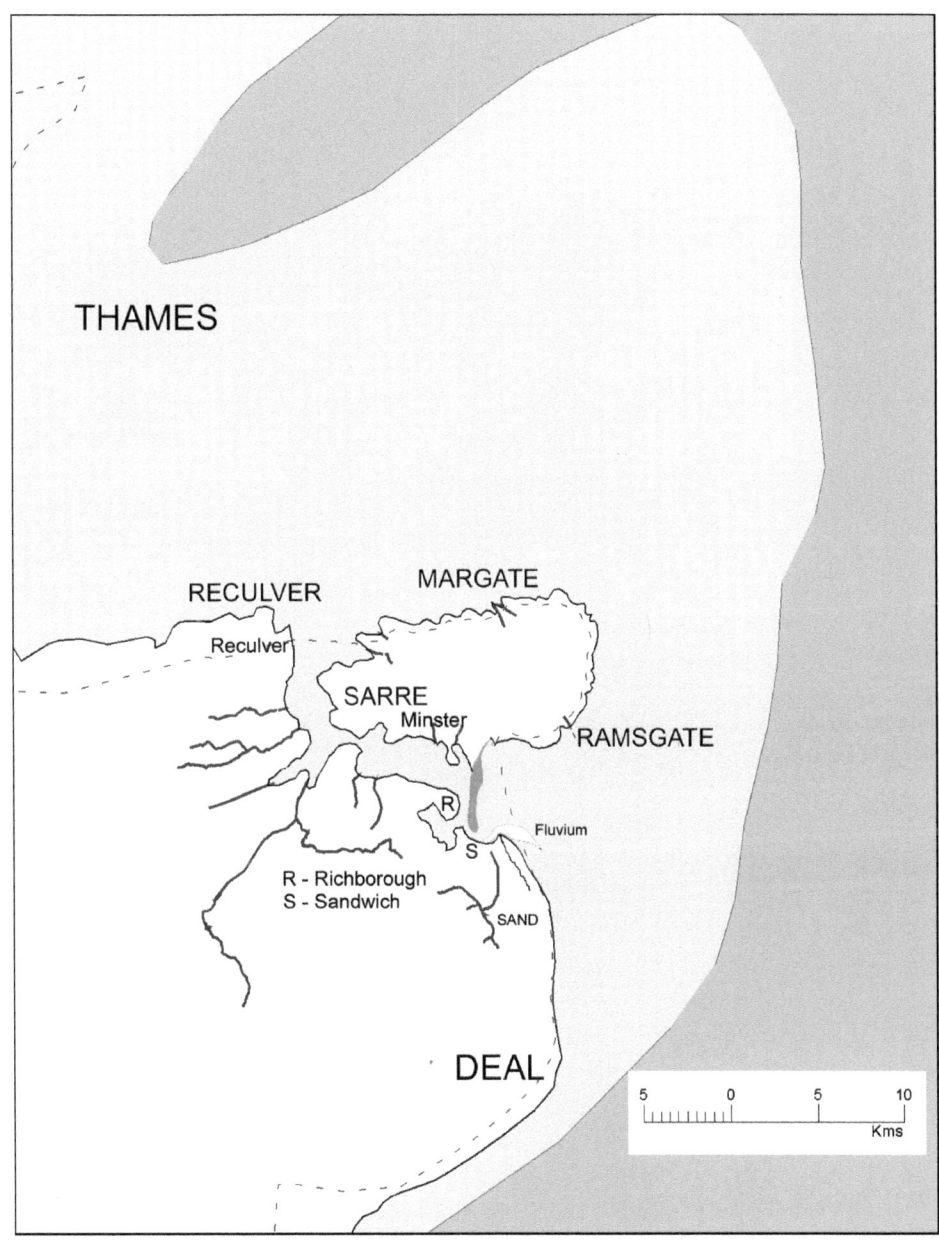

19 Conjectural reconstruction of the coastline of the Isle of Thanet in the Roman period. © *Trust for Thanet Archaeology*

The Isle of Thanet – from Prehistory to the Norman Conquest

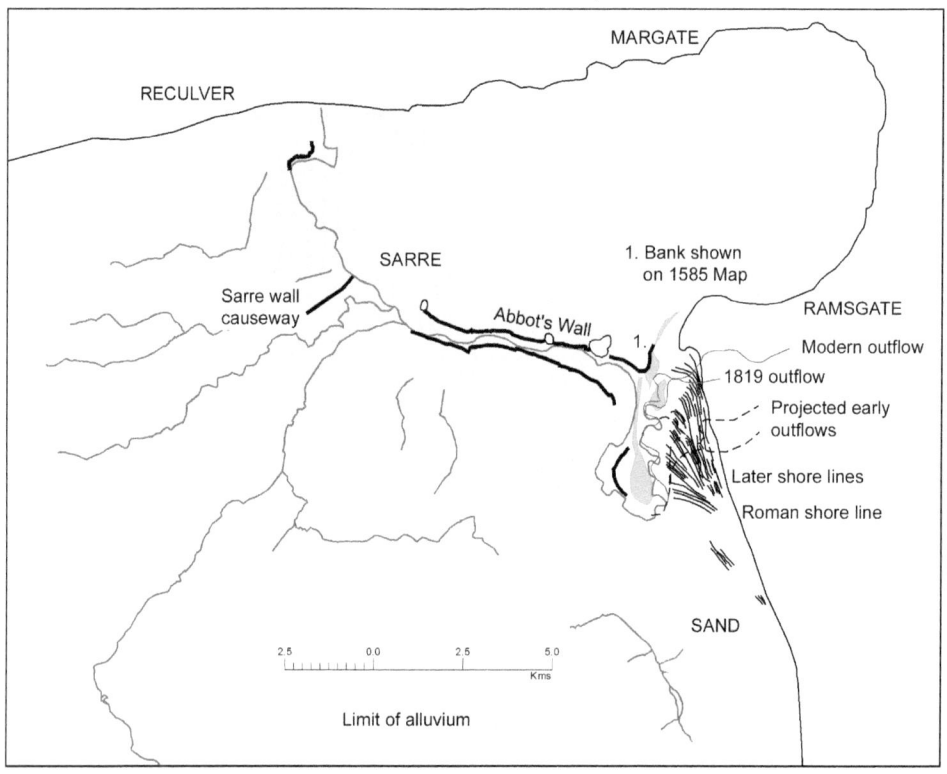

20 Post-medieval development of the course of the Stour, the Wantsum Channel and the Deal spit. © *Trust for Thanet Archaeology*

topography of the area, recorded by the Shuttle Radar Topography Mission (SRTM), has established the limits of the alluvial plane of the Wantsum at a level of approximately 1.5m above Ordnance Datum, establishing the maximum extent of the Wantsum channel reached at any point in its history. For whatever reason, the blocking of the narrow connection between the northern and eastern elements of the Wantsum caused the tidal scour to fail and the central channel to fill with silt. The sudden accumulation of debris in this area, recorded in the late fifteenth century, separated the two components and isolated the eastern part from the force of the scouring tide from the Thames estuary. The rapid collapse of the tidal system followed and the river became heavy with sand and alluvium. Within a relatively short period the process of reclamation that had been in operation since the eleventh century was advanced and the Wantsum channel became a marshy river valley drained to provide additional pasture. Although the various streams and the Great and Little Stour continued to flow through the estuary, the Wantsum ceased to be a navigable route for larger ships between the English Channel and the Thames.

4

WHAT CAME BEFORE? TRACES OF THE EARLIEST HUMAN SETTLEMENT

The scouring of the surface of the chalk on Thanet by periglacial processes generally removed the oldest deposits of geological material where evidence of human settlement at warmer periods during the Ice Age, might have been found. Palaeolithic artefacts have been found in a similar landscape on the chalk downlands around Dover and Deal (Parfitt *et al* 1996). Palaeolithic material in eastern Kent has generally been found residually in solifluction deposits and on patches of clay-with-flints geology. No formal assessment of the potential for the survival of deposits containing Palaeolithic material has been carried out on the Isle of Thanet. Few large-scale development projects have been carried out that have sampled the solifluction deposits in the periglacial valleys to a significant depth, or provided transects of the valleys. There are few finds on Thanet in comparison to the thousands of artefacts that have been found in the ancient river gravel beds in north-west Kent, nevertheless a few artefacts have been found in remnant pockets of geology on the upper plateau and in the deposits at the base of some of the periglacial valleys. This is in defiance of overwhelming odds given the incredible attrition of the land surfaces that once existed in the area.

Occasionally, exposures of the solifluction deposits have revealed artefacts of animal and human occupation from the Ice Age, indicating that a few remnants of the earliest human occupation of the area may yet be found, along with relics of the fauna of the warm periods between glaciations. The development of the town of Ramsgate over 'Coombe Rock', as the solifluction deposits are known, at the intersection of five dry valleys, seems to have exposed some of these earliest layers. George Fairholme (1837, 243), who studied the geological formation of the Isle of Thanet in the early nineteenth century, recorded that he had found ancient animal remains in a valley bottom. He used the term 'diluvium' from his assertion that they were relics of the Biblical flood:

> I have in my possession, a grinder and other bones of an Asiatic elephant, or Mammoth, which was found in this diluvium, in digging the cellar of a house in King Street Ramsgate.

Another Ramsgate observer, Captain Kennet B. Martin (1857, 84), described the deposits that were encountered in the profile of the valley when the new harbour was built at Ramsgate. The sequence he described was:

> two feet vegetable earth, one to three feet of loose boulders and shingle being a marine deposit, two feet sea sand, containing many human skeletons and animal bones ... then a substratum of stiff clay to a depth of thirty feet from the surface and deposited upon the chalk, which in this basin contains the fossil remains of the mammoth. These also rest below the clay immediately upon the chalk. Specimens of them are in my possession.

Two Lower Palaeolithic handaxes in museums at Bexley and Canterbury are recorded as finds from Ramsgate but nothing further is known of the context of their discovery. In comparison to the discovery of tools numbered in the thousands on some of the river gravel terraces further west in Kent (Scott 2004), only nine Lower Palaeolithic handaxes have been found in Thanet (*21*). No flakes or flake tools have yet been found and no tools from later periods are known (*22*).

Where the find spots of handaxes are known from archaeological sites on Thanet, they have usually been found reused within later deposits exposed on modern development sites. Handaxes have been found in later hut floors or working areas of Iron Age or Roman date at Westwood, Ramsgate and at North Foreland, Broadstairs (Perkins 1999b; Biggs 1972). Occasionally the tools have been derived from the surface of clay-with-flints, or a periglacial feature, such as at Westwood, Broadstairs (Perkins 1999a, 373; 2000a, 373). There are possibly some further small remaining deposits of the clay-with-flints geology where Palaeolithic material might be found, however the clay deposit is the product of dissolving chalk geology and the tools would not necessarily be related to the levels where occupation took place. The tools that have a find spot recorded have almost all been recovered from the intersections of dry valleys with Thanet's central plateau, possibly preserved within the upper reaches of the solifluction deposits which are being exposed by plough erosion. One axe from St Mildred's Bay, Westgate, may have been associated with deep deposits in a periglacial valley now partly eroded by the sea (Trust for Thanet Archaeology archives).

These few artefacts that we have are all of the Lower Palaeolithic, from 500-250,000 years ago, made by hominids of the *Homo Sapiens Hiedelbergensis* species and not the direct ancestors of modern humans. The tools and animal bones were deposited in an unrecognisable landscape and climate that have little relationship with the geography of the Isle of Thanet as we understand it today, but serve as a reminder of the relatively recent origin of our familiar surroundings.

The evidence for the return of human occupation to the area at the beginning of the present warm period, around 10,000 years ago, (Holocene) is equally sparse. Models of the Mesolithic settlement of Britain have depended on recreating the geological and environmental conditions of the post-glacial period. The sparse artefact assemblages that are encountered are inserted into niches in the hypothetical ecological systems that are proposed. Human occupation is taken to be integrated with these natural systems,

What came before? Traces of the earliest human settlement

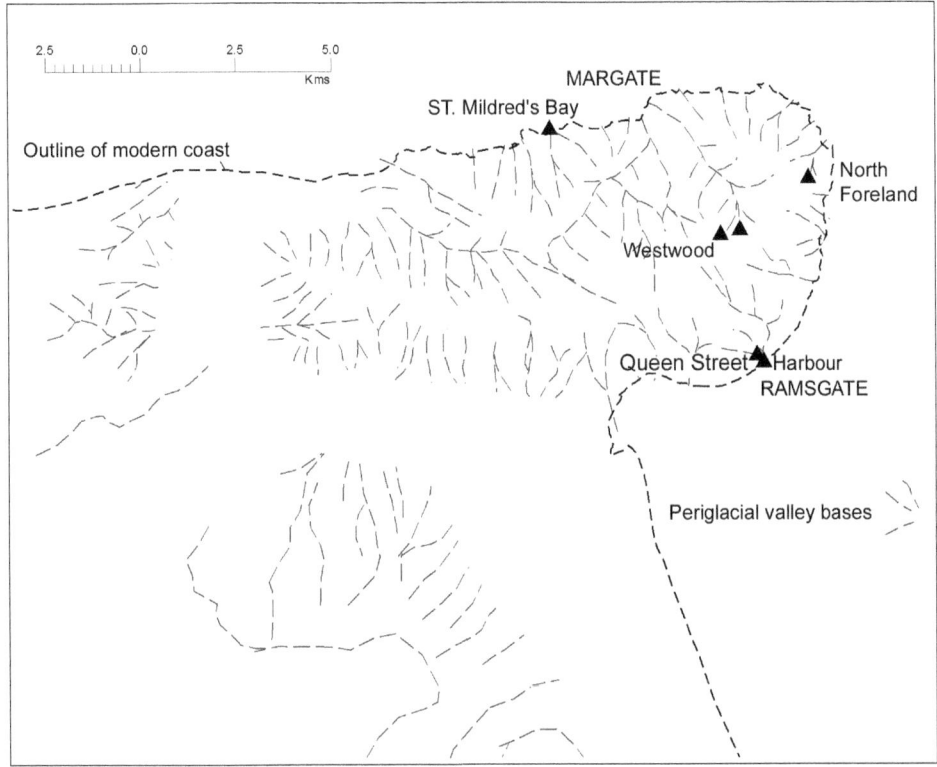

21 Location of Palaeolithic handaxe finds. © *Trust for Thanet Archaeology*

responding to the ebb and flow of the seasons in the search for adequate nutrition and resources to sustain their communities. With Britain still part of the European landmass in the Early Mesolithic it is difficult to separate a small locale such as Thanet from the broader landscape. The geographical range of wild animals and the human groups that followed them over the land would have been extensive, with broad sweeps of seasonal migrations and more varied zones in which to search for natural resources. These ranges would have decreased as the retreating ice caused sea levels to rise (Coles 1998).

As the Doggerland area between Britain and Europe was finally submerged around 6500 BC, the chalk mass of Thanet would have presented as an isolated upland area scarred by dry valleys. Although much of the area that was above the sea has been subsequently lost, the highest parts would have been the plateau and ridge that survive within the limits of the Isle of Thanet in the present day. Where the cliffs are today, the valleys would have continued their natural undulating curvature of dips and saddles to a coastal fringe some kilometres away. As the climate warmed and flora and fauna stabilised the area, the valleys would have been filled with forests and herbs growing in the deep loess deposits. To the north and east the Thames and the English Channel flowed at much lower elevations than today, extending the drainage of the glacial valleys

22 Four Acheulian handaxes from sites in Thanet. © *Trust for Thanet Archaeology*

What came before? Traces of the earliest human settlement

of the Thanet upland, with the coastal and estuarine fringes located far from the modern limits of Thanet. The chalk of the steepest valley sides and scarp of the central ridge would have been vulnerable to erosion by frost and landslips, areas with reduced tree cover caused by these processes may have formed accessible routes, allowing animals and humans to reach the high ground. The beds of springs draining the chalk may have provided cleared routes to the uplands and provided fresh water for human and animal alike. The deep glacial spine valleys would have provided access between the uplands and the coastal littoral environments of the Thames and the English Channel estuaries.

It is possible to imagine a journey through this landscape from the low chalk cliffs at the coast along the edge of a creek penetrating the dense deciduous woodland, following one of the streams up the intersecting valley, with light penetrating from the linear gaps at the stream edges where tree cover could not establish in the crumbling chalk face. The top of the valley opened out into flat plateau with sparser tree cover, where, on the ridges along the edges, the canopies of the trees in the hollow of the syncline below, could be seen falling back to the entrance of the creek and the sea beyond.

With a society so intimately dependent on the natural environment we can expect to find only fragile traces of Mesolithic occupation in such a small sample area. Environmental conditions in the past are difficult to detect archaeologically and providing a context for the material we do find presents many difficulties; the Mesolithic period has not been subject to systematic fieldwork in Thanet. Mesolithic settlement on Thanet will post-date the loess fills of the periglacial valleys, however where the upper fills have been reworked some artefacts may have survived later attrition from intensive agricultural activity. It is likely that only flint tools would survive and no structures or organic deposits. The distribution and geographical context of the few artefacts that are known suggests that areas of occupation might be identified in those parts of the island where relics of the post-glacial natural environments have been protected from later destruction. There is significant potential for the survival of early prehistoric material in the upper stratigraphy of the periglacial valleys where soil horizons have been sealed by hillwash and in areas sealed by alluvium, on the southern fringe of the syncline on the southern edge of Thanet (23).

The area between Cliffsend and Pegwell provides us with one of the longest sequences of settlement in Thanet. The present bay represents the truncated terminal of a wide gap formed by the intersection of three periglacial valleys that would have given access to the English Channel coast on the lower slopes of the gap. Erosion by the sea has exposed a geological section up to 4m high through Eocene sands and the periglacial loess. A thin black organic deposit lying over the loess and sealed by hillwash has been interpreted as a soil that formed under woodland in the hollow of the valley in the Mesolithic period. Although radiocarbon dated to 6120 +/- 250 years BP, the deposits were seen as the result of the formation of the soil under forest cover in the period between 5000 BC and 3000 BC, after which the soil was buried by hillwash (Weir *et al* 1971, 135). A pollen sample from an organic deposit in a lateral periglacial valley between Weatherlees and Ebbsfleet gives an indication of the diversity of the post-glacial forest cover in its mature state, dominated by Oak and Hazel, with Lime, Ash and Elm represented among other

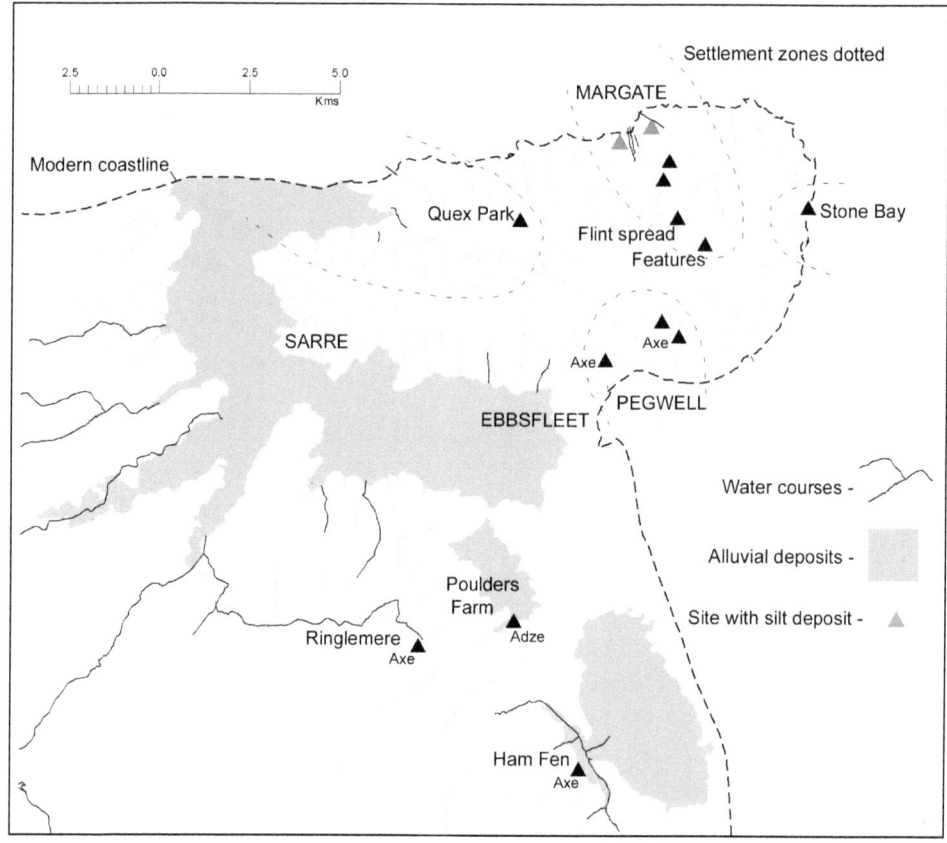

23 Location of Mesolithic finds in the Thanet and Wantsum region. © *Trust for Thanet Archaeology*

low-growing trees and shrubs including Viburnum, Buckthorn, Birches and some grasses (Hearne *et al* 1995). Molluscs from the deposit favoured damp woodland conditions and indicated an environment undisturbed by human activity. If the Middle Neolithic radiocarbon date of 3600-3100 cal BC for the material is accurate (Cook *et al* 1995, 345) then it has been suggested this forest may have been undisturbed, perhaps until salt marshes developed in the growing creek before the Bronze Age.

There is good potential for the survival of early land surfaces within the lateral valleys at the base of the central chalk ridge between Ebbsfleet and Sarre, where as George Fairholme (1837, 225) noted that under their cover of alluvial pasture:

> ... the valleys which opened into this former shallow sea being protected by their position, from the effects of wind and waves, universally remain to this day in the same entire forms, which they first presented, the very day they were first scooped out; while all those of precisely similar character ... but which chanced to open towards where the sea now beats with force, have been gradually cut short ...

The sample taken of the organic layers in the valley at Weatherlees indicates the potential for this material to provide information on the early environment.

Mesolithic flintwork has been found in valley sites on the east-facing coast. These include a large number of heavy flint axes and sharpening flakes sealed on a preserved land surface below peat at Ham Fen, near Finglesham, and a large adze probably recovered from a similar sealed surface under alluvium at Poulders Farm, north-west of Sandwich (Halliwell *et al* 1983; Ogilvie 1983). These sites tend to confirm that, if they survived erosion by the sea, the alluvium of the Wantsum channel sealed land surfaces active in the Mesolithic. The potential of the preservation under the alluvium of deposits in the Wantsum marshes might be compared to the process that protected the Mesolithic deposits at Starr Carr in Yorkshire and similar structured evidence may survive, although what is preserved would represent the exploitation of forests surrounding salt-water creeks rather than a fresh-water lake (Milner 2007).

Mesolithic settlement in the gap formed by several intersecting valleys at Pegwell Bay is demonstrated by discoveries of flintwork and animal bone, although not in association with any structures. Two Late Mesolithic flint-flaked axes have been found near the upper reaches of each of the valleys. Two small flints of possible Mesolithic date have been found in an excavation in the loess in the upper reaches of the eastern valley, indicating that intensive field walking might produce more material here (Birch *et al* 1987; Boast *et al* 2006b). Axes and sharpening flakes have been found at Ringlemere Farm, located in a similar upland position on the opposite side of the valley, near the source of the Durlock Stream (Parfitt *et al* 2007, 46).

Although significant quantities of Mesolithic flintwork were found in deposits on the southern edge of the Wantsum, they were heavy tools rather than the microliths taken to be one of the characteristic technologies of this period, it is possible that these reflect a particular activity in the region. Perhaps the forests here were dense and the tools represent periodic forays to obtain forest resources rather than the debris of a settlement.

A second potential zone of Mesolithic settlement is represented by three valleys that meet in a broad gap at Margate. This gap represents the terminal of a dendritic network that would have opened into the Thames estuary much further to the north. Excavations on a development site on the north-east facing slope of a valley overlooking the bay at Margate recorded a thin horizon of fine, dark, grey silt. The material was finely sorted and appeared to have been laid in a waterlogged environment, possibly in pools associated with the spring that once fed the network of 'meres' nearby that gave Margate its name (Hart & Moody 2005). No organic material was present in the deposit from which to obtain a radiocarbon date but Mesolithic and Neolithic flintwork were found within the material. A similar fine silt deposit associated with some Neolithic flintwork was encountered at another site close to Margate below the cellars of a demolished terrace on the north-east facing valley slope overlooking Margate Bay (Hart & Moody 2005). Other similar horizons, representing the earliest soil formation deposits above the loess sealed by hillwash in the later prehistoric period, may be present in more of the dry valleys and could be targeted by research fieldwork.

Flintwork, possibly of Late Mesolithic date, has been found at sites on the chalk promontory to the east of Margate, both as unstratified finds and residual material within Neolithic assemblages (Gardner & Moody 2005; Gardner & Moody 2006a). A substantial spread of Mesolithic and Neolithic flints are reported to have been recovered over a large area at the southern end of the terminal of a valley at Westwood (TSMR 270). Significant development has taken place in this locality in the last few decades and no systematic work has been carried out to assess the quantity or significance of the surviving flint scatters. To date no assemblages from this area have been published and valuable research fieldwork could be undertaken in surviving open areas.

The only group of Mesolithic flints found in association with an archaeological feature in Thanet were recovered from a pit with four small stake holes nearby, all filled with fine white silt. These were located on the central plateau at the south-eastern limit of the valley route from Margate Bay (Perkins 1997a, 229).

A scraper and some geometric microliths were recovered from the beach at Stone Bay, Broadstairs, in 1967. The finder, Mr Montague-Puckle, thought they might have eroded from the sand and loess fill of a hanging valley, which can be seen in section above Stone Bay (Minter *et al* 1973). This area could represent another zone of Mesolithic upland settlement, with the valley entrance far to the east. The valley has since been entirely truncated by the sea and the current access to the shore is a relatively recent gate, cut through the cliff in the post-medieval period. Much development has been carried out in this area and few assemblages of flintwork are available for modern examination; even the flintwork collected by Montague-Puckle and reported by the Broadstairs and St Peters Archaeological Society cannot now be traced.

Flints found at Quex Park, Birchington (TSMR 341; Wymer 1977), could demonstrate the potential for further Mesolithic discoveries in the loess filling the hollow of a long valley between Brooksend, Birchington and Acol. The valley has morphological similarities with the one that developed into the Wantsum channel but has been ploughed heavily since the medieval period. A single bladelet has been discovered further to the north on the upper plateau during archaeological investigations at Manston airfield in 2000 (Boast & Perkins 2001), possibly indicating that fragmentary evidence of upland settlement on the chalk plateau might survive. Perhaps archaeological work recently carried out in advance of the development of a complex of greenhouses on the north-facing slope of the valley in 2007 and 2008 will cast some light on settlement here.

At Minnis Bay a spring fed stream discharges into the sea from the cliffs and the flow of water through this valley might have been an attraction in the Mesolithic period. Similarly, it might be expected that very early settlement would be encountered in the periglacial valley that terminates at Minster where a spring flows from the slopes of the central ridge. None has yet been recorded despite fairly substantial sampling by excavation in the area near the spring and on the upper ridge overlooking the modern-day village.

Some flintworking technology continued from the Mesolithic into the Neolithic period. This presents problems for separating these periods in a narrative of the development of society in Thanet. With the typically sparse assemblages encountered on Thanet, the statistical separation of material rarely produces any characteristic distinctions in the functional range or distribution of the flintwork. Only large flint assemblages, such as were found at Chalk Hill and Court Stairs, Ramsgate (Shand 2002; Moody 2007), are of sufficient size to have the potential to separate a Mesolithic component from Neolithic material; the Mesolithic components do not appear to be significant.

The flint assemblages from a Neolithic site at Pegwell contain only a few possible residual Mesolithic pieces; no Mesolithic material is noted in the available publications of the Neolithic site at Chalk Hill located in the same valley, despite the assemblage being relatively large (Shand 2002; Hammond 2007).

The plough erosion of the upper surfaces of the chalk downs of Thanet has almost certainly damaged fragile Mesolithic settlement evidence beyond recovery, unless it was protected by the wash of later material over the loess-filled valleys. These deposits have rarely been examined in suitable samples by modern development archaeology and have often suffered damage from the industrial extraction of loess for brickmaking in the eighteenth and nineteenth centuries. The certain loss through erosion of zones of exploitation, such as the Mesolithic coastal fringe on the eastern and northern cliff areas of Thanet and the submergence of the lateral valleys of the Wantsum channel under the silts of the rising sea, imply that a comprehensive narrative of the settlement of the area, or meaningful measurements of the spatial distribution of artefacts under the current processes of discovery, are probably impossible. The heads of all the periglacial dry valleys might preserve evidence of utilisation of these distinctive landscape features in material accumulated over the loess deposits and sealed by hillwash. There is little prospect of a significant practical demonstration of the Mesolithic settlement in Thanet in the future without some form of structured approach to sampling the residual lithic scatters and exploring the valley deposits by coring, or sectioning, a sample of the periglacial valleys, in combination with geological and palaeo-environmental expertise.

A working model of the Mesolithic settlement, represented by the material encountered on Thanet, is that it is deposited on the surviving upper elevations of valley routes used to access the resources of upland areas from the creeks and estuaries below, as truncation of the mouths of the valleys by coastal erosion had not occurred in this period. The thin scatter of Mesolithic material provides a context for understanding the later development of settled communities of farmers and herdsmen in the Neolithic whose impact on the landscape left a more substantial residue. The catastrophically rapid sea-level rises, beginning around 6000 BC, had no physical effect on the chalk upland but the disruption to the ecological balance by the loss of a large landmass to the north-east of Thanet would have been significant. Although much of the technology and the lifestyle of the Mesolithic survived, the geographical context in which it took place was fundamentally altered.

5

HOW THE EAST WAS WON – THANET IN THE NEOLITHIC

The characteristics of Neolithic society are defined by the adoption of settled social conditions involving the formalisation of animal husbandry and the development of agriculture, particularly cereal production. These practices represent a transition from the consumption of the surplus generated by the natural environment, to the creation of surplus through the management of natural resources. A range of typical artefacts and monuments are taken to represent the evidence for widespread adoption of this settled way of life (Ashbee 2005, 118). These include innovations in tool-making such as developments in flint-working technology and the first use of pottery vessels. The appearance in the landscape of structures of reasonable longevity, such as enclosures and funerary monuments, are the clearest signals of the establishment of relatively settled communities that can be detected archaeologically.

In his study of prehistoric Kent, Dr Paul Ashbee pointed out that an old model of complete and irreversible social change, perhaps initiated by a wave of technologically advanced incomers, is open to serious question and that the alternative of a change that came from within existing Mesolithic populations has never been adequately explored. Social modes, he argued, can ebb and flow, with the environment and the topographical context acting as one of the forces for change. This interpretation stresses the importance of examining the social development of prehistoric people in the local context in which it took place. Continuity may be stronger in the development of prehistoric communities in Kent than succession (Ashbee 2005, 118).

> The emergence of the economic, technological and social condition that we term as Neolithic was a slow piecemeal process. Kent ... has a topography which imposes certain behavioural patterns upon human endeavour. Its terrain is at no great distance from the European mainland ... because of this contiguity and social contact, it may have been one of the first English regions where from Mesolithic selection and protection, their near horticulture, the subsistence changes that we term agriculture came about. These may have been no more than partial as it has long been recognised that fundamental Mesolithic practises endured and are a part of the various manifestations of our diverse Neolithic.

The rises in sea levels that finally isolated the British Isles from the European continent may have imposed changes and limitations on the contacts between communities living in Britain and the European continent but, Dr Ashbee suggests, there was a continuous social exchange between Kent and the continent stimulated by the changing physical landscape; the European mainland was looked to for inspiration not domination. The Neolithic was defined by innovation within established ways of life, rather than the wholesale replacement of one mode for another. The prototypes for new exploitation strategies could have a myriad of sources, some learned by experience and some communicated by other groups that benefited from a long chain of learning stretching into the distant past.

It is likely that the change to settled conditions did not happen over a short period. Human society had always sought advantage over the natural world and whenever humans intervened in nature, both human society and nature were fundamentally altered. Human interference with the systems of natural ecology would inevitably lead to the development of strategies for selection and conservation. The observation by man of the conditions in which a resource occurred in nature would lead to attempts to reproduce the conditions by artificial management such as the rerouting of animal migration, emparking of certain ecological zones and the control of hunting rights to conserve stock. If a useful plant or animal was frequently found in forest clearings then man may attempt to increase the number of clearings, and spread the seed from the plant. Wild herds could be moved around the countryside to help them find the best grazing areas, enabling a regular supply of milk, blood and meat. These strategies would naturally progress to the development of managed herds and domestic flocks. The processes for directing these systems were probably well under way within the Mesolithic period as human demand began to be asserted over natural ecology. These changes could have happened at different times in different places. The adoption of strategies for managing the environment was influenced by the way the uncontrollable forces of the physical landscape structured the range of options available.

Thanet emerged as a distinct place as the sea level rises of the Late Mesolithic isolated the British Isles from the continent and then incrementally isolated the upland area of Thanet from the mainland of Kent. The lowest-lying valley mouths became coastal fringes and large open bays, while the valleys provided access to fresh-water springs and upland areas. The Neolithic settlement of Thanet emerged as a response to the altered geography of the region. It is likely that the rising sea began to make a variety of different resources available over much shorter distances, but decreased the range over which animals and plants could be hunted.

The adjustments that human and animal populations made to the diminishing space would have been closely related; attempts to conserve animal populations would become the basis of animal husbandry. Cattle were suited to a limited range and were easily herded; goats and sheep were similarly adaptable. Game animals, deer and wild pigs probably continued to range in the forests but their numbers could easily have been reduced below viable levels. The practice of animal husbandry would lead to the necessary preservation of quality stock through careful selection, exchange of breeding stock from other flocks might become essential and seasonal culling of animals for meat may begin to occur in cycles relating to breeding seasons. Herdsmen would take into account geographical, seasonal and logistical factors to maintain the quality of their animals. Animal husbandry was as much a product of the needs of animals as the demands of humans; humans developed relationships among themselves in response to the demands of their herds (Suttie *et al* 2003).

The domestication of animals also had an impact on the landscape. Rights of access to pastures and food sources would need to be determined in the community; animals would need to be separated from crops, and at times from each other, to preserve genetic variety or for selective processing. There would also have been a search for good land that could be cleared of trees and cultivated; land that was too steep to cultivate could be used for grazing and all the time land was being lost to the sea. Evidence of these arrangements is represented in the archaeological record as the remains of field systems, enclosures and trackways. These features reflect the preferences and accommodations that were made by social groups adapting to the conditions of the landscape. Decisions made by the first farmers and stockmen persisted in the landscape and form the common threads through all the later periods (*24*).

The earliest structures regarded as characteristic of the Neolithic are long barrows and causewayed enclosures, both representing accumulations of artefacts and debris, and indicating a centre of gravity in the Neolithic way of life. The practice of communal burial in a central place is characterised in Kent by earthen long barrows and the stone-chambered tombs of the Medway valley (Ashbee 2005). Although the number of settlement sites tested by excavation increased rapidly on Thanet, no firm evidence of the funerary practices of the first settled communities has been detected. Cropmark and early map evidence have been put forward for a number of possible long barrow sites, but none of these have been tested by excavation. One site, located at Dumpton Gap and identified on early Ordnance Survey maps as a sub-rectangular bank, is now covered by a housing estate and was probably destroyed without record (Perkins 1995b, 3; 2004, 81). To date, the funerary evidence from Thanet does not conform to the rest of Kent; the individual burials that exist have been found on the periphery of settlement sites.

Causewayed enclosures are typically systems of irregular, curvilinear ditches, often arranged in concentric circuits. The ditches are characteristically separated by gaps of varying width which are located, frequently but irregularly, around the whole system of circuits. Many of these enclosures are known in Britain and several have been identified by aerial photography and excavation in Kent (Oswald *et al* 2001). Two partial plans of causewayed enclosures have now been recognised in Thanet, both located on the convex slopes of the valley in the gap at Pegwell – one of a complex of valleys that linked the upland ridge and plateau to the sea.

At Chalk Hill, Ramsgate, on the west side of the valley, the western part of as many as three concentric enclosures were identified. The outer circuits were formed by multiple pits cut along the same curvilinear path in a series of separate events (Shand 2002). On the eastern side of the valley, a short stretch of a curvilinear enclosure, with a single causewayed entrance, was excavated at Court Stairs, near Pegwell (Moody 2007; TfTA archives) (*25 & 26*).

How the east was won – Thanet in the Neolithic

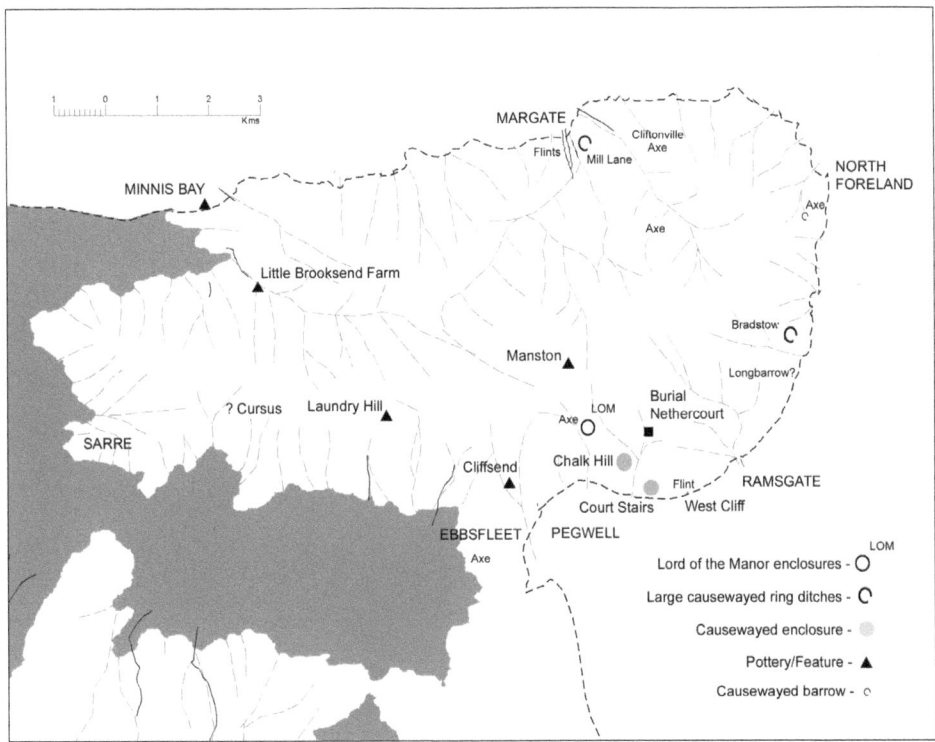

24 Map of Thanet showing Neolithic sites and find spots. © *Trust for Thanet Archaeology*

Again, a series of separate component pits were cut deep into the chalk geology to form a continuous, curvilinear feature, presumably enclosing an area to the south. The primary cuts forming the curvilinear enclosure at Court Stairs may have remained open for some time, possibly being carefully cleaned out and maintained before the earliest filling of the enclosure ditches began. The first fills were represented by fractured chalk and fine, silty loess from periglacial channels that eroded into the ditches through frost action. Pottery and cattle bones were mixed in the earliest deposits, including two partial cattle skulls found close to the base of the eastern terminal and western end of the same ditch. Cattle skulls found in the lower deposits of the enclosure at Chalk Hill have been interpreted as deliberately placed for some symbolic purpose. Those at Court Stairs were found within the material of the primary fill and could not be associated stratigraphically with a deliberate placement at the base of a feature. The larger cattle bones associated with the deposits also indicate the deposition of other major elements of the carcass and there is no particular reason why the skull should be more significant than other more substantial meat bearing joints. It is perhaps more likely that a whole animal was butchered in each of the events represented by recuts in the pits, perhaps in a seasonal celebration.

The enclosures seem to have developed in increments over many seasons and years. In the enclosure at Court Stairs, pottery, flintwork and animal bone were present in thin

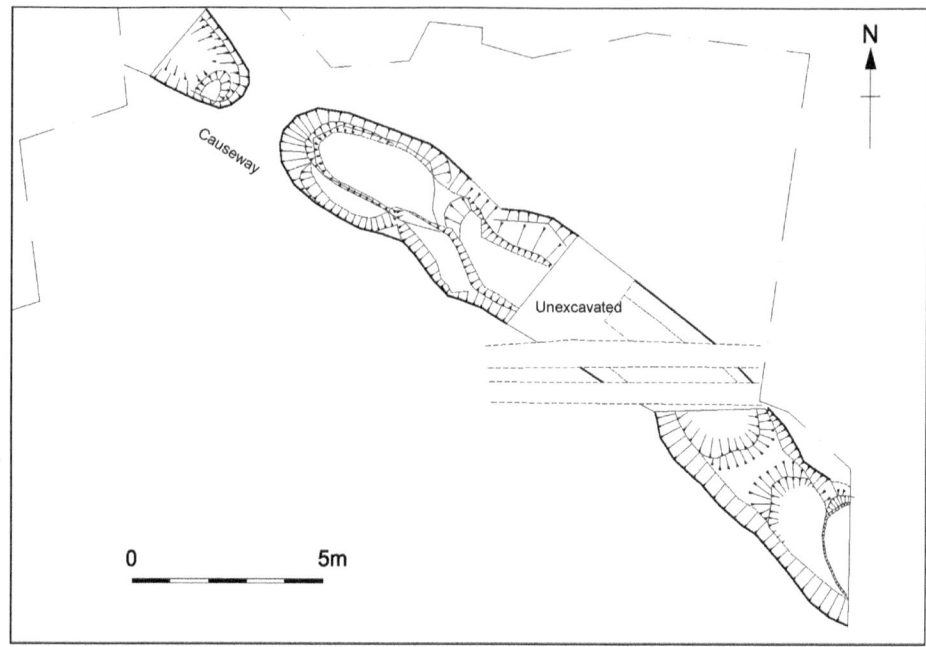

25 Plan of the segment of the Court Stairs causewayed enclosure. © *Trust for Thanet Archaeology*

bands of occupation material within pits. This occupation debris was overlain with material used to level the area before a broader hollow with sloped sides was cut. The second phase of cut also contained Early Neolithic pottery and mussel shells. A deposit of loam sealed the material before animal bones were strewn over the surface and sealed by further deposits of loam. The shape of the circuit seems to have been preserved throughout even though a later flint quarry pit was cut into the outer edge and a series of other hollows with gently sloping sides were recut across the surface. The multiple entrances and circuits of the causewayed enclosures may suggest a form of spatial control over the passage of humans and livestock.

It has been suggested that different activity zones can be recognised in the multiple circuits of the Chalk Hill enclosure, indicating another form of social structuring through division of labour. The inner circuits at Chalk Hill contained relatively few finds, while the deep pit cuttings of the outer circuit contained more abundant evidence of animal bone, pottery and flints comparable with the assemblage from Court Stairs (Shand 2002; TfTA archives). The individual, family or clan may be represented in each of the elements that contribute to the cuts and deposits in the enclosure circuits, which essentially represents an artefact of the whole social body (Oswald *et al* 2001). The relatively frequent recutting of elements of the circuits suggests refurbishment at periodic gatherings where social bonding or expressions of power may have been demonstrated. In a period with a small population and in which evidence of occupation is sparsely distributed, the prolific range of artefacts within the causewayed

26 The Court Stairs causewayed enclosure viewed from the north-west terminal. © *Trust for Thanet Archaeology*

enclosure sites on Thanet suggests either a high frequency of visits to the site or a high density of occupation at less frequent intervals. The presence of relatively large quantities of pottery at both sites may indicate the transport and storage of shared or exchanged perishable foods. Variations could be detected in the deposition of food waste at Court Stairs with larger cattle bones present in the lower deposits and shellfish remains more frequently associated with the upper fills.

Few sites have been found in Kent that could be interpreted as places of occupation, even on a seasonal basis (Ashbee 2005, ch. 5). It is possible that extended gatherings for the exchanges of stock and surpluses could have taken place at the causewayed enclosures but there is no evidence of structures of any durability. No internal features remained within the areas excavated at the Chalk Hill or the Court Stairs enclosures. The causewayed enclosures were perhaps not central places of population, but places on the interfaces between social groups, a common ground where the necessary exchanges between competing groups could be carried out. The preoccupation with the production of surplus from a range of activities might have led to a highly mobile way of life, with people only coming together occasionally at these places.

Some of the more elaborately decorated pottery forms in the Court Stairs enclosure not found at the Chalk Hill site could indicate a slightly later date or longevity (Nigel Macpherson-Grant pers. comm.). The chronological relationship between the two enclosures remains to be fully determined. Paired enclosures are known from other areas of the country, however their relative sequence and functions need careful consideration. Within the Isle of Thanet there may have been less choice for the location and relocation of these important social centres and this may explain the presence of a second enclosure on the opposite side of the valley.

There may have been other similar gathering places in the landscape. Sherds from two undecorated Early Neolithic bowls associated with two polished axes and a leaf-shaped arrowhead have been found in a clay deposit on the foreshore at Minnis Bay (Macpherson-Grant 1969). Although severely eroded by the rising sea, the site would have been situated in a location similar to the causewayed enclosures at Chalk Hill and Court Stairs. Perhaps this was a similar monument serving another community on a headland now lost to coastal erosion. The Minnis Bay site would have had access to the sea from the wide mouth of a bay formed from intersecting periglacial valleys and would have enjoyed a similar situation on the interface between upland agriculture, pasture and seashore resources. Other causewayed enclosures elsewhere in Britain have been found on the interface with a number of different resource zones (Oswald *et al* 2001, 119).

The archives of the Trust for Thanet Archaeology record a site at Little Brooksend Farm, on the valley slope opposite Minnis Bay, Birchington, where some fingernail-decorated sherds of Middle Neolithic Peterborough Ware were discovered. These sherds may indicate a corresponding site on the opposite side of the valley to that on the foreshore at Minnis Bay. The major valley intersections at Margate, Kingsgate and Ramsgate would also provide similar geographically advantageous conditions between sea and upland.

Two small pits containing sherds of fingernail-decorated pots were found at a site on the plateau near Minster (Boast 2007). Two polished axes and a large flint knife have been found on the West Cliff at Ramsgate (Hicks 1878) and sherds of an Early Neolithic lugged, carinated bowl with rim sherds of a second vessel were found at a site at Ramsgate, neither site far from the causewayed enclosures at Pegwell (Hutcheson *et al* 1998, 5). A group of pits, containing Peterborough Ware sherds, found on the slopes of a valley falling from the central ridge, indicate that Neolithic settlement was spread over a wide area on the southern side of Thanet (Wessex Archaeology 2006).

While these dispersed finds may indicate a proliferation of enclosed sites, the addition of circuits to the causewayed enclosures may reflect the aggrandisement of a communal monument as the community became larger and in greater need of exchange and social interaction. It might be possible to read the proliferation of monuments as the development of conflicting territorial groups separating and forming their own exchange centre. The archaeological sites that have been discovered so far cannot confirm these interpretations but in combination with the analysis of the landscape and other survey methods, such as aerial photographic analysis, more complex models of interaction might be proposed and other social centres identified, such as the possible causewayed enclosure at Eastry, on the opposite side of the Wantsum channel (Hammond 2007, 357).

Modern examples of rapidly changing societies demonstrate that there can be unintended consequences to adopting new exploitation strategies and the archaeological record may preserve the result of failure as well as success; for example, clearance of wooded or forested areas may have caused soils to wash away in heavy storms. The ancient soil horizon at Pegwell was preserved under a later prehistoric hillwash deposit containing Neolithic flint flakes. This has been interpreted as the effects of deforestation on the landscape (Weir *et al* 1971). Hillwash deposits sealing earlier soils containing Neolithic flintwork have been recognised in the periglacial valleys at Margate. A cache of flint found at the edge of the fine silt deposits on the slopes above Margate (Hart & Moody 2005) could imply that the area was becoming drier; perhaps the soils built up in the wet area near the springs were drained and cultivated. Forest clearance may have been carried out from nodes such as the upland ridges that were more easily accessed and where nature had already given some assistance.

While the evidence for settlement in the Neolithic period is relatively sparse, the remains of burials in the Early Neolithic are even more limited. An inhumation in a pit at Nethercourt is the only certain Early Neolithic grave from Thanet (Dunning 1966, 19). The primary crouched inhumation was laid in a large elliptical pit and covered by fragments of a plain bowl.

The burial is located on the eastern slope of the same valley as the Chalk Hill and Pegwell enclosures, and is a good candidate for a contemporary inhumation. A secondary burial was found in the same pit, probably inserted into the upper pit fill at a later date and need not be associated with the earlier burial. Three flat graves associated with the causewayed enclosure at Chalk Hill remain undated but may be associated with the site. Disarticulated human bone was found in the fills of both causewayed enclosures, represented by only a single leg bone at Court Stairs and two skull fragments in the outer enclosure ditch at Chalk Hill (Shand 2002; Moody 2007). These few features make it difficult to suggest how the Neolithic population of Thanet disposed of their dead or whether the long barrow tradition extended to all communities in the region.

A settled population would interact more frequently with people from inside and outside their immediate group, and social connections would have increased as geographical range decreased. In a society that was at a formative stage, the complexity of decoration on cultural artefacts may have increased in parallel with the development of more complex forms of interaction. Tool-making was developed into an art, and the art developed a language of symbolic expression as a fine finish was imposed over the functional aspects of some of the commonest tools, such as the carefully crafted flint sickle blade found at the causewayed enclosure at Court Stairs (27). This process was reflected in the fine polished flint axes made by Neolithic flint workers that accumulated their own symbolic veneer, as spectacular pieces were made with high degrees of finish that were unnecessary for their practical function. Eleven complete polished axes and fragments of five others have been found on Thanet. None have been recorded in primary contexts. Two of the polished axes from North Foreland and Margate show signs of pragmatic reworking of the shafts to fit new hafts and indicate that some practical use was made of these tools, perhaps after they were damaged (Hart 2005; TfTA archives). A flake from an axe from Langdale in Cumbria, found at the causewayed enclosure at Chalk Hill, is the only example of a non-flint axe known from Thanet (Shand 2002).

Axes from Ebbsfleet, North Foreland and Ramsgate were found in the fills of ring ditches, and interpretations of these depositions have included propitiatory offerings involved in rituals of sympathetic or sacrificial magic (Hearne *et al* 1995; Hart 2005; Perkins 1980a). A very large unused axe of Late Neolithic date made of non-local flint was found at Cliftonville, Margate, and may have been of more value as an indicator of the sophistication and cultural contacts of the owner than as a useful tool. Axes may have become a metaphor for the clearance of the natural landscape by the effort of man, and remained as symbols long after the land was cleared. It is only possible to guess that they were created for their own sake to display the prowess of the toolmaker or perhaps the affected dandyism of the person who owned a spectacular piece of equipment but made no use of it (28).

Aspects of the increasing decorative complexity of objects have been used as markers of key stages of progress in the Middle Neolithic period. Pottery accumulated patterned decorations so uniform that it has been possible to classify common treatments and forms into broad regional groups. This suggests that either common pottery workshops were involved or that these patterns were more broadly symbolic and were carefully copied and repeated. The patterns might have been understood in exchanges as representative of a particular commodity, producer or quality. Patterns were often created in emulation of other materials, the potters reproducing textures by impressing them in clay. The more elaborate a cultural reference, the more attractive and socially symbolic an object may have been. The purposes these elaborations were

How the east was won – Thanet in the Neolithic

27 Neolithic sickle blade from the
Court Stairs causewayed enclosure.
© *Trust for Thanet Archaeology*

put to are not clear but a form of 'advertisement' – an attempt to impress the object in the memory of another individual – may have been the motive. The causewayed enclosures seem to have continued to be a focus for the exchange and display of these goods. Sherds from a highly decorated Peterborough Ware vessel and 15 struck flints were found in the fill of a bowl-shaped pit located on the south-western limit of the circuits at Chalk Hill (Hearne *et al* 1995, 261). This could indicate that pit-digging previously taking place within the enclosure continued in later periods in a more individualistic way, but still with reference to the earlier site (*29*).

In other parts of the country Neolithic settlement has been associated with cursus-type features, large zones defined by parallel linear banks and ditches which have been

28 Large polished flint axe found at Cliftonville, Margate. © *Trust for Thanet Archaeology*

regarded as the deliberate monumentalisation of land clearance to create regular spaces, perhaps of special significance to the society. It is not clear what aspects of these spaces was particularly significant, it may have been the view created by the maintenance of a cleared space within tree cover that was of importance or perhaps the space itself was used for social activities. A limited sample of two possible cursus ditches have been excavated at Chalk Hill which post-date the causewayed enclosure (Shand 2002, 10), and a further possible cursus has been suggested at Monkton (Perkins *et al* 1994, 239). Neither has yet been investigated in any great detail so their proportions are unknown and proposed alignments are conjectural; little further light can be cast on their role in the Neolithic landscape of Thanet. At Chalk Hill the two parallel ditches appear insubstantial and might be associated with a radiating field system that also cuts across the earlier feature. A pair of linear ditches aligned north-east to south-west with irregular gaps were cut across the outer circuit of the enclosure. Recently it has been suggested that these may represent a bank barrow but with few finds they could equally represent a boundary or trackway (Hammond 2007, 361).

In the Late Neolithic a distinct new type of enclosure emerged in Thanet. Where the causewayed enclosures showed evidence of being an accumulation of small structures within a broadly defined shape and were associated with relatively large quantities of pottery and evidence of food preparation and consumption, these new monuments were cut in single circuits interrupted by only a single causeway and had little evidence of settlement activity within the circuit. They may have required the effort of a community to build but the conception was of a complete structure built in a single operation.

These large circuits have been associated with the Late Neolithic henge form, a distinctive type of circular enclosure typically with an outer bank and one or more

29 Fingernail-decorated Peterborough Ware from a site near Manston. © Trust for Thanet Archaeology

causewayed entrances (Macpherson-Grant 1977). The typical morphology of the hengiform monuments is the provision in the ditched circuit of at least one entrance. It is reasonable to assume that the gap was left because access would be required to the interior on a number of occasions, perhaps reflecting some seasonal or social cycle.

A group of three enclosures are clustered on a plateau above Pegwell Bay in an area known as Lord of the Manor, Ramsgate. It was proposed by the excavators that a ring ditch enclosure with a 30m diameter (Lord of the Manor 1), with no causeway, originated as a form of henge monument (Macpherson-Grant 1977) (*30*). A small assemblage of tiny Grooved Ware sherds was associated with the ring ditch.

The sherds from the Lord of the Manor 1 enclosure and a sherd from a pit near Monkton are the only examples of this distinctive pottery, which is closely associated with henge monuments elsewhere (Parfitt *et al* 2007, 46), that have been found so far on Thanet (Perkins 1985, 45). Two other circular enclosures, one with a broad causeway and the other with a causeway that had been artificially narrowed at some point in its development, represent the more conventional causewayed form of the typical henge monument (Lord of the Manor 11D and 111, Macpherson-Grant 1980; Perkins 1980a). The excavators could not detect a causeway in the first of these enclosures and the survival of outer banks in Thanet's heavily ploughed landscape would be very unlikely. Perhaps uniquely for a Thanet ring ditch monument, Lord of

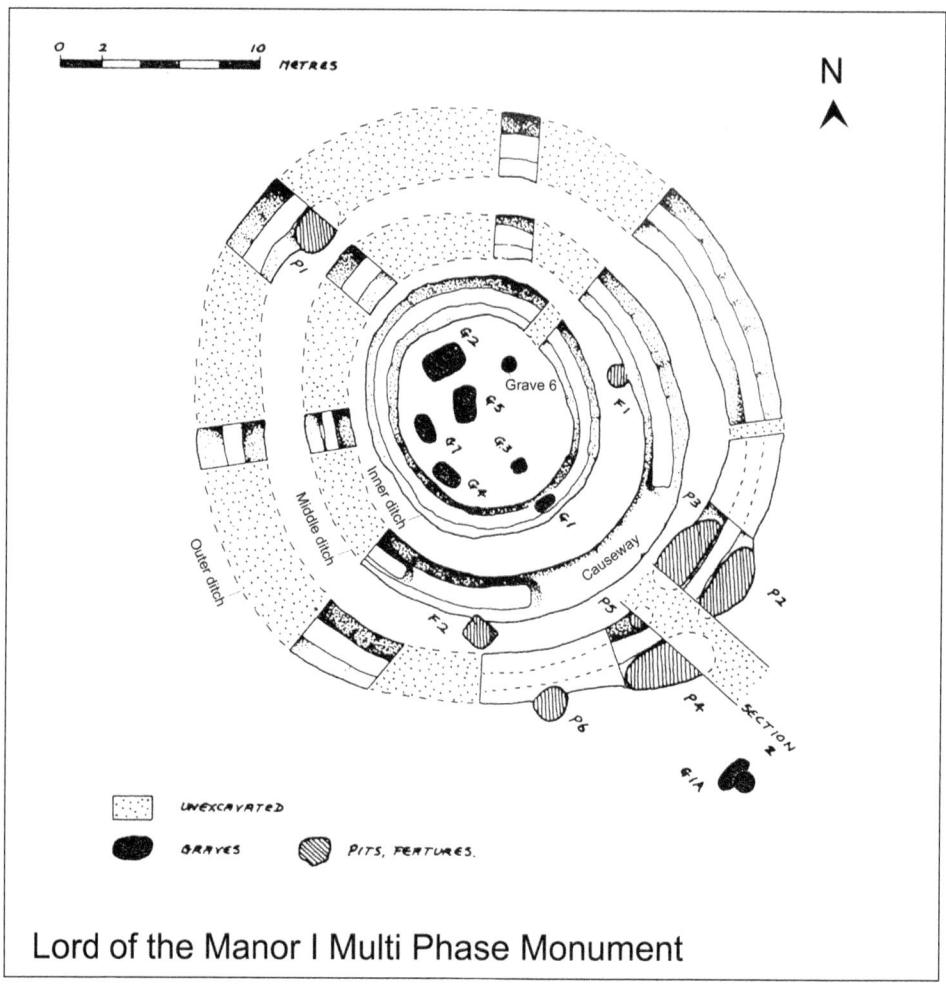

30 Plan of the multi-phase Lord of the Manor 1 ring ditch sequence. TAU 1977. © *Trust for Thanet Archaeology*

the Manor IID also had internal features including a platform of rammed chalk, a semi-circular flint bank, a hearth, occupation debris and a pentagonal post-built structure (*31*). Although the subsequent refurbishments of these three monuments had inhumation and cremation burials associated with them, the earliest phase had no funerary associations (Macpherson-Grant 1980).

Two similarly proportioned ring ditches, with circuits in the region of 25-30m, have been excavated on Thanet at Mill Lane, Margate (J. Villette pers. comm.; Philp *et al* 1974), and at Bradstow School, Broadstairs (D. Hart 2006). Thanet is well served by cropmark evidence and at least seven large circular cropmarks are known which have circuits in the 25-30m region and could represent similar hengiform monuments. These sites probably represent a continuing tradition of locating a social focus at key

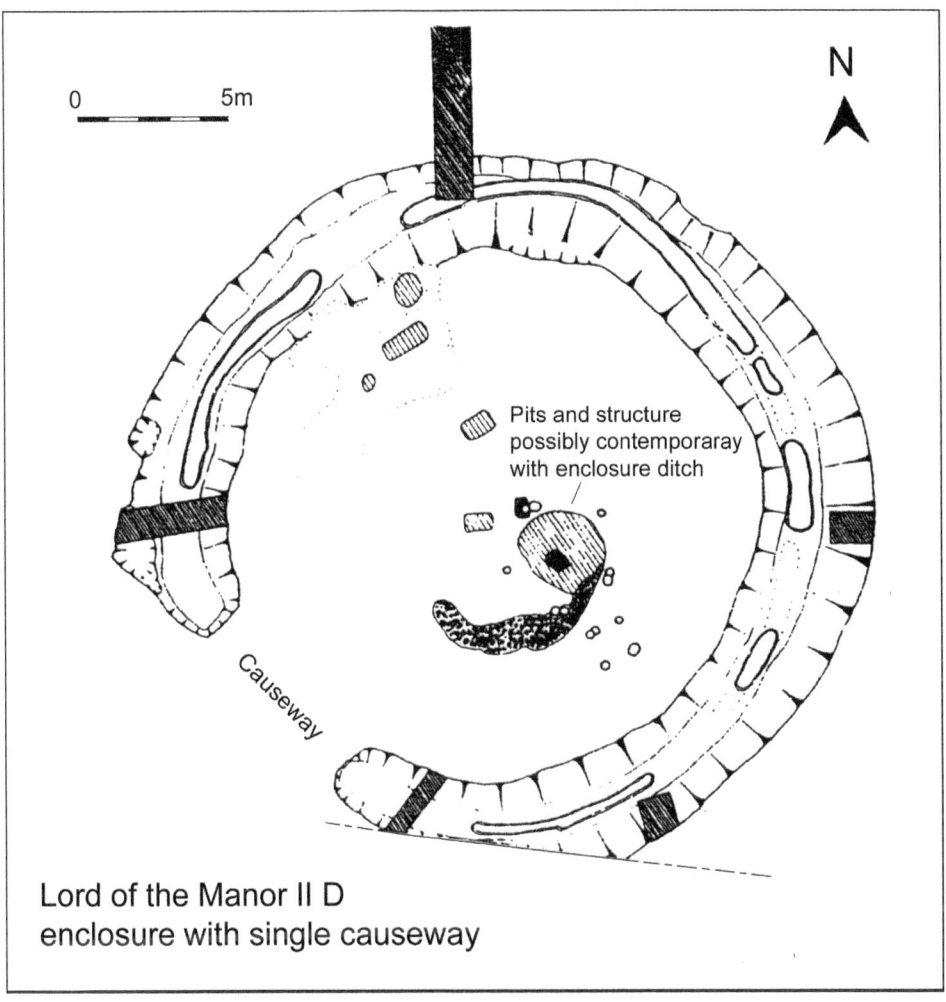

31 The Lord of the Manor IID causewayed ring ditch. TAU 1981. © Trust for Thanet Archaeology

points of interface between elements of Neolithic society represented by the upper reaches of the valleys with access to the sea. The locations of all the excavated examples provide commanding views over the bays at Pegwell, Margate and Dumpton and their locations may have been chosen for this reason.

A ceremonial function has been proposed for these enclosures although, in these early self-supporting communities, ceremony and the routine required to sustain the health of crops and livestock would have been intimately related. The lack of finds associated with the earliest phases of the monument make interpretation of their function or relationship to each other hard to establish, although the geographical position of the group at Lord of the Manor, Ramsgate, in relation to the causewayed enclosures of the valley below, suggest these enclosures should perhaps be regarded as

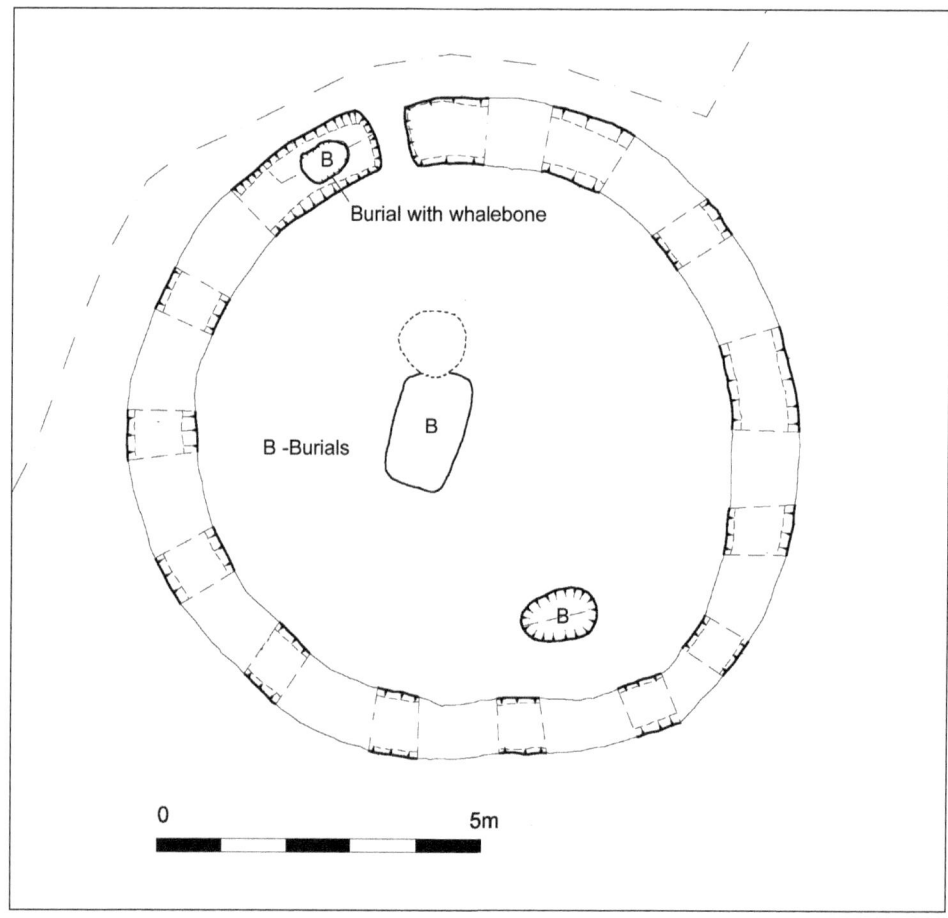

32 Curvilinear enclosure at North Foreland, Broadstairs, showing the location of burials. © Trust for Thanet Archaeology

a development of the social networks that created the causewayed enclosures and possibly represent a supplement or replacement for them in the same landscape. The longevity of the two causewayed enclosures at Chalk Hill and Pegwell is not entirely clear. Some later prehistoric pottery was associated with the upper fills at Court Stairs and the earthworks cast up in the early days of their construction would have remained a prominent landscape feature. These enclosures possibly represent a tradition of structures similar in function, but not in dimensions or richness of assemblages, to that of the larger henge monuments such as the one found at Ringlemere Farm, Woodnesborough, on the opposite bank of the Wantsum channel, which has an outer diameter of approximately 50m (Parfitt *et al* 2007).

A small irregular curvilinear enclosure, with a diameter of less than 10m excavated at North Foreland, had a narrow causewayed entrance slightly west of its north–south axis. In common with the larger examples, the location afforded spectacular views north and

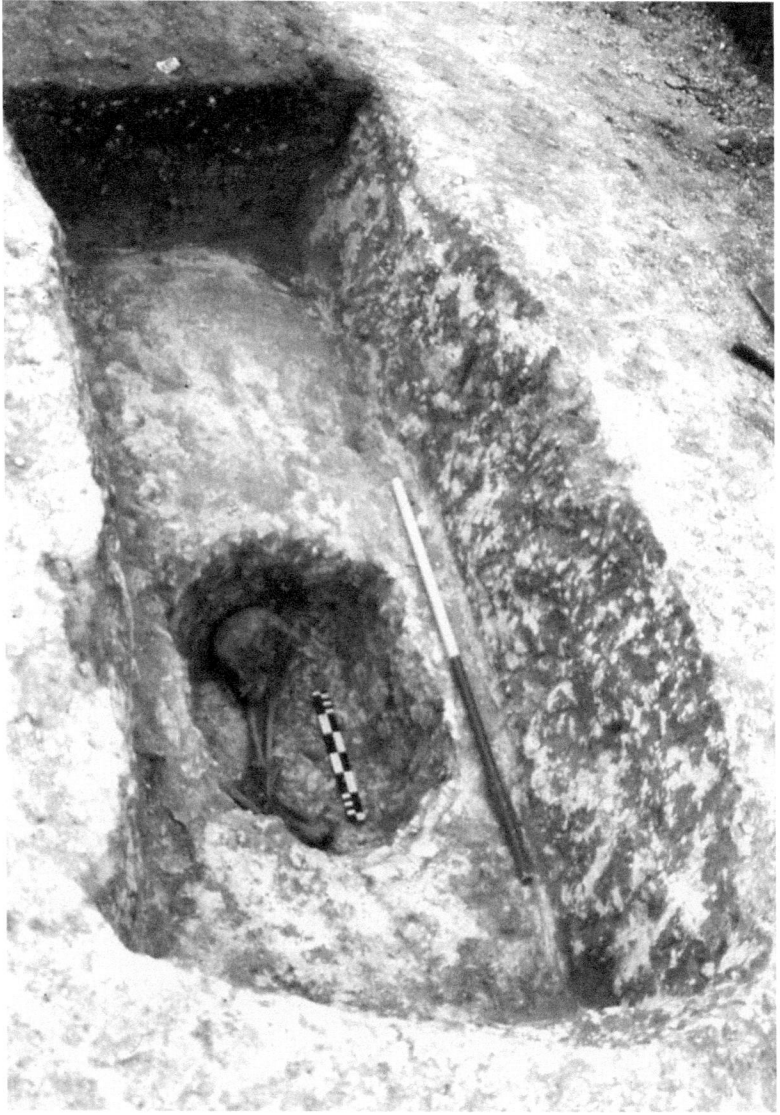

33 Burial of a juvenile inserted into the western terminal of the curvilinear enclosure at North Foreland; originally capped by a fragment of whale bone. © Trust for Thanet Archaeology

east over a deep valley and a bay below (*32*). A poorly preserved crouched burial, possibly laid within a coffin in a grave cut into the chalk geology, had been inserted slightly off-centre within the irregular enclosure ditch (Boast *et al* 2006a). This had been capped with a large piece of whalebone (*33*). This burial seems to be an exemplar of an important transition in the funerary culture in the Late Neolithic – burial of a person within a form of enclosure that appears previously to have been the focus of non-funerary social functions (Perkins 2004). This hybrid of structures created a place that was intended to be visited frequently and had now become a monument to the person who was buried within it. It also became the focus for further burials. We may never understand the significance of this event to those that created it; the combination of two distinctive archaeological structures is important in tracing the development of one of the most striking social changes in prehistoric society, the development of the round barrow as a funeral monument in the late Neolithic period.

6

BEAKERS AND BARROWS

The origin of the practice of inhumation at the centre of a round barrow has been associated with the emergence of a distinct new range of artefacts associated with Beaker pottery (*34*). The appearance of the form is often so abrupt in the record that it has been taken to indicate some form of cultural dominance, such as an invasion from the continent or the emergence of a social elite. Beaker vessels were a development in pottery technology, as well as indications of a change in cultural forms. Pottery used in east Kent and Thanet in the Early Neolithic had been manufactured with clay, incorporating a temper of burnt and ground flints; some of these fragments could be fairly large and produced a distinctive but coarse surface effect. Beaker vessels were made from clay stiffened with ground fragments of pottery, a material that potters call 'grog'. This technique had been used before with Neolithic Grooved Ware and was closely associated with the Neolithic henge monuments of this period in other areas of the country. The grog-tempered pottery could be worked into thinner-walled and finer-finished vessels with a surface on which the potter could impose intricate decoration, often using thin points or multi-pointed comb tools to create linear bands and panels filled with geometric patterns (*35*). These vessels continued the tradition of complex decoration, developed in the Middle Neolithic, onto a range of new vessel shapes, varying from squat forms to increasingly sinuous hourglass shapes and long- and short-necked vessels. The vessel forms were developed from a progression of continental prototypes that possibly reached Thanet from the Netherlands. The quality of the vessels is variable, some being finely made (Hart & Moody forthcoming) and some much cruder and irregular in shape such as the Beaker from a round barrow at Manston (Perkins & Gibson 1990) (*36*).

Beaker sherds have been associated with later refurbishment phases of some of the circular hengiform enclosures. Sherds were found in the fills of the recut ditch associated with the refurbishment of the enclosure at Lord of the Manor 1, and a large circular enclosure at East Northdown with no central burial produced a number of fresh Beaker sherds from the lower fills of the enclosing ditch (Smith 1987).

The Isle of Thanet – from Prehistory to the Norman Conquest

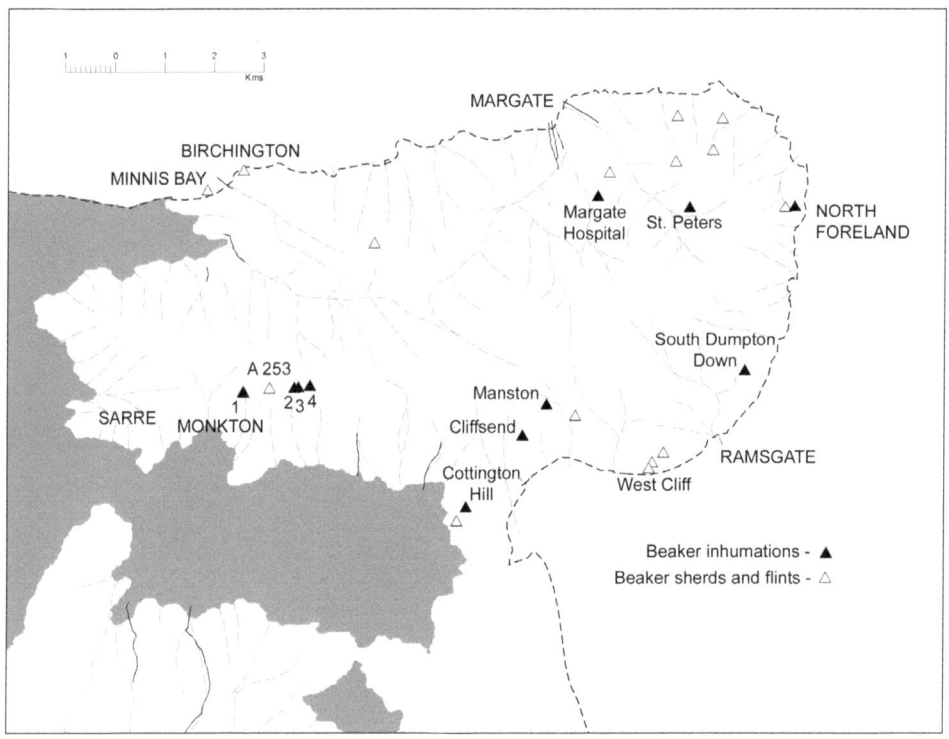

34 Location of Beaker burials and Beaker sherd and flintwork find spots. © *Trust for Thanet Archaeology*

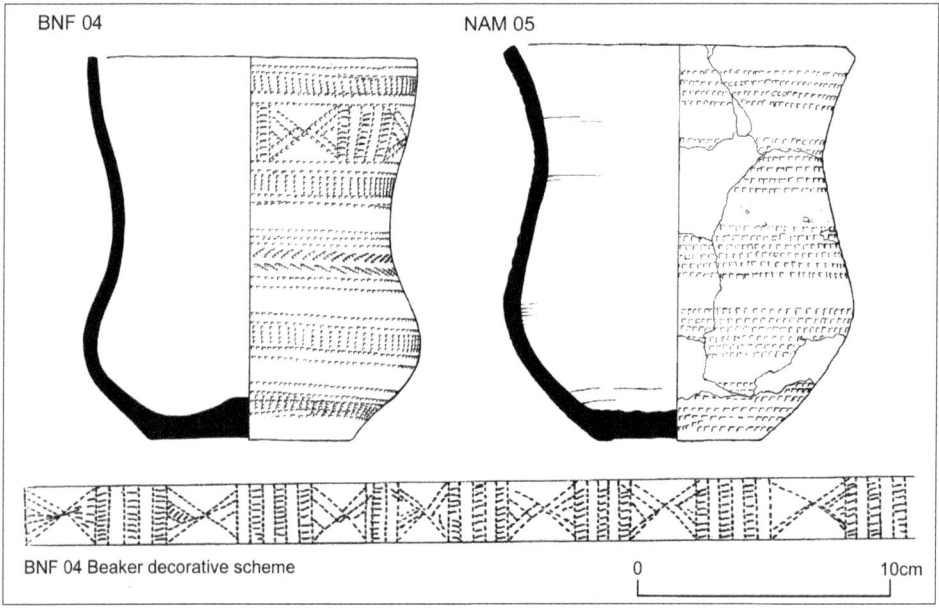

35 Decorative schemes applied to two Thanet Beakers from North Foreland (left) and Margate (right). © *Trust for Thanet Archaeology*

Beakers and barrows

36 The Beaker vessel from a round barrow at Manston. © Trust for Thanet Archaeology

Beakers are among the earliest complete pottery vessels to have been placed as grave goods alongside a body. Ten substantially complete Beaker vessels have been reported from grave assemblages from Thanet and two further vessels are known, but have not been confirmed as Beakers. The Beakers have usually accompanied a burial in a crouched position, but the placement of the Beakers in graves is varied; at North

37 Beaker burial at North Foreland Avenue showing vessel near the feet. © Trust for Thanet Archaeology

Foreland the Beaker was close to the feet (*37*), at Margate the Beaker was laid almost against the head (*38*).

The broadest date range proposed for the Thanet Beakers, based on radiocarbon dates from the burials, spans the period of 500 years between 2460 cal BC and 1930 cal BC. The earliest assemblage is almost certainly the Margate grave (2350-2270 cal BC 37 per cent), with the North Foreland burial dating to as much as a century later (2290-2190 cal BC 64.3 per cent); the three remaining dates from Monkton, Manston and Ebbsfleet cover a span between 2190 cal BC and 1880 cal BC (Hart & Moody forthcoming; Perkins 2004, 81; Perkins & Gibson 1990, 15).

Interpretation of the social function of Beakers in Late Neolithic society has ranged widely. It is not clear whether Beaker vessels of the type found in graves were in general use as domestic vessels. Larger storage vessels known as 'Potbeakers', made with the same pottery technology, are known in domestic contexts in other areas, but no vessels have been found in Thanet. Many Beaker sherds and scraps have been found in excavations but these have rarely been firmly associated with features that could explain their presence or their use. No clearly defined Beaker settlement has been discovered in Thanet that could provide evidence for the domestic use of the vessels. Beaker sherds were found in the fill of an enclosure ditch at Laundry Hill, Minster, possibly indicating a Beaker-period settlement, but the excavation was limited to a small sample and no internal features were found (Boast & Gibson 2000). Beakers may have been manufactured specially for the burial rite of the individuals in whose graves they have been found. This could be a factor in the eclectic range of vessels encountered on Thanet whose forms are comparable to others found particularly north-east of the Thames, but have little in common with the other vessels found in Thanet.

38 Beaker burial at Margate with beaker placed close to the head. © *Trust for Thanet Archaeology*

There are anomalies in the dates of the burials associated with the Beaker vessels from Thanet; forms that are thought to be early on typological grounds have produced late radiocarbon dates (Jay 1995). These problems may originate with the corpus that they have been compared with, published in 1970, it may no longer be representative of the vessels and the distribution that has been established since its publication (Clarke 1970). All of the Beakers from Thanet were discovered since the publication of Clarke's survey and the sample in the southern region as a whole has increased significantly. The varied forms and styles of the vessels from Thanet suggest that they were curated and exchanged in some way we do not fully understand, which has produced the curious mix of forms and the apparently anomalous dates.

It was suggested in an early study of Thanet Beakers that they are a phenomenon of the trading links between Thanet and the mainland of Europe (Jay 1995). However, even the relatively large number discovered on Thanet do not appear to represent a significant 'trade' in Beaker vessels, rather they may have been prestige items for an individual with connections to the emerging metal-using cultures in Europe. The likelihood that competent local craftsmen with access to continental models could easily manufacture them suggests they were made in a local context in emulation of an important class of European society with whom the Thanet elite wanted to be associated.

Several of the Beaker graves excavated on Thanet have shown evidence of a fairly complex coffin structure within the primary chalk-cut graves (Bennett 1996, 307; Perkins & Gibson 1990; Hart & Moody forthcoming; Boast et al 2006a; Gardner & Moody 2005). In all cases nothing has remained of any timber itself, but the sequence generally has a distinct outer fill with an inner deposit of finer soil covering the burial retained by the vertical interface where the timber of the grave once stood. The coffins appear to have been fairly close fitting and although reasonably regular could have been formed by something like a hollowed tree trunk rather than planking (Rahtz 1989). The grave from Margate had been set within a large elliptical pit cut into the chalk geology; the burial was placed in its coffin and surrounded with compacted redeposited chalk (*39*).

Individuals buried with Beakers are distinguished from earlier and later periods by their complex assemblages of grave goods. Items placed in Beaker graves in Britain commonly include items associated with archery, such as pierced-stone wrist guards and arrowheads, as well as bronze implements and gold ornaments. Although Thanet's graves have not produced metal tools and ornaments, other typical artefacts have been found. A stone wrist guard was found in association with a Beaker burial in St Peter's, Broadstairs (*40*) and three fine, barbed and tanged arrowheads were found near the waist of the man buried near Margate (Gardner & Moody 2005) (*41*). A secondary burial of an adult female cut into this grave also produced another arrowhead of a cruder form.

These arrowheads are a significant addition to the few that have been associated with Beaker burials in Kent (Ashbee 2005, 122). A flint knife was found with the burial at Manston (Perkins & Gibson 1990) and objects made of jet include a belt ring and a perforated button from Beaker graves at Chalk Hill, Ramsgate and Manston (*42*) respectively. Jet beads and a copper-alloy bracelet have been found near Monkton (Bennett 1995, 1996). The Chalk Hill and Manston burials are close to the Lord of the Manor Beaker-period refurbished enclosure and to the two causewayed enclosures.

The funerary rites associated with the deposition of the Beakers can only be guessed at. The clearest evidence that something more complex than simply placing a container with an offering in the grave comes from a Beaker found with an inhumation in North Foreland Avenue, Broadstairs. This appears to have been broken before being placed in the grave; a large fragment from the lower curve of the pot is missing and was not present in the grave fill (Hart & Moody forthcoming) (*43*).

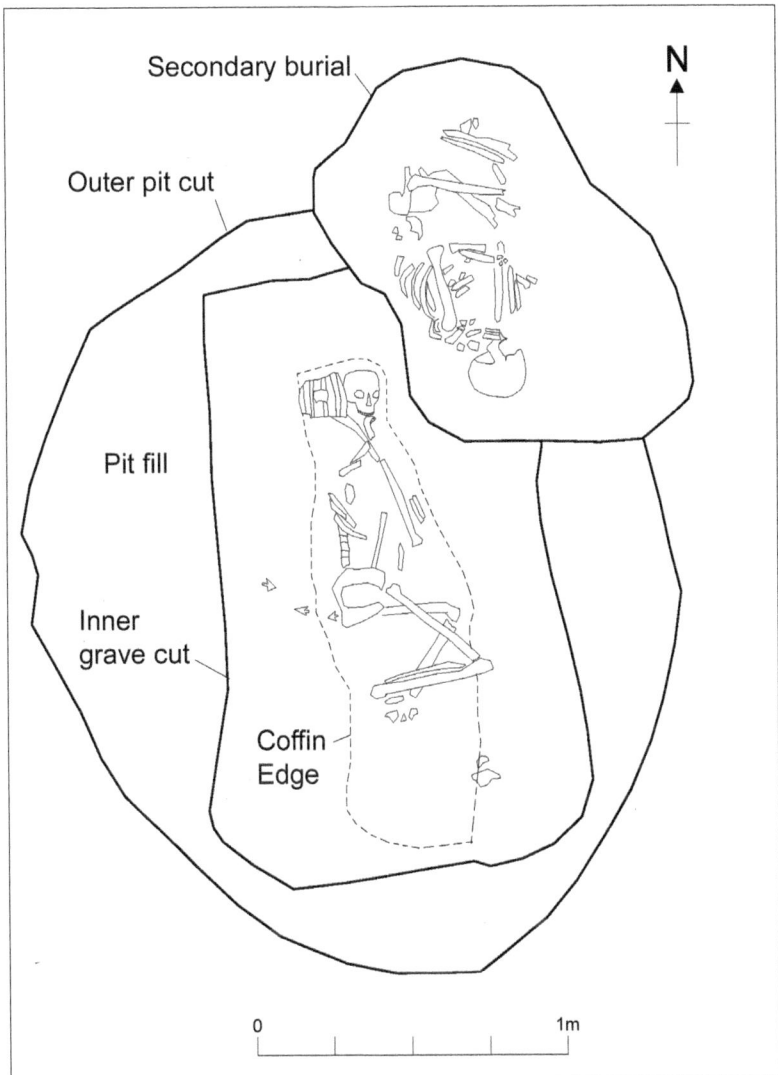

39 Plan of a Beaker burial at Margate showing the structure of the grave. © Trust for Thanet Archaeology

The development of the formal round barrow structure was not universally associated with Beakers on Thanet. Enclosing barrow ditches were present with the Beaker burials at North Foreland, Manston (*44*) and Chalk Hill (Hart & Moody forthcoming; Perkins & Gibson 1990; Shand 2002). The Beaker burial at St Peters was apparently cut by a later barrow (Minter *et al* 1973, 11) and no trace of a ditch was found at Margate. Beakers found on the A253 excavations were found in 'flat graves' with no enclosing ditch or boundary (Bennett *et al* 1996). A Beaker vessel from Cliffsend was found in a disturbed grave with no apparent accompanying features, although it was salvaged after being

42 Perforated jet button and flint knife from a Beaker burial at Manston. © Trust for Thanet Archaeology

barrow burial rite made little distinction between individuals as long as the structure and location were appropriate. The acceptance of communal burial sites may have had a much longer currency than previously suggested (Perkins 2004).

On the northern edge of the large causewayed ring ditch at Bradstow School, not far from the multiple inhumations at South Dumpton Down, a very small satellite ring ditch containing more multiple inhumations further complicates the pattern of round barrow development.

It is clear that there is no straightforward correlation between the adoption of barrow enclosures and the appearance of Beakers in the archaeological record in Thanet. Flat graves have been found both with and without Beaker assemblages; highly structured graves have been found within barrows with and without accompanying Beakers. It is possible that flat graves were marked with other forms of structure, such as a mound or cairn derived from topsoil deposits which have been lost to ploughing.

Too little is known at present of the people that were buried with Beaker vessels. The North Foreland Avenue Beaker was buried with a woman in her forties, laid on her left-hand side with the Beaker placed at her feet. The grave at Margate contained an adult male also laid on his left-hand side, with the Beaker placed next to his head and three arrowheads at his waist. Analysis of some of the inhumations in the flat graves at

Beakers and barrows

43 The Beaker vessel from North Foreland Avenue. © *Trust for Thanet Archaeology*

44 Ring ditch enclosing Beaker burial at Manston. © Trust for Thanet Archaeology

North Foreland has shown that some of the body positions could not be achieved without at least binding the legs of the individual into place. As far as the processing of a body for burial in the Late Neolithic and Early Bronze Age is concerned, the point of death and burial do appear to have been separated, but it is only possible to speculate if bodies were perhaps moved from their places of death back to a burial site associated with their family or clan. It is also possible that bodies could be curated and placed, sometimes out of sequence, with relatives or clan members. The secondary burial of a female over the Beaker at Margate might be that of a wife expected to go to the same grave as a husband, or a stranger who associated herself with the grave long after. These questions could only be answered by examination of large samples of data, which are lacking in even such a well-explored area as Thanet.

It is very likely that each generation might only have seen a very small number of Beaker burials in relation to the size of the population. Some individuals were buried under the mounds of round barrows, without the grave goods associated with the Beakers. Others were laid in the unadorned flat graves that clustered around the barrow groups. Some graves appear to have been added to existing burial monuments, perhaps representing a founder family member with whom later generations wished to be associated. The social dimension of the development of these individual graves was more complex than simply the veneration of an individual. Families of social status groups retained a special interest in their clan, cult or family member and wished to be associated with them even beyond death.

More information is needed on the diversity of the Thanet population during this broad period by taking data from all known sites together in one large group and then individual dating could be applied to the horizontal stratigraphy of the site plans. Sampling on a large scale of the bone isotopes from Early Bronze Age and Beaker burials is at time of publication being undertaken at the University of Sheffield and this might clarify the relationship between the people buried with Beakers and other grave assemblages. Burials from the North Foreland and Dumpton groups are being examined by this project (University of Sheffield 2007). Inhumation in barrows continued to become a defining characteristic of the Bronze Age and many more were constructed in Thanet. How many of these are associated with other forms of burial or reuse in later periods is open to question.

Although a relatively large number of round barrows have been excavated on Thanet, they represent only a small proportion of the numbers we can establish from aerial photography and we struggle at present to fully understand the development of this phenomenon in Late Neolithic and Early Bronze Age society.

7

BRONZES AND BOATS

By the Early Bronze Age the rising sea and coastal erosion started to define Thanet as an island, bounded by chalk cliffs. The area was separated from the mainland by the two sea water creeks on the north and eastern sides and linked to the mainland only by a narrow causeway at Sarre. By around 2000 BC, the full force of storm waves driven by south-westerly winds were eroding the coast from Deal to Cliffsend and a shingle beach was forming. Flints accumulating in the entrance to the eastern creek formed a mass that would become Great Stonar and a flat beach extended to Pegwell Bay. As the beach grew, breaking the force of the waves before they reached the bay, the Ebbsfleet peninsula was protected from further direct erosion from the sea. At some time in the Bronze Age the two tidal creeks on the north and east of the island met and the tidal flow between the north and eastern mouths was established. The exact date at which they were joined cannot be clearly established but it can be assumed it was soon after the Stonar shingle formed. The west to east tidal flow of the channel deposited sand and silts behind the beach and kept a passage open through the shingle, near Sandwich, where the sea discharged into the broad (Pegwell) bay between Cliffsend and Deal. The formation of a tidal lagoon behind the Stonar Bank and the cutting of channels by the spring-fed streams through the growing tidal mud flats started in this period. The sheltered sand beaches on the Ebbsfleet peninsula and mouths of the springs along the banks of the lagoon would have been points of entry to the interior of Thanet for sea and river craft. The fringes of the Wantsum below the central ridge were increasingly subject to the influence of salt water conditions and areas of former woodland were becoming salt marsh and mud flats at the outer limits of the tides (Hearne *et al* 1995); by 1300 BC land surfaces within the Lydden valley on the southern edge of the channel were being submerged (Lydden Valley Research Group 2006).

The chalk cliffs on the outer edges of the island would already be important landmarks and their periodic falls a matter of concern. On the north-east and eastern sides of Thanet some of the valleys that had provided the earliest routes to the upland plateau would have become impassable; slopes that had previously been accessed at beach level became cut off as the cliff-line formed. The upland of the eastern side of the island would only have been reached from the deeper valleys, accessed from the broad bays and smaller gaps which had formed at Birchington, Margate, Kingsgate, Ramsgate, Dumpton and Pegwell. Other open bays would have formed natural harbours and provided opportunities for the development of offshore fishing and coastal trade; the coastal zone could be expected to provide much of the resources of food and vital salt. These new occupations would provide valuable substitutes for the loss of the once familiar environment caused by the rising sea and disruption of traditional trackways. Communities becoming dependent on new technologies and trade would increasingly need to exchange their surpluses and obtain resources that now could not be generated by the natural environment. The route from Sarre, following the central ridge and then curving to follow the plateau, would have linked all the accessible routes to the coastline and would have become important to the trade network. The paths were probably already established in earlier periods as drove routes to the crossing point at Sarre but, as alternative ways were cut off by the sea, the upland route would have assumed new importance.

One influence on the placing of settlements and monuments would have been the formation of new vistas across the open sea from places like the promontories at North Foreland and the bays at Stone Gap and Joss Bay on the east of Thanet, and they would become more significant over time. As maritime trade increased, the observation of the sea from high points would become more important.

Much of the way of life of the Neolithic probably continued into the Early Bronze Age. In the absence of evidence, we cannot prove that any significant alteration to the economic and social foundations of the settlement of the landscape took place. Herding of cattle and sheep and the continued clearance of forest for cereal crops were the economic backbone. As round barrows became a significant element in the culture of the Early Bronze Age, it is possible to detect some significant changes that must have considerably altered the material conditions of life. The locations of the monuments in the landscape were the result of a complicated interaction between the symbolic meanings the barrows conveyed about memory and cultural identity, and the competing economic factors that structured the landscape (45). The choice of location could reflect any number of social and environmental factors. It is possible that, even with a mixed landscape of woodland, grazing lands and fields, the steep ridges of the valleys on Thanet would stand out as clear spaces. They may have been sparsely wooded as the deep loess deposits gave way to thin soils on chalk around the valley tops. The sites chosen could have been too steep to cut away the vegetation to make fields or to use as grazing land. Alternatively these unusual but familiar spaces may have been chosen for their relative isolation. The community might have been able to afford to give over land that was not easily cultivated to the raising of large monuments. The density of features in some areas suggests that each barrow was raised in reference to other monuments and to the pathways that were familiar to the community. The landscape would become progressively clearer, making the visual referencing between old and new monuments more significant.

The study of round barrows on Thanet has taken place over a century or more of archaeological investigation. Cropmarks, identified by aerial photography, have greatly added to the accumulating evidence that very many of these monuments were built on

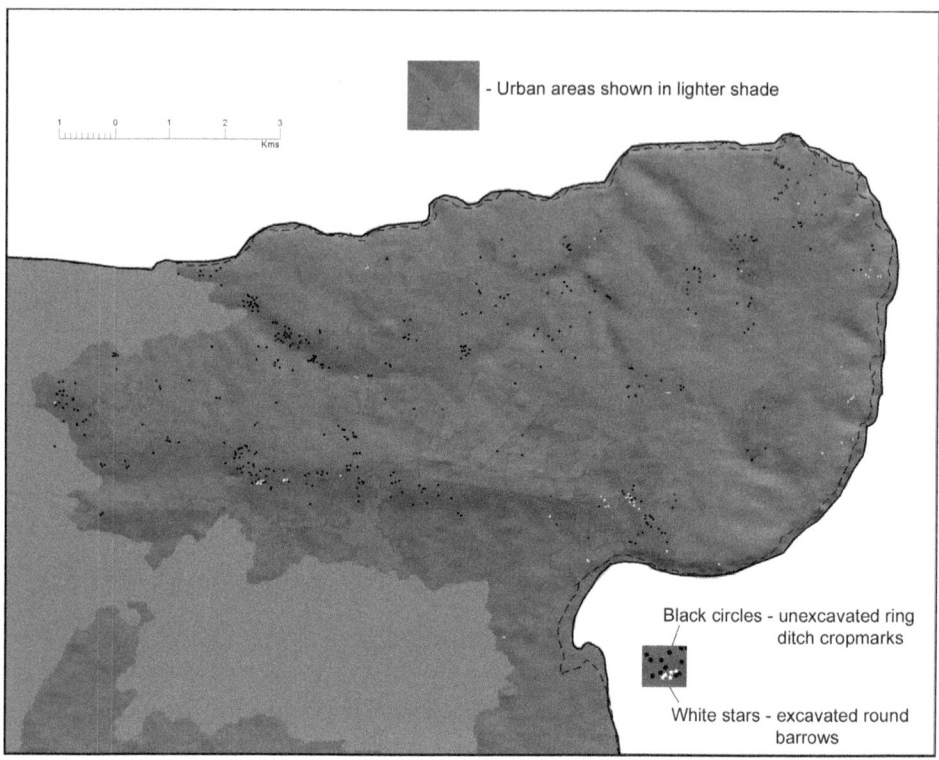

45 The locations of unexcavated and excavated ring ditch cropmarks on Thanet. © *Trust for Thanet Archaeology*

Thanet. Plotting the locations of the circular cropmarks, formed by the ditches of round barrows, and the locations of excavated monuments has provided some evidence about the choice of sites and the impact they had on the landscape (Perkins 1999b). Although many are untested by excavation, samples have been taken through the densest concentrations and it has been shown that the cropmark distribution probably underestimates the number and complexity of the features represented (Bennett 1995; 1996). The clusters recorded by aerial photography seem to be a reasonably accurate indication of the areas that were chosen as sites for the location of barrows. These appear to reflect some common ideas in Bronze Age society about what areas of the landscape were suitable. It does not appear that any particular aspect was preferred, but promontories and the steepest slopes of valleys at high elevations appear to have been favoured. Where these sites are accessible in the present day, it is striking that they provide such impressive views and this must have been a factor in their location.

The sites of the earlier hengiform enclosures had been chosen for their position within ancient transit networks and commanding views over the major valleys and bays. The barrow monuments that developed emulated some of these choices. They competed for suitable locations that fitted the prevailing ideas of what were appropriate locations, often producing dense concentrations. It is possible that funerary barrows were located in relation to the

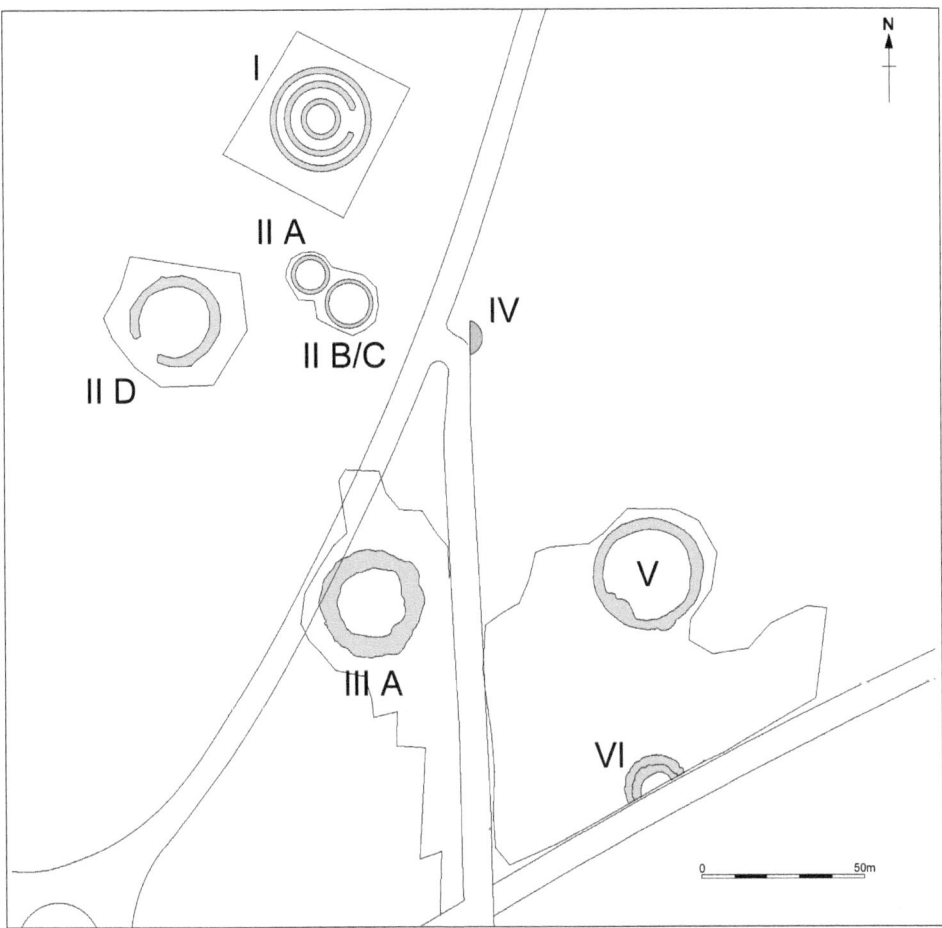

46 The Lord of the Manor barrow and enclosure complex. © Trust for Thanet Archaeology

earlier circular hengiform enclosures and founding groups of these are associated with round barrow clusters at Lord of the Manor, Ramsgate (*46*), and at Bradstow School, Broadstairs.

Attempts have been made to classify the likely form and date of the ring ditches represented by cropmarks according to their size (RCHME 1989). The smallest barrows in the aerial photographs were considered likely to have been of Anglo-Saxon date. However, the discovery of a ring ditch with a diameter of only 5.5m surrounding a group of four inhumations at Bradstow School, Broadstairs (Hart 2006), has raised doubts about imposing a lower threshold size on Bronze Age monuments. The multiple inhumations in the round barrow at South Dumpton Down were not far away (*47*) and these two sites demonstrate that there were more variations in the form of round barrows than has generally been recognised (Perkins 1999b).

A recent survey of archaeological archives and excavations by the Trust for Thanet Archaeology has shown 56 ring-ditched structures to have been excavated on Thanet,

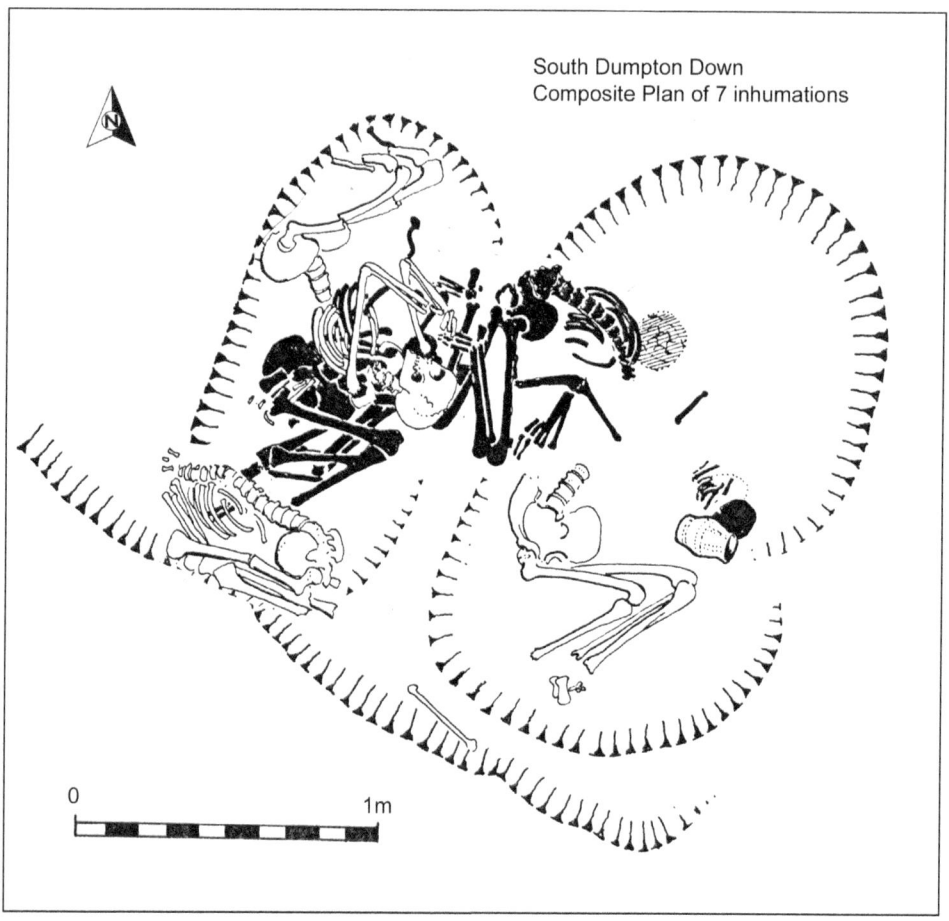

47 Multiple inhumations at South Dumpton Down. © Trust for Thanet Archaeology

starting with the exploration of graves at Hackemdown Banks in 1745 and 1765 during a popular craze for barrow-digging (Fisher 1779, 94). The majority that have been exposed in archaeological investigations have not previously been recognised by aerial photography as they lie in areas developed for housing around the coastal towns in the period before the Second World War. This has proved a useful test of the distributions implied by aerial photography.

Not all of the ring ditches can be identified simply as round barrows. Excavation has revealed variation in the components of these features showing that their functions are not fully understood. Some round barrows seem to be monuments to individuals, but many of the excavated ring ditches do not have a primary burial enclosed within the ditches; it is possible that these served some other purpose. Secondary inhumations were present in a large barrow at North Foreland and in one of the terminals of the hengiform barrow in the same group (capped with a large fragment of whalebone; Boast *et al* 2006a).

The ring ditches with no inhumations may have been the focus of different forms of funerary activity. The ditch fill could have been used to build a mound over a chamber built on the original ground surface or over the funeral pyre of a single person. However, the excavated barrows on Thanet have been heavily truncated by ploughing and most of this evidence will have been lost.

The sample of excavated round barrows in Thanet is so large that a full analysis of these might be used to establish a norm for these monuments applicable to a wider region. David Perkins has identified parallels with barrows known from the Yorkshire Wolds, where many monuments with multiple phases were recorded in the nineteenth century (Perkins 1995b). The evidence points to the progressive development of round barrows as monuments over many centuries. The complex elements of round barrow sites are a product of the choice of location, significant to the social body, rather than a preconceived idea of a formal structure. Once the ring ditches and mounds were established, a complex sequence of interpretations of their significance was made. Barrows could be reused for pragmatic purposes, reinterpreted according to prevailing ideas or curated as symbols of the memory of the past. The secondary inhumations extended the symbolic meaning of a barrow from a monument to an individual, into one for a wider group such as the immediate family of the earliest burial, or a broader social set. In the landscape the raising of a barrow over the first burial was an act of personal commemoration, but the presence of that memorial, among many others in the landscape, was the expression of a society's collective respect for its dead.

It is likely that, even in Thanet, where there is evidence for a large number of round barrows, burial under a barrow was limited to a few. We are left to question who the barrows were built for and what range of reactions there was to the construction of the monuments. An experimental reconstruction of a barrow at Monkton (*48*) has given an indication that considerable labour was required to raise the monument but the circumstances under which that labour was extracted can not be presumed (Jay 1993). With the pride of every warrior who raised a barrow over his venerated leader came the physical exertion and perhaps the resentment of a peasant or footsoldier who had to dig the hole. If priests or learned members of a society were venerated by the barrows, perhaps their followers made their exertions willingly to commemorate their acts and learning. A pilgrimage to the barrow could then have been part of the philosophical or liturgical calendar. The complex of ceremonies may have been comparable with the medieval veneration of saintly burial places; we will probably never know.

Distributions of flintwork and bronze tools are the main evidence for settlement during the Early Bronze Age in Thanet. Features of this date have generally not been substantial and little structural evidence can be assigned to the earlier part of the period. Residual flintwork is frequently encountered incorporated in the fills of the round barrow ditches, from which we can detect a background of settlement material. Excavations at Manston have produced Early Bronze Age pottery and flintwork that could represent occupation contemporary with the nearby Lord of the Manor complex of enclosures and barrows (Hutcheson *et al* 1998; Boast *et al* 2006b). Fine flint tools, such as a flint knife discovered on West Cliff at Ramsgate in the nineteenth century, show the skill of flint-knappers in the Late Neolithic and Early Bronze Age (Hicks 1878). The tool

48 Full-size replica round barrow constructed by Thanet Archaeological Unit at Monkton

appears to prefigure the form of Bronze daggers and swords and may reflect the adaptation of a long-practised technology in the face of the importation of the first bronze tools.

Occasional stray finds of barbed and tanged arrowheads have been found, indicating they were put to a practical use as hunting tools or weapons, as well as being prestige goods in graves (Gardner & Moody 2005). A cremation in a food vessel, inserted into the Lord of the Manor 1 enclosure, was also accompanied by a barbed and tanged arrowhead (*49 & 50*). The same enclosure also contained a rare Early Bronze Age perforated cup, associated with some burnt bone, showing that it was already an adaptable monument (*51*).

Man's impact on the landscape, which is demonstrated by the amount of land cleared for barrow building, was reflected in the range and quality of tools that were becoming available. The axe remained the most common tool form. A few early bronze tools have been found in Thanet; a flat axe, which may have accompanied a flanged axe in a hoard, was found at Gore End, Birchington (Perkins 1999b, vol 1, 63) (*52*).

A flanged axe was found in Northdown near Margate and another decorated with dense incised markings was found at Ellington, Ramsgate (*53*). These occasional finds perhaps represent the elite equipment of a society still heavily reliant on its traditional tools made from flint, which had been effective for many centuries (*54*).

There is evidence for the intensive clearance and division of land into field systems and enclosed areas associated with agriculture emerging in the Middle Bronze Age. Many of these archaeological features are difficult to date and may have persisted into the Late Bronze Age and even formed the basis of land divisions in the Early Iron Age. Field systems

Bronzes and boats

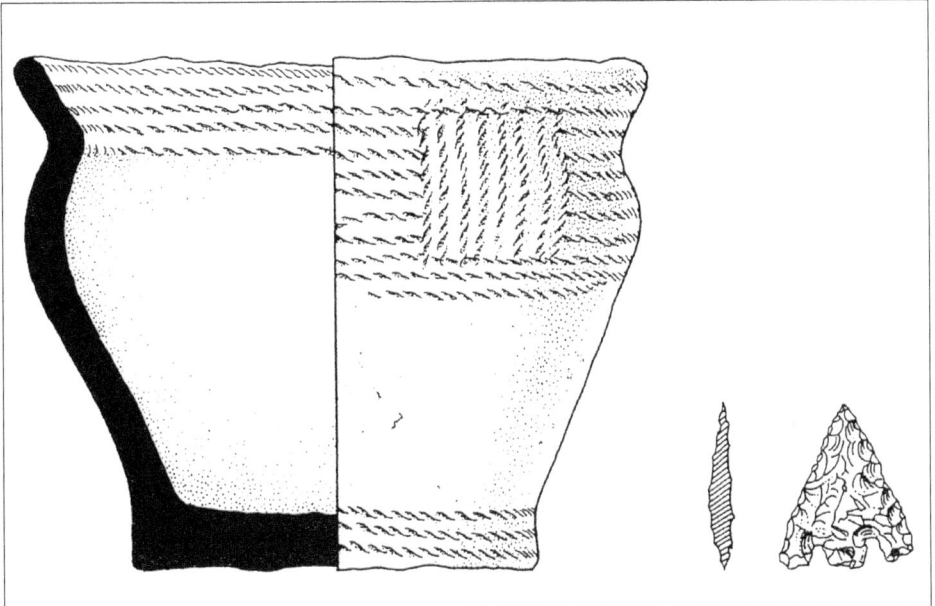

49 Food vessel and barbed and tanged arrowhead from Lord of the Manor grave 6. © *Trust for Thanet Archaeology*

and agricultural settlements associated with Middle Bronze Age pottery have been found in a number of locations. Possible field ditches have been found at St Nicholas (Perkins 1980c, 25), Birchington (TfTA archives) and Margate (Hart & Moody 2005). Three sites at Manston have produced evidence for agricultural settlement. At the easternmost site, a square of postholes with additional linear posthole groups may represent a roofed structure associated with some irregular linear field ditches (Hutcheson *et al* 1998, 5).

The ditches of an open field system and a linear gully produced a number of Late Bronze Age sherds from sites north of Manston airfield (TfTA archives, Swale and Thames Archaeology (SWAT) archives). A drove way, partly overlying the earlier field systems, rises from Pegwell Bay and follows a route that would take it from the region of the Lord of the Manor enclosure complex south-west of the structure and onto the high ground of the plateau (Boast *et al* 2006b) (*55*). A lozenge-shaped enclosure at South Dumpton Down possibly represents a small collection of post-built dwellings within a large ditch for holding stock within the settlement (*56*). At Margate, a deep boundary ditch contained Middle Bronze Age pottery and a human skull in its lower fills (Boast 2007). Other contemporary enclosures associated with field systems have been found at Westwood and Chalk Hill, Ramsgate (Gollop 2004; Shand 2002).

Hoards of more-developed bronze tools of the Middle Bronze Age have been found in greater quantity. The number of pieces is an indication of the revolutionary effect of the new technology on the trade in the raw materials of copper and tin, and the distribution of manufactured objects as commodities. Two hoards of palstave axes have been found very

The Isle of Thanet – from Prehistory to the Norman Conquest

50 Lord of the Manor grave 6 with cremation burial in situ. © *Trust for Thanet Archaeology*

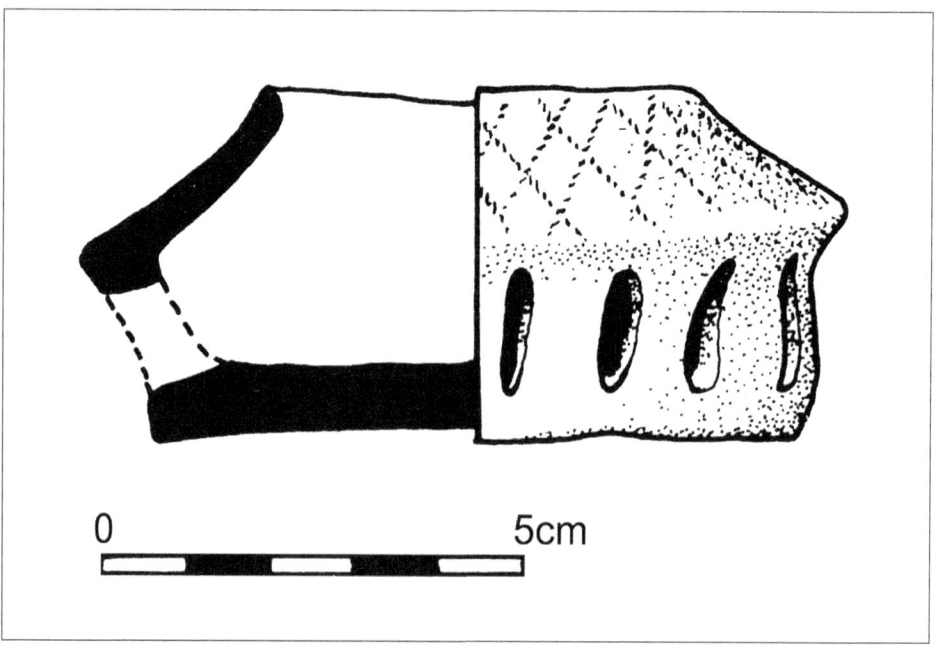

51 Early Bronze Age perforated cup from Lord of the Manor. © *Trust for Thanet Archaeology*

Bronzes and boats

52 Early Bronze Age flat axe from Gore End, Birchington. © *Trust for Thanet Archaeology*

close together at St Mildred's Bay, Westgate. The first was discovered in 1724 by a farmer cutting a sea gate through the cliffs near Motherwicks and the story of this discovery is well known (Lewis 1736, Ashbee 2005). The second hoard was associated with settlement features on the foreshore when unusual weather conditions scoured sand away from the chalk of the wave-cut shelf. Organic deposits were preserved by the waterlogged conditions and features excavated included pits with wickerwork lining (57).

The ten palstaves in the second hoard were found in a row with their cutting edges vertical within the clay fill of a submerged ditch sealed under the sand. The axes appeared to have been packed in organic material including birch bark and grass. When compared with the palstaves in another Late Bronze Age hoard found on the foreshore at Minnis Bay, two axes were found to have one match and one had two matches amongst the group; it is likely that these matching axes were cast from the same moulds (Perkins 1988a, 248). The careful packing of these axes demonstrates that the tools were a traded commodity as well as functional items.

A further hoard of 14 palstave axes was found in a brickfield near Birchington in the remains of a globular fineware bowl of the Deverel-Rimbury tradition. This unusual vessel was stamped with two bands of concentric impressed rings above and below a band of scored horizontal lines (58).

A cruder bowl with rough horizontal banding placed in the centre of a round barrow at King Edward Avenue, Broadstairs, shows that the decorative scheme could be applied to coarser vessels of this period. Vessel fragments with similar stamps have been found at Margate, St Nicholas, Ramsgate and Manston, but do not occur elsewhere in Kent (Boast 2007; TfTA archives; Boast *et al* 2006b; SWAT archives; Gollop 2004). Only a few of the characteristically decorated sherds were found on these sites but the presence of the palstaves in the vessel suggests that they may have been used for a different range of activities than the typical urn vessels of the same Deverel-Rimbury pottery tradition

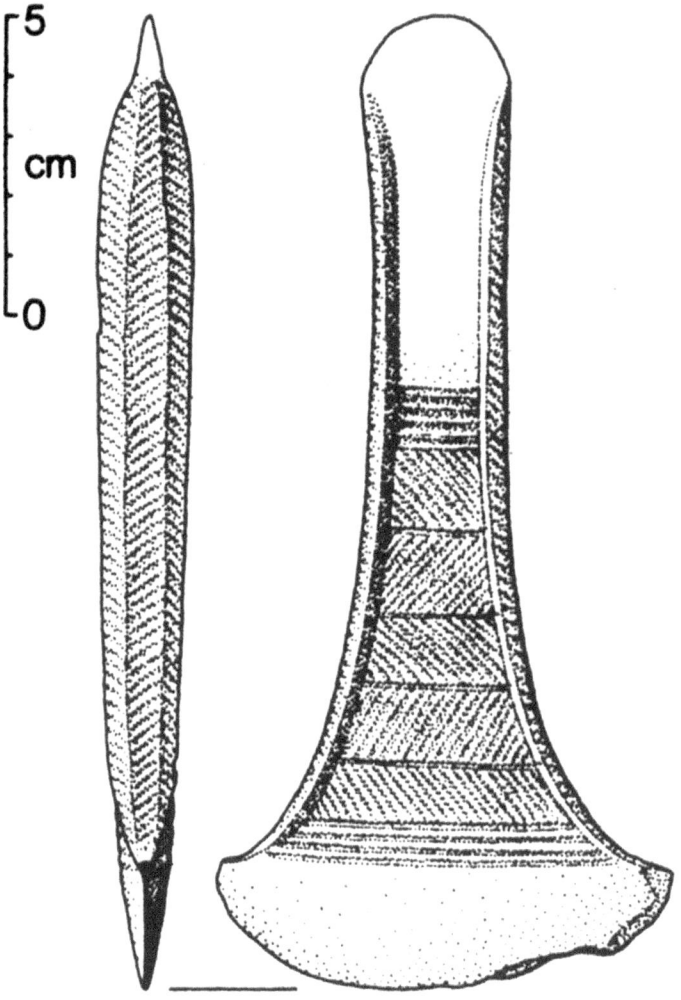

53 Highly decorated flat axe from Ellington, Ramsgate. © Trust for Thanet Archaeology

used in cremation rites. The ring stamps may repeat, in pottery, the effect of riveted metal vessels from the continent. They could indicate that local potters had experience of a range of vessels of continental style, or that the vessels were imported. They might have been traded alongside the palstaves that were contained in the Birchington bowl.

The very large number of bronze tools that has been recovered points to some revolutionary changes in production and consumption in the Middle Bronze Age. The evidence comes to us from hoards gathered for various purposes, sometimes pristine objects in trade consignments, some casually lost, others gathered up as stock for reuse

Bronzes and boats

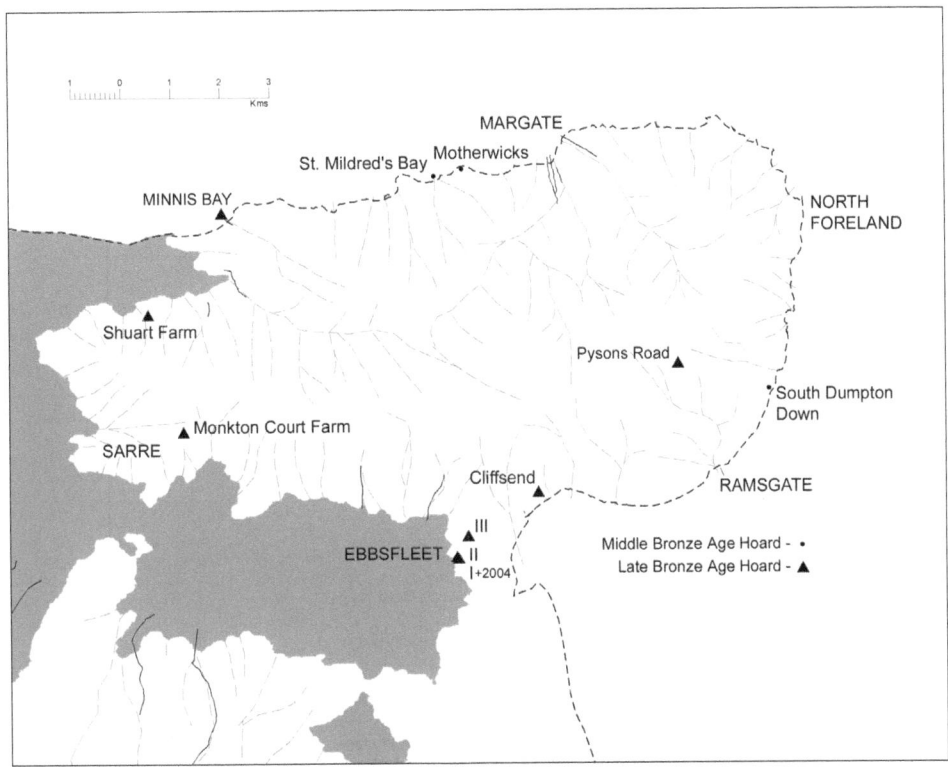

54 Distribution of Bronze hoards in the Isle of Thanet from all phases. © *Trust for Thanet Archaeology*

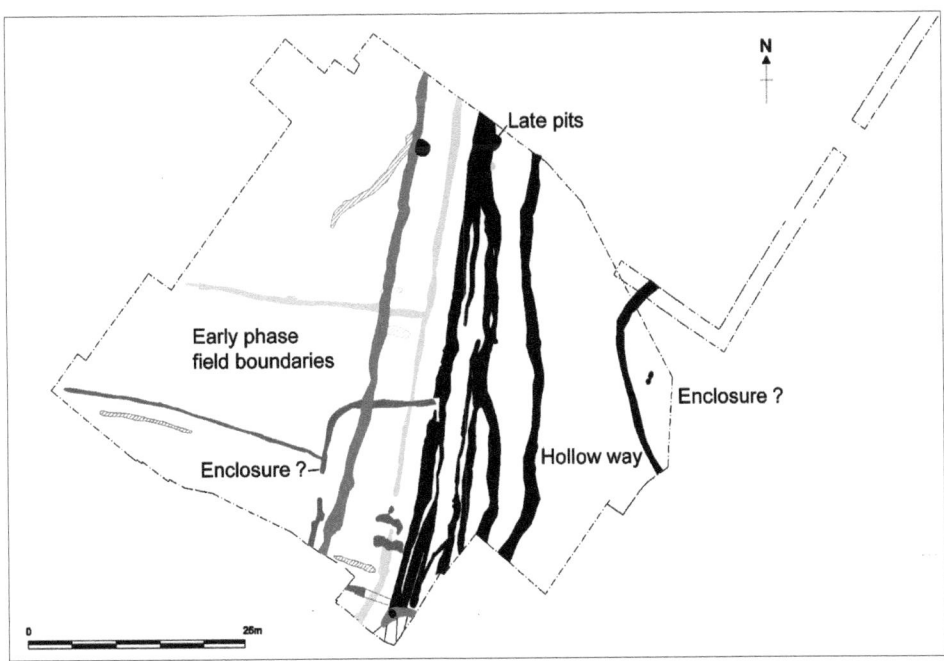

55 Middle Bronze Age trackway at Manston. © *Trust for Thanet Archaeology*

The Isle of Thanet – from Prehistory to the Norman Conquest

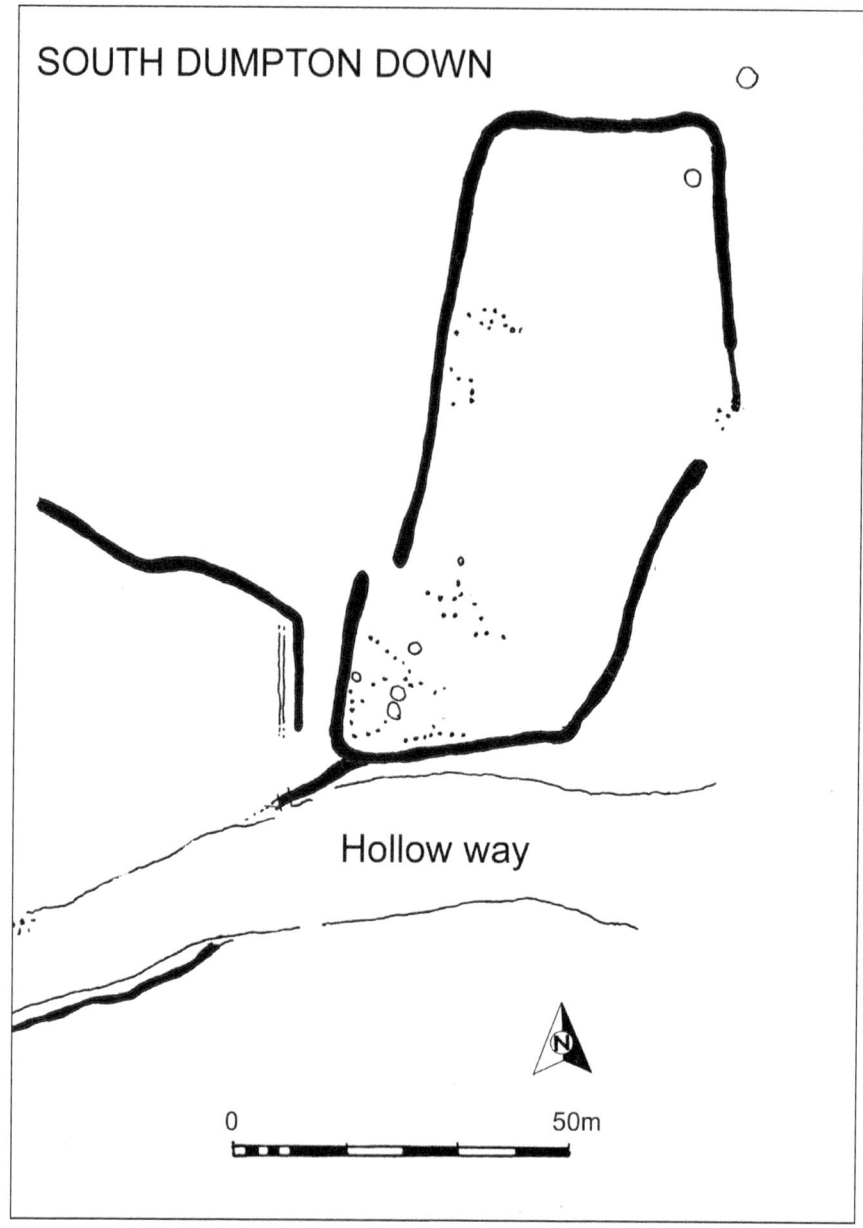

56 Middle Bronze Age enclosure at South Dumpton Down. © Trust for Thanet Archaeology

or 'bullion'. The latter might represent a stash of wealth that could have been recovered but for some reason never was. Some were gathered together for a more symbolic disposal (Perkins 1999b & Barber 2003). The systematic manufacturing of bronze tools indicates a major change in the way that human effort was being directed in society. The discovery of a Bronze Age boat at Dover dated to around 1550 BC (Clark 2004) has

57 Pit with preserved wickerwork lining at St Mildred's Bay. © Trust for Thanet Archaeology

increased our understanding of the purpose of these tools and what imperatives there were for making so many of them. The implications of the technology of the Dover Boat are of considerable importance in understanding the development of an emerging coastal community such as on Thanet where so many Bronze tools and tool hoards have been found.

Attempts to recreate parts of the boat indicate that these bronzes were tools of work, required for massive carpentry operations.

> ... reconstructing a section of boat to the same design gave us some interesting information about the original Bronze Age boat. If ten woodworkers were involved, it would have taken them a month to shape all the timbers and assemble the boat. This does not include all the time needed to gather and prepare the moss, yew withies and tool handles that would have been used.
>
> www.dover.gov.uk/museum/boat/building.asp

Until further evidence is found, it is not possible to know whether the Dover Boat represents in itself some special effort of construction and whether it would have been accompanied by other boats of greater or lesser sophistication (Clarke 2004; 2005). The

The Isle of Thanet – from Prehistory to the Norman Conquest

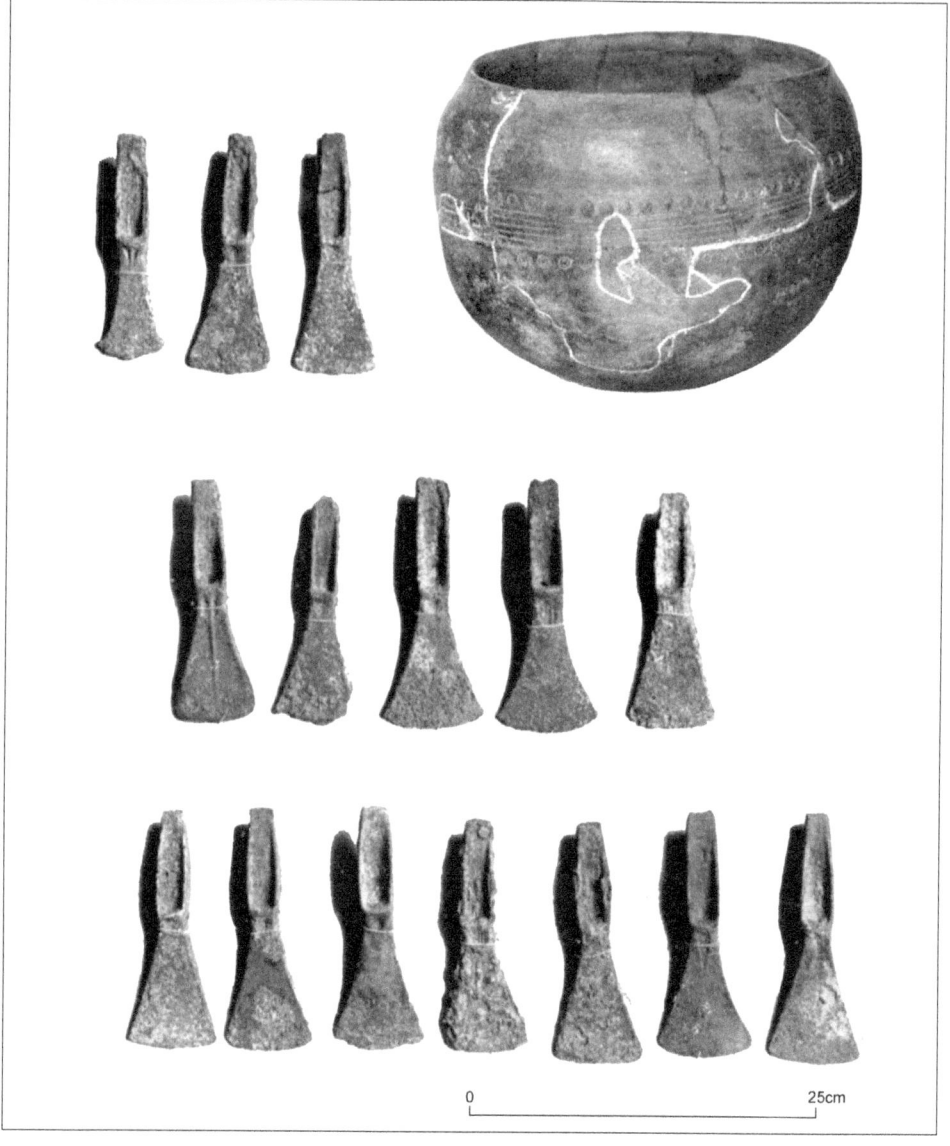

58 Birchington palstave hoard

Dover Boat has emphasised that maritime trade and boat-building technology in particular are key elements of the development of Bronze Age society. Specialised carpentry skills would have been developed on the construction tasks. In deducing the complexity of the process that went toward building the Dover Boat, the proliferation of axes, adzes and chisels in bronze hoards can be placed in context.

The complex range of construction activities would need specialists to manage the process; the assets of the natural environment would have to be surveyed and choices of raw material made. The intellectual stimulation of a project like the construction of the Dover Boat and its effect on the organisation of the society that built it would have been profound. The analysis of the boat-building methods raises questions about who would have controlled such technological innovations and what social organisation developed around the processes. The Dover Boat can also be seen as a work in progress; elements of the design, such as the formation of the loops that hold the separate parts in place by cutting away a mass of wood, are examples of experimental over-engineering. They are indicative of an expedient solution to a problem that was not elegant but functional. The massive timbers required indicate that, in the long run, the boat builders would run into problems with resources that would require less wasteful and expensive approaches that would depend on the natural inventiveness and skill of the constructors. The boat can be seen as a metaphor for the development of Bronze Age technology. Even if the boat was a one-off it would have required an epic programme of trial and error, perhaps denuding the landscape of its best trees and stripping other crafts of their raw materials. Such sacrifices are often demanded by great leaps forward. If the Dover Boat was a routine product of the Bronze Age boat yard it is a shadow of the complex world of work, apprenticeships, tool development, design and technological innovation that would have been needed to complete them.

Dr David Perkins has raised the issue of the social implications of cross-Channel trade on the development of a maritime class, such as Channel pilots who developed an understanding through experience of the rigours of the sea-crossing and knowledge of currents and tides (Perkins 2006). These issues become paramount to the narrative for the Isle of Thanet where natural processes at this time were combining to make knowledge of the marine environment an important survival skill among the population. Nature was forming the bays, harbours, channels and lagoons of the east Kent coast; man was making the sailors, boat-builders and fishermen.

The distribution of Middle Bronze Age hoards is biased towards the coasts of the north and south-east of Thanet, whereas, apart from the Minnis Bay finds, Late Bronze Age hoards have been found more commonly on the west and southern coast along the edge of the Wantsum channel. This distribution is also reflected in the incidences of Late Bronze Age hoards on the southern bank of the Wantsum, reflecting the increased importance of coastal and riverine trade through this route (Perkins 1991b, 263).

Technological innovation often causes revolutionary changes in a society over a relatively short period of time. With specialist skills came the separations of roles in society for which a complex exchange system of labour and resources needed to evolve. With the recruitment of boat-builders, shipwrights and sailors to the process, societies were no longer able to depend on the labour of every individual to produce food and other resources from traditional agriculture. Trade and exchange could substitute work for food, new sources would be available from the sea, and salt would ensure that food could be transported over long distances. A Trevisker Urn from Cornwall, found in the fill of one of the ring ditches excavated at Monkton, represents a by-product of links established with the tin trade routes of the West Country and in turn their ancient connections with western European trade. Along with the seafarers and boat-builders, specialised agricultural communities may have developed. Freed from the requirement to feed a whole community, they could specialise in particularly productive crops and production for exchange.

Trade contacts with the continent also brought new funerary practices; Urnfield cremation cemeteries begin to be associated with the earlier round barrow funerary monuments. In the Middle Bronze Age, barrows seem to have served as communal cemeteries with cremations dug into pits within the central mound. Many of the excavated ring ditches have additional concentric circuits, suggesting that they were refurbished for this secondary purpose, usually in the Late Bronze Age. A barrow at Broadstairs with two ditches (*59*), contained a central pit with a cremation urn shaped like a small barrel and decorated with a band of fine scored lines (*60*) (Hurd 1913, 10).

The flint-tempered bucket urns characteristic of this period are frequently associated with the refurbishment of, or insertion into, round barrow monuments, as seen in the cutting of additional circuits within existing barrows and the insertion of unurned cremations into other monuments (Hurd 1913; Fisk 2003). Sherds of the coarse flint-tempered pottery generally used in these cremations (Deverel-Rimbury type wares) are associated with some of the ring-ditched enclosures. Late Bronze Age cremation vessels were associated with round barrow ditches at East Northdown (Smith 1986) and an inhumation was cut into the base of one of the ring ditch circuits.

On the West Cliff above Ramsgate, pits containing groups of inverted urns placed over small fragments of cremated human bone were located near a small ring ditch capped with a cairn of flint nodules (*61*). Sherds of another small pot in the same fabric were sealed under the flints in the shallow circular gully (*62*). The cremated bone sealed under one of the vessels produced a radiocarbon date of around 1400 cal BC (Boast & Moody 2003). The people buried around this small cairn lived only a century or so after the Dover Boat had been constructed and may in their lives have seen similar vessels, sailed with them, or even built them on Thanet's own shores.

Two other finds within the great intersection of valleys of Ramsgate indicate the significance of trading links in the Middle Bronze Age. A large urn found on the slopes of a valley contained a series of distinctive bronze pins whose parallels are found in the Picardy region of northern France (Hawkes 1942). A ribbed bracelet and three engraved armlets associated with a North German metalworking tradition were discovered with a skeleton between Hollicondane and Dumpton (Payne 1896). The context of these armlets can be established now with some certainty as their find spot was described in enough detail to place it on a steep-sided slope with a spectacular view overlooking the Ramsgate valleys. Cropmark evidence indicates that a series of barrows, including one excavated above Dumpton Gap (Philp *et al* 2002) followed the steep edge of the valley face along a contour. The finds were probably associated with a barrow in this series now under the modern cemetery at Ramsgate (Ashbee 2005) where there is a particularly commanding view over the gap at Ramsgate as far as Deal, albeit over the rooftops of houses.

At South Dumpton Down, a 'Quoit headed' pin with a large ring at the top of the shaft was found in the fill of a contemporary enclosure ditch. A hoard of unused

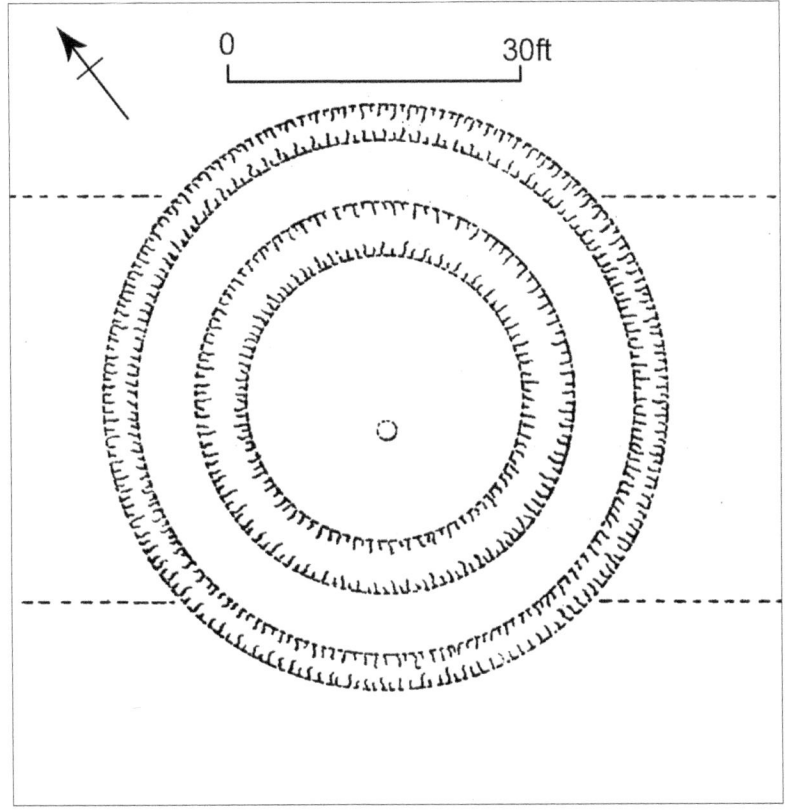

59 Round barrow at King Edward Avenue. *After Hurd, 1913*

palstave axes as found in a pit cut through the enclosure ditch, deposited when it had been almost completely filled (*63*).

The association between these Middle Bronze Age hoards and finer ornaments and trade goods indicates that the result of this technological specialisation was increased interaction with similarly developed societies on the continent.

Dating Late Bronze Age settlements has been difficult, as there are few sites where specifically Late Bronze Age pottery types have been associated with distinctive settlement features. Some fabrics are considered transitional between the Bronze and Iron Ages and are often found on sites where features from one or the other period are predominant. The degree to which uncertainty prevails in identifying sites of this period reflects the essential continuity of the settlements. A site significant to the development of the maritime role of Late Bronze Age Thanet is located at Monkton Court Farm, at the head of a short periglacial valley south of the central chalk ridge. Further down the slope the intersection with other valleys forms a wide gap. This area may have formed a deep water basin when the Wantsum channel was formed, an ideal location for a small landing place or even a boatyard on the tidal channel. Four bronze

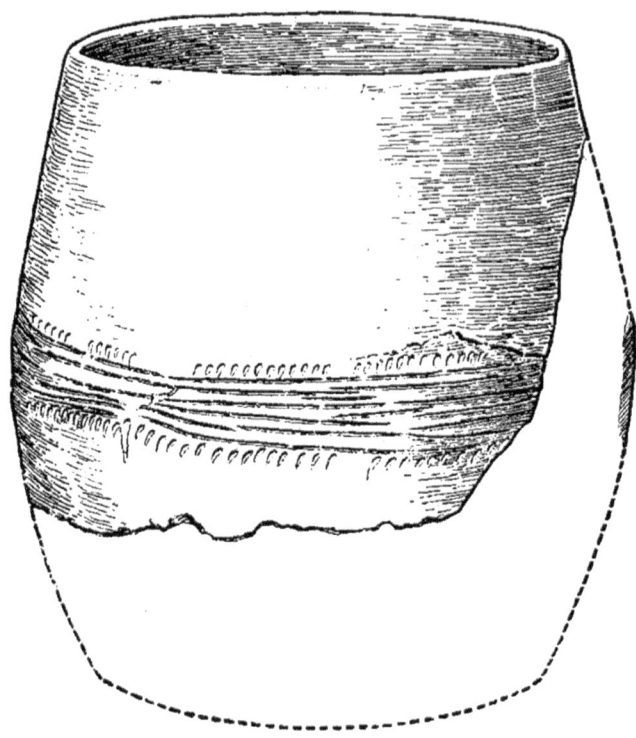

60 Small barrel-shaped cremation urn from a barrow at King Edward Avenue. *After Hurd, 1913*

hoards were found within a small area at the top of the valley. Features found in the area were difficult to define but seem to represent floors and hollows associated with dwellings. Hearths were present and a perforated clay plaque found on the site may be kiln furniture. A significant assemblage of pottery typical of the range of the transition from the Late Bronze Age to the Early Iron Age pottery types was present (Perkins *et al* 1994).

The Bronze hoards of the Late Bronze Age are easier to identify as they are frequently large and the range of items in them more complex, including weapons, cast tools and objects made of sheet metal reflecting the increased sophistication and range of the metalworkers. Generally, ingots and lumps of raw bronze are present, indicating that the material may have been gathered for recycling into new objects. Some axes of early forms have been included in large hoards with later Bronze Age material, indicating that older tools might circulate for some time. If the larger, late groups represent gatherings of raw material for reworking, older types of tool found with them may have been scavenged from burials, tips or older workshop relics. Early tools only survived because they escaped the demand in later years for scrap bronze to make whatever new objects were currently required.

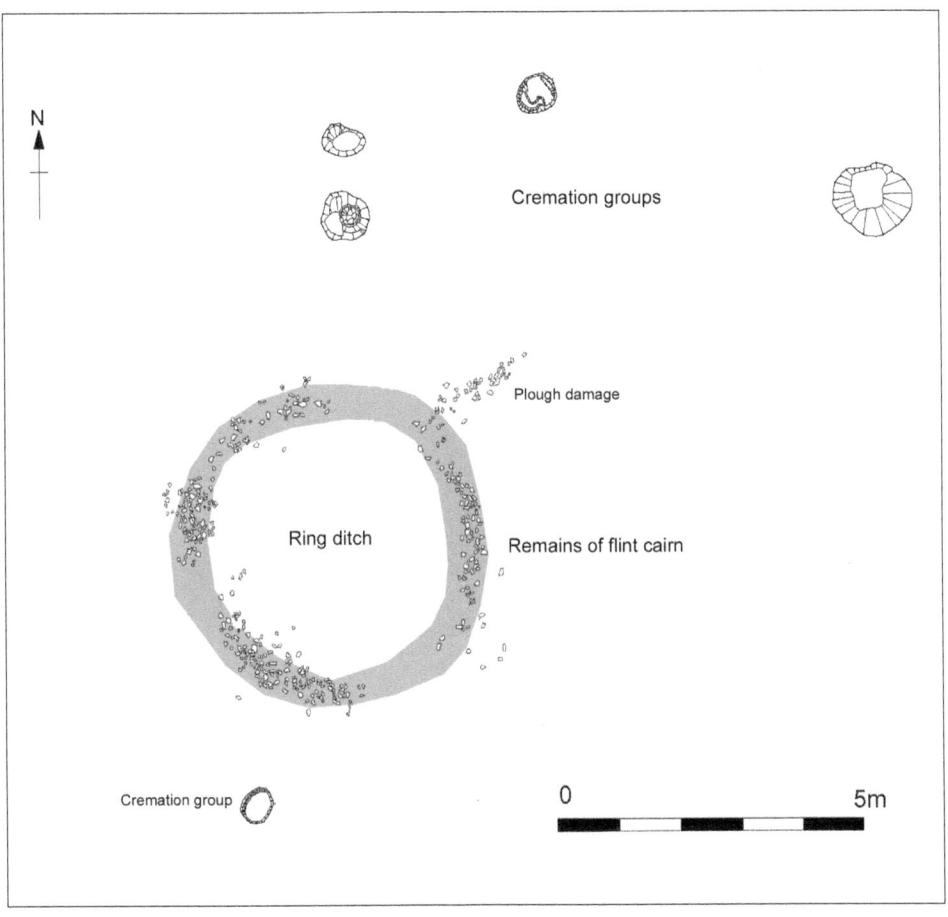

61 Cremation groups associated with a small ring ditch and a flint cairn at West Cliff, Ramsgate. © Trust for Thanet Archaeology

Another element of the Late Bronze Age hoards is the proliferation of (often) military equipment and fittings with their echoes of ancient literature, and the Bronze Age world of Greece — shields, swords, armour and chariot fittings. These hoards show the working of fine sheet metal and reveal a sophisticated range of objects wonderfully demonstrated by the Beck find (*64*). This hoard, with 73 pieces weighing 13lb 10oz (6.18kg), was discovered in 1938 in a pit close to a spring on the foreshore at Minnis Bay after strong tides had scoured away sand covering the beach. A subsequent excavation explored Late Bronze Age features on the foreshore containing preserved timber structures and waterlogged material included rush or straw thatching material and an important assemblage of ceramics (Worsfold 1943). The finds were associated with an inundated settlement located on the western side of a periglacial valley. In the Bronze Age the spring had entered a bay cut into the chalk further to the north-west.

62 A flint-tempered vessel found inverted over cremation at the site at West Cliff, Ramsgate (the vessel is shown inverted). © *Trust for Thanet Archaeology*

Bronzes and boats

63 South Dumpton Down palstave hoard and ring. © *Trust for Thanet Archaeology*

A very large number of bronzes have been found in the area of Ebbsfleet, likely to have been a sheltered beaching area in the lagoon behind the Ebbsfleet peninsula. The find spot of the largest and earliest recorded hoard (65) was reported by George Payne in 1895:

> Mr. W.H. Hills of Ramsgate kindly placed in my hands a hoard of bronze weapons and implements which had been discovered on a farm at Ebbs Fleet near Minster. The hoard consisted of 181 pieces, weighing about 60lbs [27.21 kg] and comprising palstaves, socketed celts, spear-heads, portions of swords and celts, belt fasteners, portions of a dagger, a knife, and a quantity of lumps of copper. These objects formed the stock in trade of a bronze founder, who went about from one settlement to another casting implements on the spot and taking old worn and broken ones as payment for new.
>
> Payne 1895

Four further small groups of bronzes have since been found on the Ebbsfleet peninsula in archaeological excavations associated with a wastewater treatment plant, and at Cliffsend in excavations for a housing development (Wessex Archaeology 2006, 48; 2005, 23). Fragments of bronzes from a dispersed hoard have also been found at Minster and may be associated with another landing place on the spring-fed stream (Kent Archaeological Society Archives).

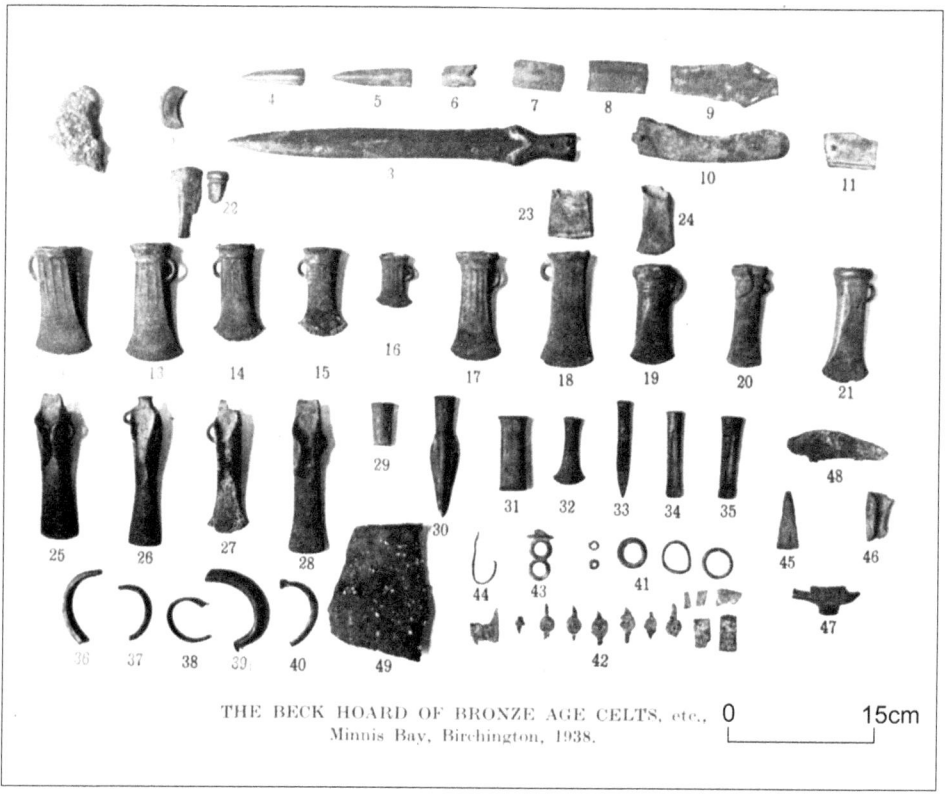

64 Late Bronze Age hoard found by James Beck at Minnis Bay

With the specialisation of social groups along divisions based on particular areas of skills, labour, trade and economic production, came the struggles of power and politics. Labour could be directed and organised to the advantage and enrichment of one faction or another.

The direction of bronze-working technology to the development of weapons is attested by the numerous spearheads and sword blade fragments that have been found in the hoards. The mass production of these objects in a series of common types suggests the widespread organisation of armed groups. It is difficult to say what form organised military groups would take; they may have been closely associated with community groups such as a family or clan, or organised at a higher level by village or by regional levies. The politics and warfare of the age have left nothing but the debris of their struggles as clues for us to piece together the causes and justification of its social conflict. These communities are the ancestors of the tribes that were met by Caesar in the first century BC and the societies he described with its tribal conflicts may have their origin in this period.

There is increasing evidence of violent conflict or extreme judicial punishment in the period of transition into the Iron Age. The burial of several individuals with unhealed

Bronzes and boats

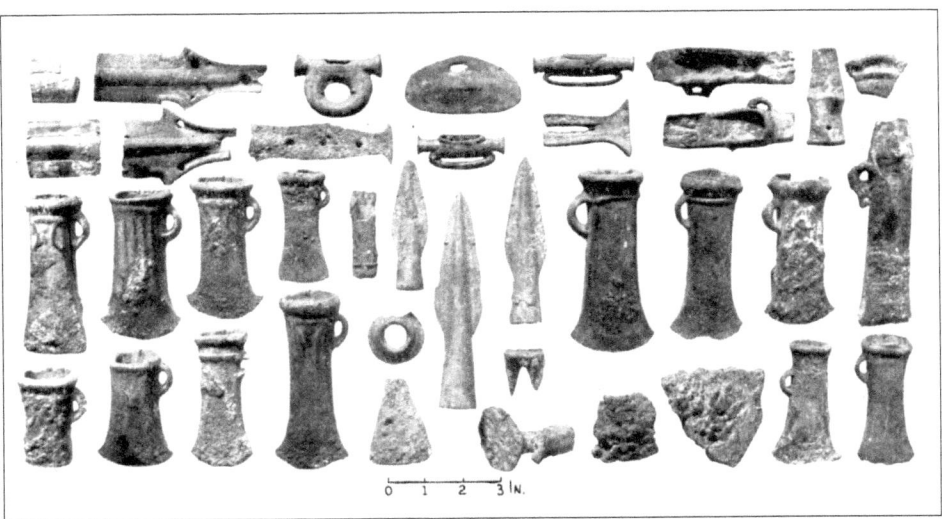

65 The Ebbsfleet Farm hoard. *After R. Jessup*

sword cuts, and evidence of violent death were found at Cliffsend (Wessex Archaeology 2005). The placement of these burials in the large pits of abandoned clay quarry workings is a stark deviation from the formal and ceremonial burial of the past age and prefigures the diverse burial practices found in later Iron Age sites on Thanet. The association of human remains with animal carcasses and evidence of dismembering has generated dark tales of symbolic sacrifice and the arrangement of post mortem messages to the rest of society. Like the pirate's skeleton in *Treasure Island* that was laid on the beach pointing toward hidden treasures, or the highwayman hanging in the gibbet as an example to others not to follow his wicked ways, these burials have been read as mysterious acts full of symbolism (Greatorex 2005, 2). However, we know nothing of the life of these folk buried in their quarries and hollows. History teaches us that the innocent and vulnerable are usually victims in conflict between the powerful, and we should be careful not to regard these arrangements as indicators of the health and moral trajectory of a society.

It has been suggested that the deposition of some hoards could represent 'leave-taking deposits', buried when closing a settlement after people have moved on from it (Perkins 1999b). Perhaps this has more of a metaphorical than literal truth in it, as the mechanisms through which a society moves on from both its spatial location and its economic foundations are complex. Tools do serve symbolic roles in society, as extensions of man's power over material things, however these symbolisms are accrued from a living interaction with the objects through work and craftsmanship, rather than the veneration of the tool in the abstract. There may have been many forces at work when tools were lost or abandoned and we should take care not to elevate one of these roles over any other without careful consideration. The hoards are symbolic, perhaps, of leave-taking from one social mode to another reliant on different technologies, new social relationships and with an altered spatial distribution.

8

ISLANDERS –
THE IRON AGE IN THANET

By the sixth century BC the erosion of the chalk cliffs around Thanet had produced tall, almost impassable cliff edges in all but the deepest valley intersections. Other than the broad bay harbours at Margate and Ramsgate, several smaller bays and creeks still allowed access to the sea on the north and eastern coasts at Kingsgate, Joss Bay, Stone Bay and Dumpton. Several of these would have provided harbour for fishing boats and coastal traders, as well as sea-going trading ships. The north coast between Margate and Birchington was well populated, but the soft loess filling the valley network eroded very quickly along a low straight cliff edge between Margate Bay and a rise north-west of Birchington. Here a promontory between two valleys at Gore End was being cut away by the sea; this may have been one of the only long stretches of accessible coastline suitable for saltings and for beaching small fishing boats. The chalk cliffs developing around the fringe would not have been as high around some of the inlets as they are at the present day. The north-east face of the central plateau would have presented as a tall cliff at White Ness and North Foreland, even though the valleys between probably reached down to the sea.

A ferry or ford at Sarre provided a link between the mainland and the well-developed trackway across the central ridge (*66*). The route crossed passages along valleys sides that connected the bays and harbours to the upland areas. The main route across the plateau may have been linked by a branch that followed a roughly level route across the north-western part of the island from Monkton to Margate. Cropmarks of trackways consistent with this route are visible at Woodchurch, south-east of Birchington (TfTA Archives). Herds of sheep and cattle shared the valley routes as drove ways to pastures and markets. By the Iron Age the Wantsum channel would have been deepening, with the lateral valleys presenting as salt marsh and mud flats up to the tidal limits. Several of these valleys would have allowed vessels to beach near to small settlements along the southern slopes of the central ridge at Minster, Monkton, Durlock, Ebbsfleet, St Nicholas and Brooksend. Larger vessels could enter a safe harbour through the gap at Stonar and anchor in the central channel or beach along the sands on the Ebbsfleet peninsula. There were small communities on a headland between creeks off the southern entrance to the Wantsum at Richborough and at Sandwich (Cunliffe 1968; Parfitt 2004; Holman 2005).

Islanders – the Iron Age in Thanet

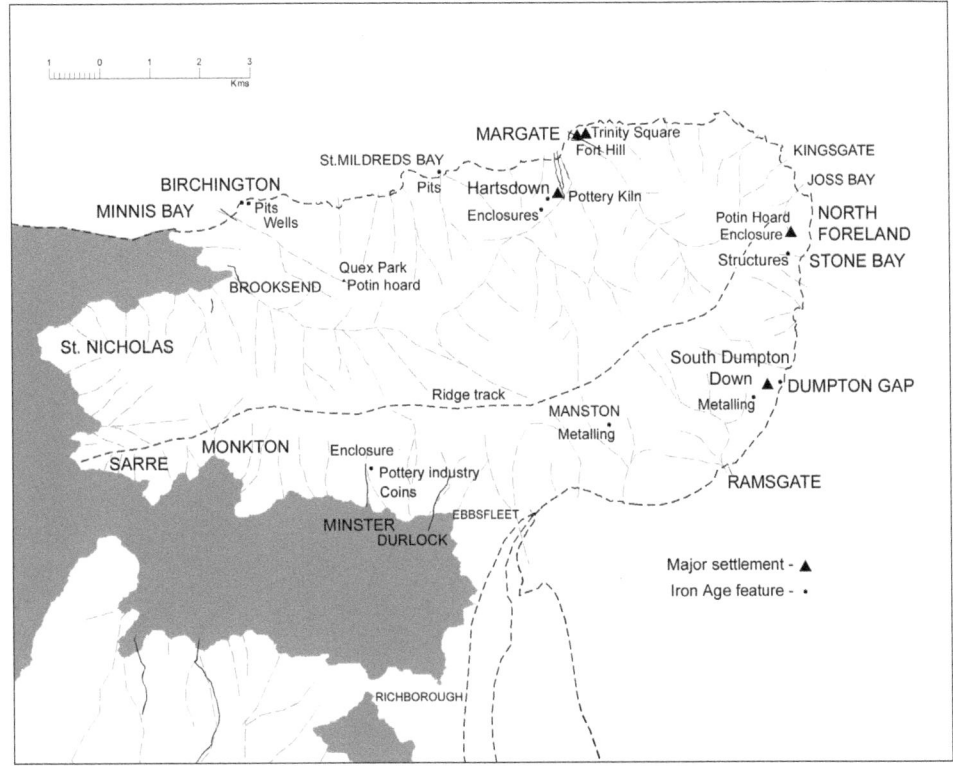

66 Location of Iron Age settlement sites and features on Thanet. © *Trust for Thanet Archaeology*

The transition to a distinctive Iron Age around the sixth century BC is probably no more than an arbitrary division, as the social conditions of work and settlement under which iron tools replaced bronze had been laid in the Late Bronze Age. Transitional forms of ceramics dating to between the tenth and seventh century BC, spanning the interface between the Bronze Age and Early Iron Age, have been identified. These are widely distributed on Thanet and in the east Kent region (Macpherson-Grant 1994). Many sites of essentially Late Bronze Age date are associated with ceramic sherds of these forms; they have been described in detail at Minnis Bay (Worsfold 1943) and Monkton Court Farm. Pottery of this date has been recognised on sites at Margate (Perkins 1996) and Ebbsfleet (Hearne *et al* 1995; WA 2006, 42). No excavations have produced extensive settlement evidence exclusively associated with these forms, and they appear in the record generally as the latest material on sites of essentially Late Bronze Age date. The transitional pottery forms discovered at Monkton Court Farm were found in association with hoards of Late Bronze Age date (Macpherson-Grant 1994). Pottery of this period was present in quarry ditches cut into a Bronze Age ring ditch at East Northdown, the last phase of alteration to this monument, and in the upper fills of a Bronze Age round barrow ditch at North Foreland (Smith 1986; Boast *et al* 2006a). No further activity took place at the site at

North Foreland for some 300 years. The first Early Iron Age features date to the fifth century BC.

A stratified society had emerged in the Bronze Age based on the specialisation of social roles. At that time, the economy provided a source of demand for skilled carpenters and shipwrights, bronze- and ironworkers, sailors, traders and also a class of professional or semi-professional soldiers. By the Iron Age, the division of society by occupation was ingrained. The foundations of regional identities were set, with power bases forming under the influence of very ancient territorial and social traditions. The market for foodstuffs enabled agricultural production to be directed toward generating tradable surpluses rather than subsistence. Salt-makers, working around the coast of Thanet, provided the preservatives that would allow foods to be stored and traded over greater distances without tainting.

Pollen samples from Weatherlees have indicated an increase in clearance and agricultural activity beginning in the Iron Age, probably reflecting increased grain production (Hearne *et al* 1995, 311). Clearance of timber on a large scale in the Bronze Age probably opened up more land for grazing and grain production, and by the Iron Age the landscape may have been more open and exposed than it had ever been before. The pollen samples also indicate a background presence of woodland species. With a developed maritime tradition it is likely that natural resources of large timbers and natural forest cover were no longer available, any woods that were preserved on the island would have been carefully managed and controlled, possibly with a strategic supply, for construction purposes.

The evidence for Iron Age settlement on the uplands of Thanet is dominated by the artefacts of large-scale livestock and grain production and by the network of trade routes that went with this rural economy. The settlement around the coastal margins also shows evidence for the trade of goods and cultural influences with the continent. The two largest upland sites that have been excavated at North Foreland and South Dumpton Down appear to be new establishments, replacing earlier Bronze Age landscapes dominated by round barrows. It is a common pattern in the British Iron Age for sites to develop in defensible landscape zones, producing nucleated hillfort communities represented by classic sites such as Maiden Castle or Danebury (Wheeler 1943; Cunliffe 1991). The Iron Age settlements at North Foreland and South Dumpton Down have generally been interpreted within this framework (Perkins *et al* 1998) (67). Analysis of the components of the Iron Age settlements in Thanet in their landscape context supports a different model of a more mobile society, where the sites excavated represent zones of specialised functions, linked by paths to the main trackway across the island, thereby joining all the coastal and uplands zones in a single network.

The settlement at North Foreland occupies a distinctive landscape feature: a plateau on a promontory with a steep slope on either side. A complex of linear ditches on the northern side of the promontory has been observed in aerial photographs. The ditches have been interpreted as a defensive enclosure, possibly following the contours of the promontory, encompassing the settlement on the plateau (Perkins *et al* 1998). The ditches have been sampled by excavation (Hogwood 1995) showing them to be of limited depth

Islanders – the Iron Age in Thanet

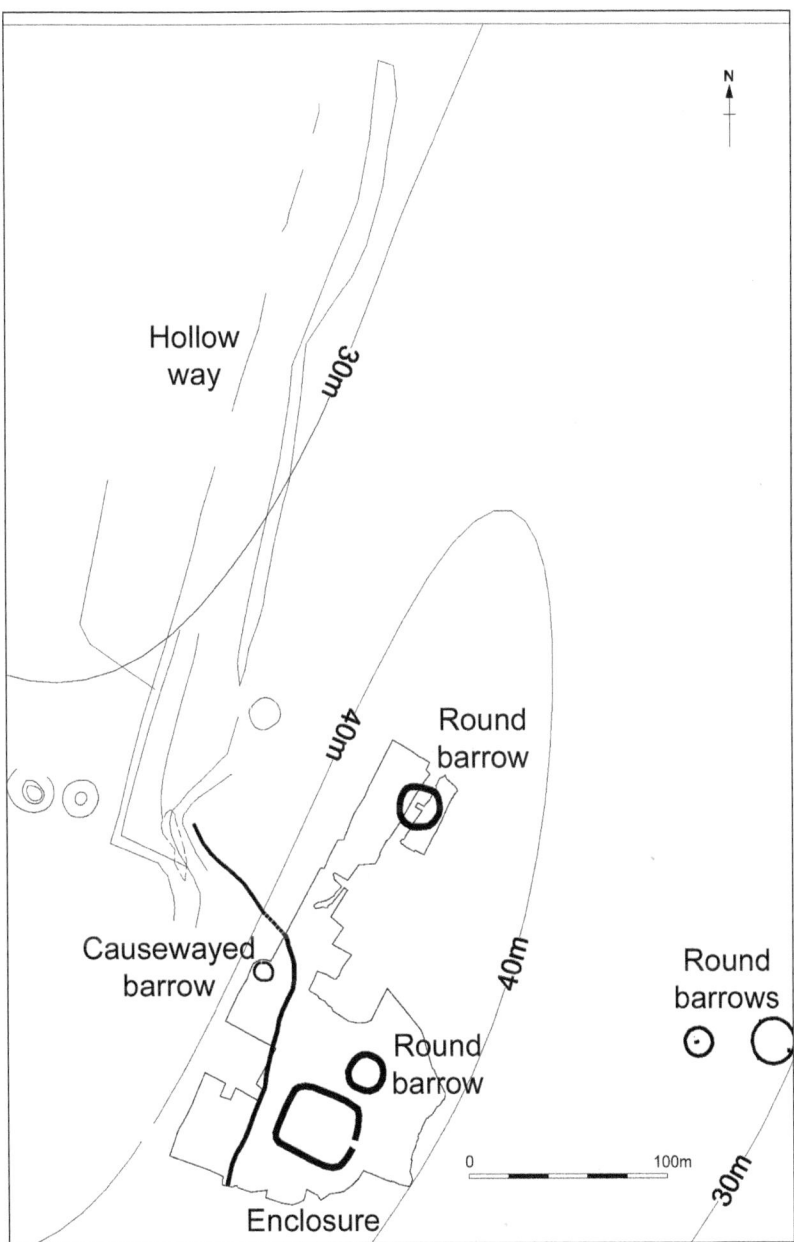

67 Cropmarks and excavated features on the North Foreland promontory. ©
Trust for Thanet Archaeology

and of more than one phase, with ceramics dating from the Iron Age to the Roman period. Overlaying the aerial photographic plots and the archaeological data on a topographic model has produced evidence of a more complicated system operating within the landscape. The linear features are more appropriately interpreted as the ditches of a hollow-way climbing in a curvilinear path up the north-facing slope of the valley (*68*).

The route is paralleled by a sunken lane (Elmwood Avenue), still in use on the other side of the same valley, and other routes on Thanet (Boast *et al* 2006a). This hollow-way route probably evolved as a drove way linking Joss Bay to the upland plateau and from there to the central track across the ridge toward Ramsgate and Sarre. Multiple-tracked hollow-ways tend to form on steep rises, where different routes up the slope are taken by traffic according to the conditions and their ability to climb the slope. Parallels to a hollow-way of this type on the central ridge were excavated on the steep slope of the ridge near Monkton and are likely to have formed in the same way over a similar period of time (Bennett 1995; 1996). Rather than a nucleated site, it is likely that the settlement features at North Foreland were a node on a transport route from the coast at Joss Bay toward the upland plateau.

At South Dumpton Down a very broad linear feature extended westwards from a point in the east where it had been truncated by the cliff-line across the settlement. This feature is also the result of the cutting of a number of linear ditches, eventually forming a broad hollow-way. This would have risen through the site in a similar curving trajectory toward the plateau as the ditches at North Foreland (Perkins 1995b). A series of ditches to the east, dating from the Early Iron Age, appear to define large rectangular field boundaries and a smaller trackway, established at right angles to the hollow-way. Other linear features may also be tracks rising from Dumpton Gap to intersect with the main east to west route. The new enclosure superseded a Late Bronze Age enclosure of more irregular lozenge shape. The excavators noted that the Bronze Age ditches were less substantial than the Iron Age ones, indicating that it was an entirely new layout. A nucleated Late Bronze Age farmstead was replaced by a more extensive stock- or grain-raising system with integrated tracks linking it to the main route across the ridge.

Further linear ditches and possible trackways of Iron Age date were found in the same valley as far as the plateau (Minter *et al* 1973, 14; Philp *et al* 2002). Although the whole network cannot be definitively linked in plan, it is likely that the landscape was divided regularly between large fields and stock enclosures laced with drove ways up the valleys. The trackways appear to have been surfaced in places. Patches of metalling, in a hollow discovered at Upton along the route of the main track across the plateau date from the Late Iron Age. This observation probably indicates that important interchanges were prepared with hard standings, if not paved (Moody 2007). At Manston, the ditches of a hollow-way, probably dating to the Late Bronze Age, were later sealed by spreads of small flint pebbles and broken fragments of pottery in the Iron Age (Boast *et al* 2006b) (*69*). Metalled areas were also recognised in the sections cut through the hollow-way at Dumpton and further west up the slope (Perkins 1995b, 16; Philp *et al* 2002).

A large settlement developed on the chalk slopes around Margate Bay in the Iron Age. On the eastern side of the bay a number of ditches, pits and structures dating from the Middle to Late Iron Age have been excavated. These have all been encountered in sites within the town and it is difficult to interpret the overall layout of the sites (Perkins 1998d). Linear ditches are present that might indicate field boundaries similar to the sites

Islanders – the Iron Age in Thanet

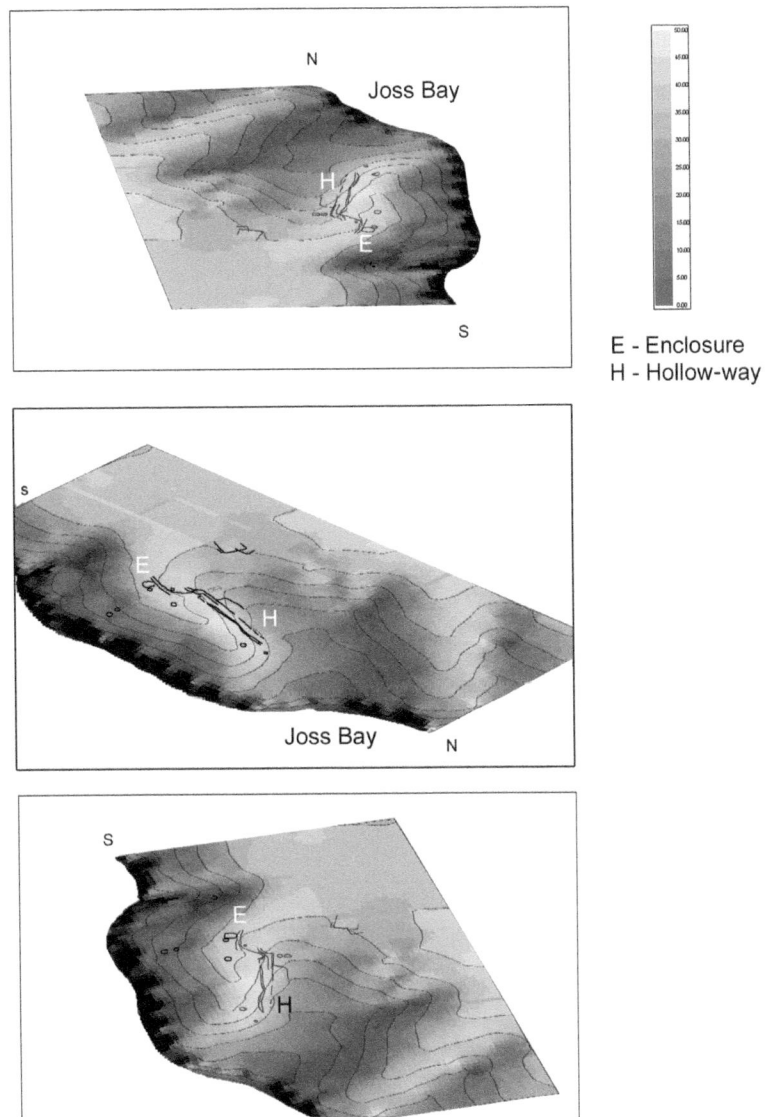

68 Elevation model of the North Foreland peninsular, showing features in relation to topography. © *Trust for Thanet Archaeology*

on the south-east of Thanet. At Hartsdown, on the western side of Margate, the lower slopes of the valley once carried the spring-fed Tivoli Brook. Excavation and aerial photography have shown that the western slopes of the valley were occupied by enclosures and field systems. These have been partly sampled and appear to date broadly from the Late Bronze Age to the Late Iron Age (Perkins 1996; TfTA Archives). This

69 Flint pebble metalling at Manston. © Trust for Thanet Archaeology

further reinforces the pattern of rectilinear enclosures linked by small local tracks to the upland routes.

The pattern of enclosed settlements and trackways can be compared to the ladder settlements of Iron Age and Roman date that are found along the slopes of valleys in the Yorkshire Wolds (Stoertz 1997). Settlements are interspersed at regular intervals, sharing the resources of upland pasture and streams that run through the valley bases. In Thanet, the streams are fed by springs in the chalk and generally emerge near the heads of the valleys. Thus settlement tends to be slightly more concentrated around the deep valleys with access to the sea. The Yorkshire examples are more often spaced regularly through long gullies.

Several sites on the northern Thanet coast have produced evidence of occupation in the Late Iron Age. The erosion of the coastal fringe between Margate and Birchington has been extensive and probably advanced in the Iron Age, resulting in a low cliff. Well bases and pit remnants have been encountered on the foreshore at Minnis Bay and St Mildred's Bay where the sea has scoured away the sand (Powell-Cotton *et al* 1939; Worsfold 1943; Perkins 2001a). Well shafts, large quarries and even cemeteries of Late Iron Age or Roman date can be seen in section on the cliff faces at Birchington (TAU 1986). Evidence of further settlements has been gathered in the excavation of pits and burials close to the cliffs between Birchington and Margate (Boast 2004a). Erosion probably progressed too fast in these areas to establish large enclosed settlements on the valleys.

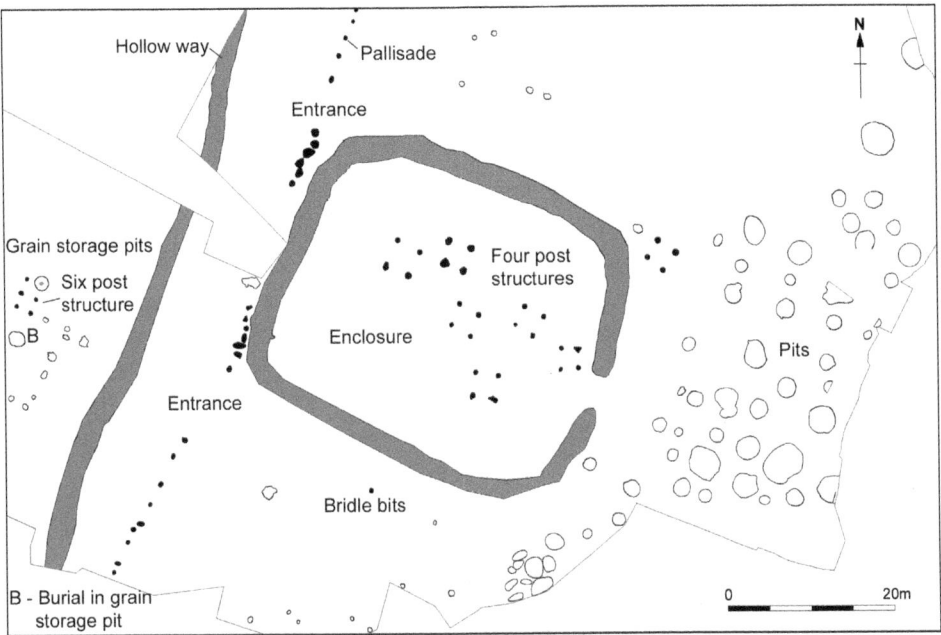

70 Iron Age features on the North Foreland promontory (all phases). © Trust for Thanet Archaeology

The range of features on the enclosed sites generally includes subdivisions and structural evidence, allowing some discussion of the distribution of functions within sites and between settlements. Occupation at North Foreland and South Dumpton Down was spread over considerable areas. Pottery and other finds were present in the fills of cut features, allowing separate periods of occupation to be distinguished.

Large, regular, circular storage pits cut into the chalk are typical Early Iron Age features on sites on Thanet and in Early Iron Age sites generally. The pits are sometimes vertically sided and neatly cut, but can also often have undercut sides giving them rounded bag shapes. These pits had been used to store some element of the annual grain harvest below ground, in combination with post-built structures used to store some grain above ground. Two large pits dating from the fourth to fifth century BC were the earliest features of the Iron Age settlement at North Foreland (*70*). A thick deposit of charred grains including barley, spelt, emmer and oats remained at the base of one of the storage pits. A basalt saddle quern fragment found among the charred grains at the base of the pit indicated that suitable stones were traded, probably as ballast in ships from the West Country using the Wantsum channel. Fragments of hand querns have been found within Iron Age features at many sites on Thanet.

Several deep, straight-sided storage pits were present at South Dumpton, dispersed irregularly within the rectangular boundaries (Perkins 1995b; Minter *et al* 1973, 14). The earliest storage pits were sparsely distributed and may have served to keep the whole of the stored element of the season's harvest for a community or a family. Excavations at Fort Hill and Trinity Square at Margate have exposed complexes of circular pits similar to that at South Dumpton Down and North Foreland. A feature at Trinity Square appears to have been a large, circular grain storage pit with the upper levels cut away to create an irregular hollow. A series of stake holes surrounding the feature may have formed a windbreak around the hollow. Similar adaptations to grain storage pits are known from the enclosed Early Iron Age site at Little Woodbury in Wiltshire (Bersu 1940). At Hartsdown, a dense concentration of Late Iron Age storage pits and linear gullies were found on the north-west facing slope of the valley overlooking Margate Bay (*71*). These probably represent one of the series of small enclosed settlements arranged along the sides of the valley (TfTA Archives).

Inhumations have often been found within the backfills of the large storage pits which are associated with the early phases of many of the settlements. These burials appear informal; the skeletons are often in positions that indicate that they were not carefully laid out after death. At Fort Hill (*72*) and Trinity Square, Margate, burials were crouched on their fronts and face-down respectively. Several other skeletons have been found in similar positions in other storage pits (Perkins 1995b). One grave within an enclosure at South Dumpton Down contained the skeleton of a young girl with her head resting on a small dog (Minter *et al* 1973, 15). These inhumations have been interpreted as representing people excluded from normal society, banished with the rubbish of the settlement (TfTA Archives). However, the association with the grain stores may have had a more symbolic resonance to the communities. Three small blue glass beads (one very decayed) were found at the neck of an adult woman buried in a grain storage pit at North Foreland (*73*). These prestige items indicate that perhaps this type of burial was a more formal rite than has previously been suggested. The burial may have been a secondary cut dug into the fill of an existing pit. Perhaps the remains of the pit above ground were interpreted as some other form of structure, such as a small barrow mound or cairn, which was socially acceptable for reuse as a prestige burial monument.

The enlarged grain storage pit at Trinity Square, Margate, contained an inhumation buried face-down within the original fill of the feature. Two further inhumations, cut through the upper fill of this structure, were perhaps of Romano-British date. The only examples of inhumations in conventional graves of Early Iron Age date were five burials excavated on a small development site at North Foreland, probably cut into an earlier round barrow. One was accompanied by a sherd of incised decorated pottery which has parallels with the Early Iron Age pottery of the Marne area of France (TAU 1981).

In the Middle Iron Age the intensity of settlement at North Foreland increased. In the second century BC, a ditched enclosure with a rounded rectangular plan and a single causewayed entrance was built in a key location at a constricted point in the promontory. One of the ditches of the hollow-way, rising through the valley, takes a sharp deviation through a natural hollow in the promontory to pass the enclosure at the north-west end.

Parallel to the hollow-way ditch, a line of posts was erected with gaps either side of the enclosure ditch. A zone relatively clear of features around the outside of the enclosure suggests it may have had an outer bank. The fence and the enclosure could

71 Circular grain storage pit at Hartsdown, Margate. © Trust for Thanet Archaeology

72 Inhumation within a grain storage pit at Fort Hill, Margate. © Trust for Thanet Archaeology

73 Inhumation within a grain storage pit at North Foreland, Broadstairs. © Trust for Thanet Archaeology

be part of a stock-management system, controlling and selecting from herds that were driven through the valley to the bay below. The enclosure may have been used to hold stock for sale or to be slaughtered within the hilltop site. The enclosure was located at a key point to take advantage of passing stock and may have been the site of a specialised livestock or meat trader.

As specialised elements of the community required others to produce the surpluses that sustained them, the demand for trade goods in the Late Iron Age increased. Trade and exchange is dependent on both the movement of goods and the cultural acceptance of tokens of exchange. From the fourth century BC, gold coin became the standard for the storage of wealth throughout the Mediterranean world. The European Celtic world adopted the model of the Greek gold stater of Philip II of Macedon as a symbol of compatibility with the tokens of this ancient nation, thereby associating their coinage with the success and longevity of the Greek trading formula. Copper and tin alloys became the tokens of smaller exchanges. Gold could be interchanged over the trading networks of the European continent, whereas small change was largely guaranteed by the local customs and confidence. A recent comprehensive study of the Iron Age coin distributions in east Kent by David Holman has recognised that coins were adopted at an early stage in the east Kent area. Thanet followed a similar pattern to the mainland of Kent in that coins were in use at an early period somewhere between 150 and 100 BC. The most common Iron Age coins were made of potin, a copper and tin alloy. The two earliest forms of these coins, Kentish Primary and Flat Linear Potins, were probably made in Kent in large quantities (Holman 2005). The North Foreland promontory has produced 81 Iron Age coins in gold, silver and bronze as well as potin, which were the most abundant, and are represented by the earliest Kentish Primary and Flat Linear types. A pit at the north-eastern edge of the excavation contained a hoard of 62 Flat Linear Potins distributed in its upper fills (Boast et al 2006a; Holman 2005, 19).

Concentrations of coins have been found on Cottington Hill on the Ebbsfleet peninsula, located at a key point near the Wantsum. A very large Potin hoard containing several hundred coins, with many more possibly dispersed among the men who discovered them, was found at Quex Park, Birchington, in 1853. The coins appeared to have been packed in some form of container (Barrett 1893). Another trading centre might exist here that has not yet been investigated by archaeologists. Small numbers of Iron Age coins are known from other sites indicating the widespread adoption of coinage in Thanet (TfTA Archives). Not all trade would take place in the open market or through the exchange of coinage; large-scale transfers of goods between groups could be negotiated by community leaders and regulated by customary agreements. These would not be reflected in the patterns of coin use. Coins might only be used on the margins of the developing economy where there were no customary arrangements. Their distribution indicates locations where direct marketing of goods took place and where exchanges were between groups with no previously established relationships of trust.

Iron Age settlement sites are the first in Thanet where a common range of post-built structures can be recognised. The interpretation of the function and sequence of these structures depends on interpreting the superstructures represented by postholes. The common four- and six-posthole groups found on Iron Age sites in Thanet are comparable with those found within the enclosed hilltop settlements in other parts of Britain. The structures that the posthole groups represent can be interpreted in various ways to indicate the different functions taking place within a settlement. Several experimental reconstructions have been made, such as those at Butser Ancient Farm. Four-posted buildings have been interpreted as granaries where threshed grains would be stored ready to be used over the winter and spring (Cunliffe 1991; www.butserancientfarm.co.uk). A storage area was constructed on top of, and supported by, a set of four posts, each post being capped by a large flat stone to prevent rodents from climbing up and over into the grain. The four-post structure may have been used to store grain ready to be used, while silos containing threshed grain for seed corn were sealed below ground.

Six-posted structures are harder to interpret. Usually their dimensions are too small to be regarded as a barn for storing grain still on the stalk, unless the year's harvest was distributed around smaller buildings. Some buildings may have been finished more elaborately; at North Foreland fragments of a thick plaster of chalk paste were found. This material had been applied over a framework of stakes and wattles whose impressions were visible in the blocks of plaster. Squared edges and corners suggested that these were carefully finished and might have been related to a domestic building (74). It is possible

74 Chalk plaster lining found within a storage pit at North Foreland. © Trust for Thanet Archaeology

they were remnants of a lining for the pit itself, prepared for storage of seed grain by carefully plastering a lining of timber.

The proliferation of these features coincides with the introduction of coinage in Kent. The storage pits and post-built structures were elements of a complex cycle of grain production. The grain that was to be used through the year was to be kept above ground. The seeds for sowing the following year were sealed in the underground pits where they would keep well. The post-built structures may have stored grain that could be traded.

A large number of four- and six-post structures can be recognised at North Foreland and these seem to supersede the function of the stock enclosure. Structures were being found inside and outside the enclosing ditch, suggesting that it may have been retained as a compound. Two more four-post structures were found on the slope of a valley at Stone Bay, dated by a potin coin to after 150 BC. This may indicate the western extent

Islanders – the Iron Age in Thanet

75 Six-post structure excavated at Fort Hill, Margate. *Trust for Thanet Archaeology archive* © *J. Villette, reproduced by permission*

of the North Foreland settlement or the start of another settlement focus, at the head of this valley to the west (Moody 2007). A six-post structure has been recognised on a site on the eastern side of the bay at Fort Hill, Margate (Perkins 1998d) (*75*). Although postholes were present at the South Dumpton Down settlement, typical four- or six-post structures were not present in large numbers and there were alignments of structural postholes in other linear configurations not clearly interpretable as buildings.

A dense concentration of pits located at the eastern side of the North Foreland enclosure entrance suggests that intensive occupation was separated from the grain storage area. The pottery in the fills indicates a first-century BC date for the excavated sample. With little stratigraphy to separate phases of cutting in the concentrations of smaller pits on the sites, it is only possible to classify the features by the variety of sizes and forms. With dense pit groups, posts that might be arranged in circular or rectangular structures are obscured by other, randomly placed pits and truncation by other substantial features. Posthole groups interpreted as structures have to be extracted carefully from the plans. Some of the pits in the complex might be structural, others may be domestic rubbish pits. In one of the pits on the south-western edge of the enclosure, two sets of iron bridle bits were recovered from the base. It is not clear whether these were thrown away, suggesting the pits were at the margin of settlement, or deliberately placed in the pit, which might indicate the pit area was less peripheral to the community (*76*).

No convincing plans of Iron Age round houses have been recognised on Thanet. These are usually characterised as regular post settings representing the structure, with

The Isle of Thanet – from Prehistory to the Norman Conquest

76 A bridle bit from pit at North Foreland. The picture shows the object and a reconstruction.
© *Trust for Thanet Archaeology*

circular drip gullies around the outside. Reconstructions using four-post buildings as the central supporting framework of roundhouses have been made. In these the rafters are arranged in a circle spreading from a square sill beam at the top of the long corner posts. Six-post structures could represent a similar arrangement, with an extra pair of posts supporting a porch entrance to the round house. The alternative reconstructions of the buildings of the Iron Age make the interpretation of the pattern of settlement problematic. A large group of four-post structures, such as were encountered in the North Foreland area, could be considered to be evidence of a densely occupied village. If the buildings were granaries and barns then communal storage is a valid interpretation, with the population housed in an undiscovered area. Only further analysis of the spatial distribution of the structures on the sites will help to resolve this issue. In the absence of contradictory evidence, the North Foreland structures can be interpreted as an above-ground grain storage zone for a wider settlement. This would be a busy place: each day the granaries would be visited for grain to grind into flour. Although not the home of the Iron Age people, it was a place central to their community. Other craft activities may have taken place on the site and a large chalk loom weight and a spindle whorl found at North Foreland and Stone Bay are evidence that textile production at least was practiced, perhaps as a domestic craft. Another pierced flat stone from North Foreland could be a loom weight or possibly a weight to sink a fishing net.

The pottery assemblages in Early and Middle Iron Age sites in Thanet include several continental influences. Thanet has many examples of vessels that have been treated with an external slip of clay to create a distinctive 'rusticated' finish, a style with parallels to vessels from the Marne area of France. This pottery has a restricted east Kent distribution (Perkins 1999b, 125-6). Rusticated pottery of this type has been found at North Foreland, Ebbsfleet and Margate. Some plain pottery from the same sites was finished with a coating of haematite, an iron oxide compound, creating a red surface on the outside of the vessels. In some Early and Middle Iron Age vessels, the red staining was used to pick out elements of patterns on the surface of the pottery.

Fineware bowls, with painted red and white finishes, were also present and have close parallels in the Pas de Calais area (*77*). Among the vessels recovered in excavations by Dr Arthur Rowe in 1924 at Tivoli, Margate, were two Middle Iron Age pots decorated with geometric patterns in the distinctive La Tène style (*78*). Although the vessels were probably the products of local industries, continental styles and vessel forms were well represented at Margate. Similarly decorated vessels with the pattern picked out in red paint have been found at Fort Hill on the eastern side of Margate (Rowe 1925; SWAT Archives) (*79 & 80*).

Iron Age settlement sites with the range of structures found at South Dumpton Down, North Foreland and Margate are rare in Thanet. Geophysical survey at Minster produced the plan of a large circular feature enclosed within a rectangular boundary similar to that at North Foreland. The location of this site, adjacent to the spring, suggests it may represent some form of temple. Limited sampling of the area suggests that it may date to the Late Iron Age (Kent Archaeological Society Archives). In one of the few opportunities there has been to explore the features along the northern coast, pits of

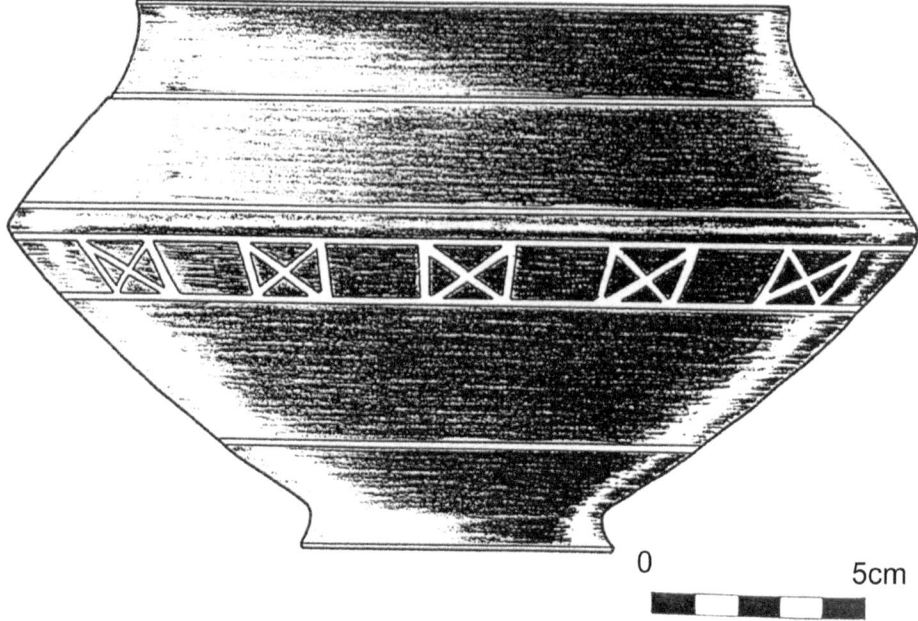

77 Reconstruction of an Iron Age polychrome-decorated vessel of the type found at Margate. © *Trust for Thanet Archaeology*

rectangular and circular plan, associated with small gullies, were excavated on a small site at Birchington (Boast 2004). A deep circular shaft on the site may have been the upper part of a well, matched by features eroding from the cliffs only a few metres away (TAU 1986, 4). Many other Iron Age features have probably been lost to the sea.

Throughout the later part of the Iron Age, communities in Britain felt the influence of the expansion of the Roman Empire in various ways, ranging from the physical intervention of Julius Caesar in 55 and 54 BC to the effect of demand for trade goods from the Romanised European countries. In the Late Iron Age a distinct range of fine, wheel-turned vessels, decorated with cordons, scratched chevrons and combed and furrowed decoration emerged in east Kent and are found in considerable numbers on Thanet (*81*). These vessels had strong continental influences and sites of this age display a complex mix of imported prototypes and varying degrees of local copying of the style (Pollard 1988). Due to the immediate continental parallels in northern France and Belgium, this pottery was associated with an influx of 'Belgic' people from that area in the Late Iron Age, in response to the Roman conquest of Gaul. Due to the general continuity of settlement on the sites and the long history of contact with this area it is not clear whether this movement of people actually happened, or whether the increasing trade with Roman-influenced Gaul brought more of these vessels into the late communities in Thanet. At North Foreland there was much less activity in the area that could be dated to the Late Iron Age, 'Belgic' period. The distribution of coins also

Islanders – the Iron Age in Thanet

78 Front and back views of a vessel decorated with La Tène style patterns found at Tivoli, Margate

79 Mid to Late Iron Age pottery vessel of La Tène II phase, *c.*250-125 BC. Decorated with iron oxide pigment. © *Trust for Thanet Archaeology*

indicates a reduction in activity on the site in the mid first century BC (Holman 2005, 20). If the site represented a specialised functional zone within the grain production cycle it is possible that these moved to another location without the implication that there was any major change to the population or the economy. Pottery and coin evidence suggest that the hollow-ways at both North Foreland and Dumpton continued to be used well into the Roman period.

80 Reconstruction of the La Tène II vessel from Margate. © *SWAT Archaeology*

In the Late Iron Age, coinage began to be marked with names signifying the authorities under which it was issued. Later Iron Age coins carried the names of their local issuers in the Roman style, creating the earliest historical records of the leaders of Kentish society. Dubnovellaunos, Vosenos, Tasciovanus, Eppillus, Cunobelin and Amminus are known from the coins that were endorsed with their names (Holman 2005). There is little further documentary evidence of these people and historians are left to ponder who they were and what roles they had in society (Cunliffe 1991). Coins increasingly served to integrate Britain with the economy of the European continent, emulating Roman forms and inscription until they were subsumed by a common coinage after the Roman invasion in AD 43 (Holman 2005; De Jersey 1996).

There is evidence of a shift in settlement to new sites in regular rectangular enclosures in the Late Iron Age (*82*). Features associated with a rectangular enclosure at Dumpton Gap produced pottery ranging from Late Iron Age to early Roman date (Hurd 1913; Boast & Gardner 2006) (*83*). A polygonal enclosure of similar proportions was partly excavated at Manston and produced a pottery assemblage restricted to the Late Iron Age period, with no later Roman ceramics (Perkins *et al* 1997). Other enclosures of similar proportions have been recognised by aerial photography in the north-east part of Thanet, at North Foreland and Reading Street (Thanet Archaeological Society Archives) and also at Sarre, Woodchurch and Birchington, in the western part of Thanet. Although the aerial photographic plots are usually taken as indicators of enclosures of Romano-British date, it is clear that many of Thanet's Roman sites have direct precursors in rectangular enclosures of Late Iron Age date (RCHME 1989).

Islanders – the Iron Age in Thanet

81 Late Iron Age vessel decorated with cordons and scratched chevrons. © Trust for Thanet Archaeology

These sites may have been late farmsteads that were to become the earliest Romanised settlements on Thanet.

Two bone weaving-combs and triangular clay loomweights have been found at the Dumpton Gap enclosure (Boast & Gardner 2006; Hurd 1913) indicating domestic textile production. At Minster evidence has been found of a Late Iron Age pottery industry. Misfired water vessels in two fabrics, one in the form of a storage jar, as well as the other jars and necked bowls, were found in Late Iron Age features during the excavation of the Roman villa at Abbey Farm. In the years before the Roman invasion, 80 per cent of the pottery used at Minster was of very local production (Lyne 2006). A pottery kiln of Late Iron Age date was found on the banks of the Tivoli Brook by Dr Arthur Rowe

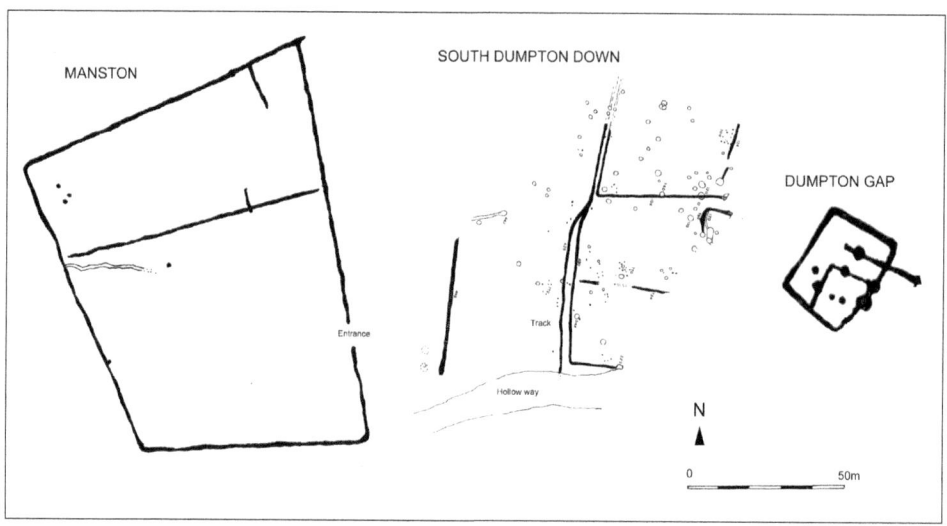

82 Iron Age settlement enclosures from Manston, South Dumpton Down and Dumpton Gap. © *Trust for Thanet Archaeology*

in 1924 (Rowe 1924). Both Minster and Margate were close to supplies of fine loess deposits, where the abundant water supply from the springs nearby could be used to make potting clay from the local material. At Hartsdown a large complex of circular quarry pits were cut through the loess deposits running through the valley to Margate. These may have been for clay extraction and may have been associated with the Tivoli kiln. Late Iron Age quarries encountered between Westwood and Margate were cut into chalk in search of seams of flints for construction purposes such as posthole packing, or heated and crushed to use as temper in potting clay. At Dumpton Gap several quarry pits were found close to the enclosure and may have been used to extract chalk to make plaster for structures on the site (Boast & Gardner 2006).

No formal Late Iron Age cemeteries have been recognised in Thanet but occasional inhumations have been encountered with pottery of early first-century date. A burial at Hartsdown, in a regular rectangular grave accompanied with a Terra Nigra platter, appears to date to the Late Iron Age or to early in the Roman period (TfTA Archives). Isolated inhumations accompanied by Romanised Late Iron Age vessels have been encountered and it is possible that some of these, or other unaccompanied examples, might be interpreted as formal Late Iron Age burials. Some of the grave groups from Ramsgate, summarised by Robert Hicks in *Archaeologia Cantiana* in 1878, probably date to the Late Iron Age rather than the Roman period as he proposed. Comb-decorated vessels, a large cordoned urn, a large platter and two Butt Beakers all indicate that Late Iron Age cremations or occupation pits were disturbed in the area (Hicks 1878). Late Iron Age cremations inserted into isolated pits were encountered in excavations for new roads at Dumpton Gap (Hurd 1913). Other vessels found in the urban expansion of Thanet's towns in the nineteenth century, attributed to the Roman period, may rather belong to the Late Iron Age.

Islanders – the Iron Age in Thanet

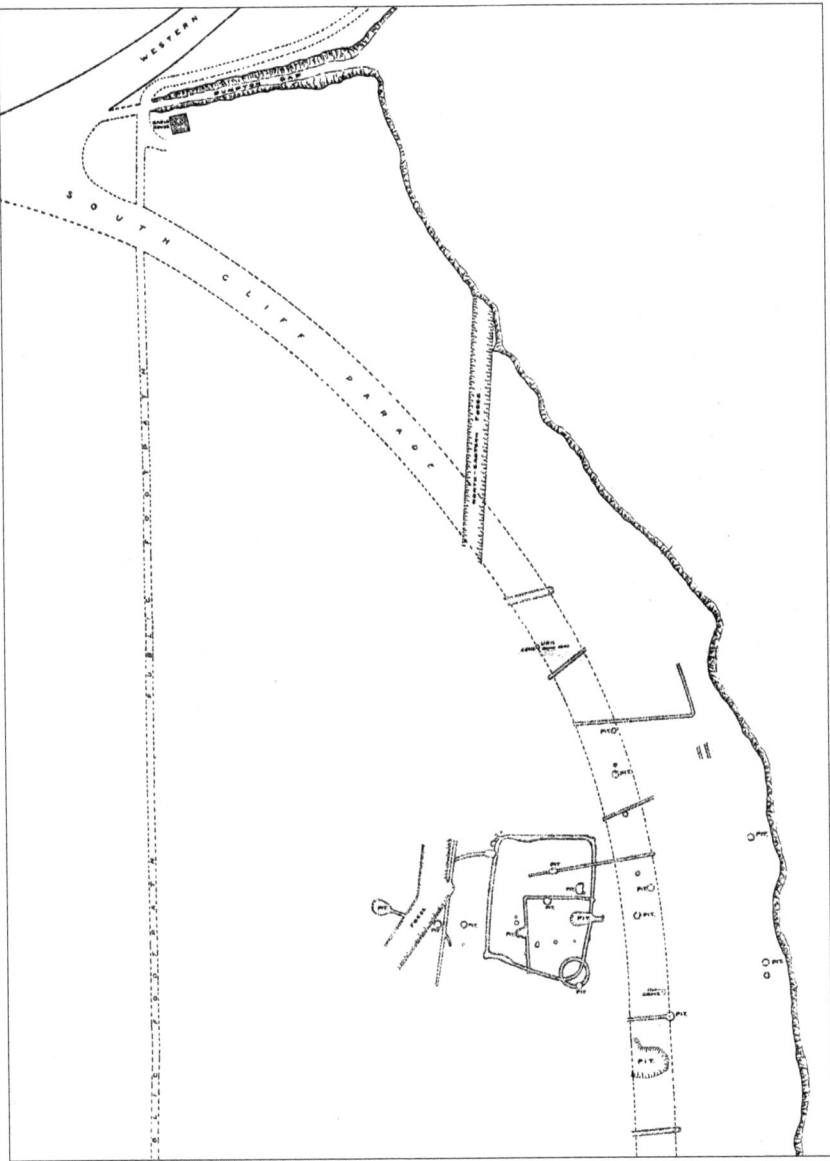

83 Late Iron Age settlement at Dumpton Gap. *After Hurd, 1913*

On the eve of the invasion of Britain by the Roman Army, the Late Iron Age inhabitants of Thanet lived in a sophisticated community. Their local pottery industries had adopted Romanised styles from mainland Europe. Their coinage was exchangeable with European, and even Roman coins and their industries were producing trade goods for the European markets. Settlements were characterised by small enclosed farmsteads with regular rectangular plans surrounded by productive fields and woodlands. Sea-going ships regularly came and went from the Wantsum channel and the coastal havens at Margate, Joss Bay and Ramsgate, as well as from numerous small bays and coves along the cliffs that served the communities based in each valley. Flocks of sheep and cattle would have been a common sight, grazing on the slopes, or being driven along the wide drove roads that linked each community to the harbours and the ferry over the Wantsum at Sarre.

9

AN IMPERIAL OUTPOST – THE ROMANS IN THANET

The invasion of Britain by Claudius in AD 43 is essentially an event that occurs in an Iron Age context. The landscape, economy and social conditions of Late Iron Age Britain were what attracted the invasion. The conquest would not have been as significant if the British population had not been so similar to the tribal groups of Gaul which had been absorbed into the Roman Empire, and were already integrated into the system of payments that Rome extracted from the provinces of its Empire. Most of the published historical accounts of the Roman invasion of Britain agree that the exact location of the landings cannot be established with any certainty. There are now two competing positions, one proposing a landing in the Solent, and the traditional and currently favoured theory placing it at Richborough, a small hill formed by an outcrop of Eocene sand within the Wantsum channel. If the Roman invasion was centred on Richborough, Thanet would have been placed in a central position in the history of Roman Britain. There is evidence for early defensive ditches on Richborough Hill dated to around the right period for the invasion. At a slightly later date, a supply base with large granaries was developed (Cunliffe *et al* 1968). There is no evidence, however, for the immediate events of the invasion in the historical or archaeological record. The historical sources we have for the Roman conquest of Britain are useful for understanding the process at a strategic level and over long periods of time. It is difficult to give a narrative account of the Roman settlement of Thanet; it is easier to follow the effects of the invasion as they can be seen in the archaeological record (*84*).

The geographical implications of a landing at Richborough are worth considering briefly. To reach the coast between Deal and Thanet, the fleet would have crossed from Boulogne to the coast near Dover before waiting for a favourable tide to sail for the coast, off Thanet, and then to force a passage through the Wantsum channel (Perkins 2006). The ships would have entered the Wantsum through a gap between Sandwich and the flint headland at Great Stonar. Several points along the channel were suited to a landing and had operated as trade ports in the Late Iron Age. The settlement at Archer's Low had occupied a low platform, built up on an alluvial sand bar over a period of 70 years and a high number of imported coins and evidence of Late Iron Age pottery

The Isle of Thanet – from Prehistory to the Norman Conquest

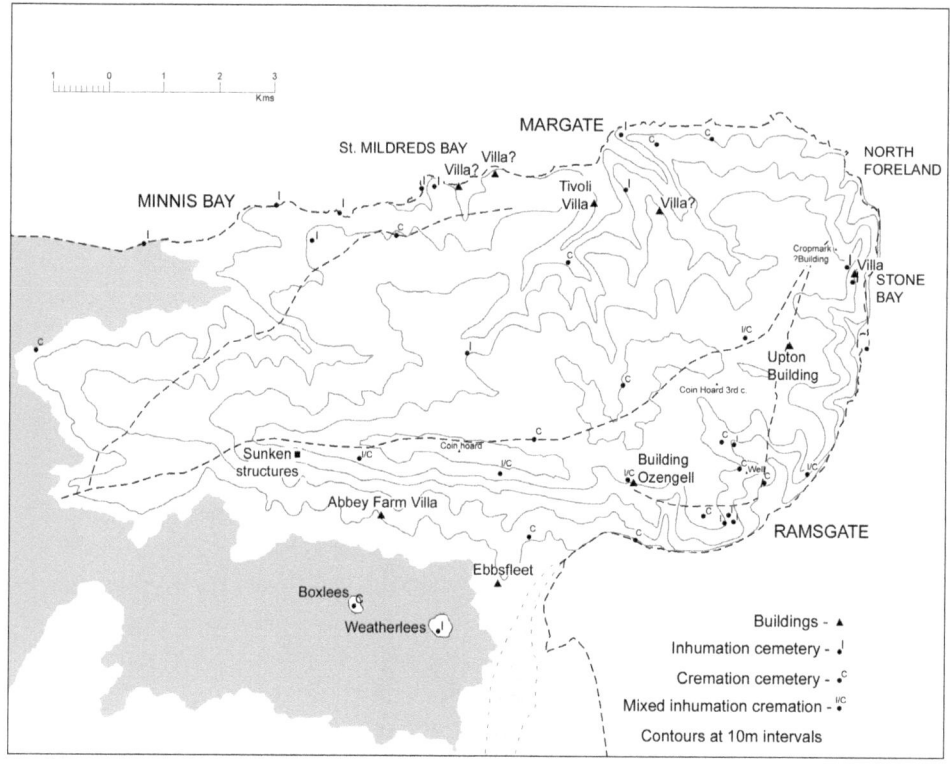

84 Location of Roman sites on Thanet. © Trust for Thanet Archaeology

indicate a similar settlement at Richborough (Holman 2005, 10). If the fleet entered here, it would have sailed up through a deep water channel in the centre of the valley. On each side there were shallow creeks and salt marshes, where the mud of the estuary would occasionally have been scoured out by a spring-fed stream, wide enough to sail through to small landing places on the northern side of the Wantsum channel at Durlock, Minster or Monkton. At Sarre, a crossing point across the Wantsum probably linked the main routes across Thanet to a similar drove road on the main land.

The logistics of the Roman invasion fleet have rarely been considered in detail and the landing of 20,000 men from four legions with a similar number of auxiliaries (approximately 40,000 in total) would have been a complicated process. Although it is recorded that the invasion fleet was separated into three divisions it is not known how many vessels were in each division and what troops or equipment would have been chosen for the first landings. There were many possible landing places on the sand spit between Deal and Sandwich where a large number of boats could have been beached to disembark in rapid order, while other craft entered the tidal channel directly. On the bends in the channel, against Richborough and Ebbsfleet, sand beaches built up against the shingle and it would have been possible to beach vessels and unload men, animals and equipment there. There is surprisingly little, if any, physical evidence known for the

An Imperial outpost – the Romans in Thanet

arrival of so many soldiers and their equipment along the banks of the Wantsum channel, but then this scenario has not, as yet, been directly investigated. Some ships may have made a direct passage through the channel to the north mouth of the Wantsum estuary and the surrounding area, the shores would have been a solid mass of beached vessels and these might have formed the first invasion camp. The headland at Richborough would have needed no more than a screening ditch to be excavated as a cordon against any attacker who attempted to reach the shores. There were already well-established settlements at Ramsgate and North Foreland and along the northern coast at Minnis Bay and Westbrook. A well-connected community was also well established at Margate, so the invading Romans encountered a more sophisticated and developed range of native communities than is conventionally assumed.

Given the size of the operation, it is unlikely that a single location can be identified for the Roman landings. More probably, the ships landed where they could, in the network of harbours, beaches and trading ports on the east and western sides of the Wantsum and troops secured themselves, by units, over a wide area. No single camp would have been large enough for the invasion troops; it would be more profitable to investigate the wider landscape for temporary marching camps and piece together the first period of the invasion from these results. Many cropmarks of rectilinear enclosures are known in Thanet and on the chalk lands of the eastern North Downs from aerial photography; some may prove to be the temporary camps of the invasion force. Given the need for the general security of the invading troops, ports and population centres on Thanet would inevitably have been included in early operations. The inter-visibility between the high points of the central plateau at North Foreland, Ramsgate, Margate and the high points around Reculver and Richborough, would have formed the ideal basis for a signalling network and coordination of naval traffic. The small ports in the bays around the island would also have made excellent secondary landing places. The main track from Sarre linked all significant points on the island and must have been an immediate objective in the early stage of the invasion.

Historical accounts suggest that the Roman legionaries were reluctant to board their ships due to a fear of crossing the unknown ocean and had to be humiliated into the ships by an Imperial freedman sent by Claudius (de la Bédoyère 2006, 28). Considering the quantity of men and equipment required to mount the invasion, not to mention the planning for the security and provisioning of the army in the aftermath, it is very unlikely that this story applied to the whole fleet. The invasion ships probably co-opted a core of experienced sailors who, perhaps, had crossed these routes many times before and had even operated as Channel pilots from the southern side of the English Channel (Perkins 2006). These men would have known where the best landing places were and where the troops could establish their first base for disembarkation. It is likely that both sides knew their enemy well and preliminary contacts with sympathetic groups may have already been made. If not, the Romans may have employed a form of 'gunboat diplomacy' where the first Roman ships forced their way into the harbour regardless of the ships of traders and noblemen that were undoubtedly moored there and waited to see how strong the response was. The invasion may have been a show of force and not an actual assault. If the invasion was directed at another location further west, some action must eventually have been taken, in any case, to secure the Isle of Thanet in advance of the construction of the supply base that stood at Richborough between AD 45 and 85.

The principal features of the supply bases were large timber granaries served by gravel roads. Of course the grain in them, used to supply the Roman Army, would have been extracted in some way from the surrounding countryside. The Roman State in Britain was founded on the assumption of the right of the Emperor and his representatives to extract tribute from the traditional land owners. In some areas of Britain the transfer of these rights to the Roman State was enabled by the submission of local tribes prior to the conquest. The traditional rights held by the indigenous population were ended by military conquest. They were then delegated back to the population, in a Romanised model of their own society, by the organisation of rural areas around a principal town. Ultimate power was retained by the Roman State through the right of conquest. The absorption of the province of Britannia into the Empire brought it from the periphery of the Roman markets, where it had been in the Iron Age, into the centre. The establishment of Roman power above traditional rights ensured that money invested in the region would see the same rates of return and guarantees of security that prevailed in the established parts of Empire. The population could be confident in the use of Roman coinage. It was backed by a powerful state that demanded its tribute in its own silver and gold coin. Ultimately the role of the Roman Army in the country was to extend and enforce the system of tribute, from which it derived its own supply of disposable wealth in the form of pay and donatives. Mini towns formed around the military populations to supply goods and services during extended occupations.

When the Roman State set the level of tribute, a measure of the relative difference between the productivity of land and the rate of taxation could be estimated. A market value for land could then be established and the rights of ownership traded. It is not clear whether there was a market in land in the Late Iron Age period; the specialisation of production roles would have led to some investment to ensure the production of certain commodities, but much land use would have been governed by traditional rights and exchanges. It is possible that the signs of early nucleation in the Late Iron Age sites on Thanet reflect some early changes in land ownership. After the invasion, the disposal of land was regulated according to an evolved system of property law and it could be sold by traditional owners. Towns, fortresses and trading centres were all developed as functions of an economy based on the produce from landed estates.

The network of communications, established over hundreds of years, was utilised by the Roman State. The riverine routes from the northern and southern ends of the Wantsum channel linked the ports of Richborough, Minster, Fleet and Sarre to the limits of the tidal Stour at Fordwich. From the northern mouth of the Wantsum, the Thames could be reached without having to make the hazardous journey around the North Foreland and the Goodwin Sands. The old track across the ridge and plateau linked the farms and villages of Thanet to a central route.

The most substantial evidence for change in the settlement patterns of the Roman period on Thanet is the appearance of buildings that reflect the architectural methods

An Imperial outpost – the Romans in Thanet

85 Central range and west wing of the Abbey Farm Villa overlooking Minster and the alluvial plain of the Wantsum channel. © Trust for Thanet Archaeology

brought by the Romans from the many cultures of the Empire. Many buildings were constructed on Thanet during the Roman period in stone, flint, concrete and timber (Perkins 2001a). David Perkins listed five buildings tested by excavation in 2001, to which must be added a new building at Stone Bay, discovered accidentally, but anticipated in the analysis of the accompanying distribution map (Perkins 2001a, 48, fig. 2). The list of buildings was generated from a range of evidence; some were found in controlled circumstances and have been sampled by excavation revealing something of their structure and development (Moody 2007). A few are known only from antiquarian records or have been identified by spreads of distinctive building materials, such as ceramic roof tiles. Occasionally, pits and ditches have been found with very rich artefact assemblages that indicate the presence nearby of a major occupation centre, usually a building. Other buildings have been identified from cropmarks where ground plans can be determined with some accuracy. Some common traits were found in the locations of the buildings, often they occupied platforms on the edge of the slopes of valleys and the flow of springs may have been diverted to provide supplies of water to them.

The most extensively investigated Roman building in Thanet is the winged corridor villa at Minster (*85*). Built on the site of an earlier Iron Age settlement, the building was located on a plateau on the eastern slope of a periglacial valley (Perkins & Parfitt 2004) (*86*). The main range was placed within a walled compound at the break of slope of the valley, overlooking the banks of the Wantsum channel. A spring, running through the base of the valley, was diverted further up the slope to supply a piped water system for bathhouses within the villa complex (Perkins & Parfitt 2004, 33; Parfitt 2007). The main villa was built in the late first century AD and was occupied for 200 years into the late

The Isle of Thanet – from Prehistory to the Norman Conquest

86 Plan of the Abbey Farm Villa in its topographic context. © *Trust for Thanet Archaeology*

third century, when it was demolished entirely. At the eastern corner of the compound, a two-chambered house had a small heated room, in the south-western corner of the surrounding corridor. On the opposite western corner of the boundary, a matching house underwent several adaptations to convert it into a bathhouse with heated rooms and a piped water supply. It was later demolished and a new structure cut through the earlier foundations to restore the symmetrical arrangement of the two corner buildings. The earlier bathhouse was replaced by a purpose-built, detached one on the western edge of the corridor surrounding the outside of the villa.

The Abbey Farm Villa is very significant in understanding of the settlement of the Isle of Thanet in the Roman period. The main building is likely to have been constructed before AD 70 in the last decade of the use of Richborough as a supply base. In around AD 85, a huge monumental arch was erected at Richborough, symbolically marking its official status as the gateway to the new province of Britannia. Towns were established at Richborough and Reculver and it is likely that the harbours and inlets of the Wantsum prospered with the main port at Richborough. It is very likely that there was no single port but various landing places for different types of traffic, and Minster was the ideal location for a building with facilities familiar to visitors used to continental luxuries, as it stood on an existing landing place. There may have been further significance to the building as springs were often places of religious significance and the waters piped through the structure may have been considered to have some beneficial properties. The painted plaster, mosaic fragments and personal items that were found at the Abbey Farm Villa have demonstrated the arrival of a Romanised way of life to Thanet. It is possible that this building stood among villages and farmsteads essentially unchanged from their Iron Age roots, but this building demonstrated, in an emphatic way, the changes that Roman settlement would make.

At Stone Gap, close to the North Foreland peninsula, the cellar and a few wall foundations of a building indicate the site of another small villa, probably built in the late first century AD. This structure was cut into hillwash on the slopes of the valley, peppered with pottery and domestic debris eroded from the enclosed Iron Age settlement nearby (Moody 2007) (*87*). The square cut of the cellar had been lined with flint cobbles, and within this sunken room, a sequence of small kilns, possibly bread ovens, had been built over a period of time (*88*).

Several worn millstone fragments and threshing waste, recovered from structures in the Stone Gap building, indicate that the Romanised community continued the same large-scale grain production that had been practised by the Late Iron Age occupants of this site and the North Foreland settlement. Food waste also confirmed the continuation of sheep and cattle herding. The building was probably served by a small haven in the bay at Stone Gap that has now been lost to the sea. The vista from the site over the sea to the south-east is extensive and the building may have been placed specifically for its landscape setting. On an east-facing slope, south and west of the Stone Gap building, cremations and inhumations have been recorded on several different occasions indicating that the burials are contemporary with the building which dates from the late first to the third century (Hurd 1913; Wilson 1983).

Many Roman buildings on Thanet have been severely damaged by many centuries of ploughing and their presence is often only established when structures cut deep into the ground are exposed. The villa at Abbey Farm could only be traced in plan because its deep foundations had not been entirely ploughed away. In places no more than a few centimetres survived to record the presence of walls. A chalk-lined cellar and some

87 The Roman building excavated at Stone Gap. © *Trust for Thanet Archaeology*

88 The latest oven set within the cellar of the building at Stone Gap. © *Trust for Thanet Archaeology*

of the stones from boundary walls were all that remained of a building on the central ridge near Lord of the Manor, Ramsgate (Perkins 1983). George Dowker sampled the remains of a building on the North Foreland promontory in the nineteenth century. His records indicate that it was a cobble-built range measuring 40ft long and 7ft wide. Only remnants of a floor and a little dateable material were encountered (Tucker 2007a). Elements of the Roman building at Stone Road, not far from Dowker's site, were represented by only a single course of rounded cobbles surviving from the lowest level. At Upton, a short length of wall foundation had been placed over an earlier quarry pit to provide a stronger foundation and this was all that remained of any structure that might have been present on the site. The small building, on the south-east corner of the Abbey Farm Villa compound, was similarly truncated to only one or two layers of cobbles.

At Margate, a Roman building known as the Tivoli Villa, was discovered when new roads were laid out in 1924 (89). Only brief notes of the discovery of this building, a single photograph and a sketch plan, survive although Roman finds from the site are at Margate Museum. Dr Arthur Rowe, who excavated the site, recorded that painted plaster had been found and that there was evidence for tessellated floors in the building. Recent excavations over the site have confirmed the presence of painted plaster (Thanet Archaeological Society Archives). In a similar way to the Stone Gap structure, the building was cut into extensive hillwash deposits containing pottery from the nearby Iron Age settlements. The flint walls encountered may represent only the foundation cuts of the original structure built up in unmortared flints. The measurements of the range recorded suggest the excavated parts may be a series of rooms from a much larger structure (Rowe 1924).

Two early reports of Roman finds from the Broadstairs area indicate that another building stood at Dumpton Gap. John Lewis (1736) illustrated a number of Iron Age and Roman coins he had in his collection and noted that he had found coins of Constantine and Domitian from the beach under the cliffs near Broadstairs. In the 1850s, Captain Kennett Martin of Ramsgate noted that:

> … about a mile from Ramsgate pier, at Dumpton stairs was also the remains of a Roman wall, which is now entirely gone, but Roman coins are to this day occasionally found between that point and Ramsgate harbour, and fragments of Roman pottery also.
>
> Martin 1857, 85

Roman tiles and pottery were found in the excavation of the large enclosed Iron Age site at Dumpton. Recent excavation of the upper fills of pits within a Late Iron Age rectangular enclosure produced Roman roof tiles and first- and second-century pottery from the upper fills, suggesting that a building was present but has been lost to coastal erosion (Hurd 1913; Boast & Gardner 2006)

Fragmentary cobble walls and spreads of occupation material at Cottington Hill, Ebbsfleet, represent a small Roman building, perhaps a secondary structure rather than a main range (Jay 1990, 237). The Roman settlement succeeded an Iron Age occupation

89 Dr Arthur Rowe's excavation photograph of Tivoli Villa showing wall foundations and the new road c.1924

area that produced many coins. Although this building and its associated features appear modest, it may be part of a larger complex as recent excavations have demonstrated that Roman cut features are present over a much wider area (WA 2006). The cropmarks of large rectangular enclosures and possible building ranges almost certainly indicate that a greater number of structures are present on Thanet than have been discovered so far (RCHME 1989). A large enclosure recorded at Sarre could contain a small fort or marching camp. A rectangular enclosure cropmark is located on a platform overlooking the valley above Joss Bay, close to the North Foreland Iron Age settlement and trackway, and only a short distance from the Roman building at Stone Bay. Geophysical survey of this enclosure suggests that building remains may be located within it. Roman burials have been found close to the site, and brooches and other finds associated with large pits have also been found in the same area. It is very likely that a fairly large settlement complex was located in this key location.

The site of a Roman villa is marked at St Mildred's Bay, apparently destroyed during the construction of a hotel in the 1870s. Although the area is now built over, recent excavations nearby produced some scraps of Roman roof tile (Boast *et al* 2006c, 1.3). Building material was recorded at the site of the Sunken Garden at Westbrook, when it

An Imperial outpost – the Romans in Thanet

90 Leaf-shaped pendants of copper/zinc alloy, found in deposits filling a well at Abbey Farm. Height 44mm. © *Trust for Thanet Archaeology*

was built in 1931. Scatters of Roman building material on a number of other sites indicate the presence of structures nearby. Another interesting possibility is that building remains and a Roman cremation at Boxlees Hill, in the Wantsum channel near Minster, could represent some form of navigational aid, such as a lighthouse (Perkins 2001a, 56).

Structural remains and small finds from the excavation of Roman sites have filled in some detail of the range of objects that were in everyday use, and occasionally, special finds indicate greater personal significance. The decorative finishes on the structures have allowed the reconstruction, in part, of the cultural world of Roman Thanet. From the objects encountered in excavations, some small fragments of the histories of people who lived on the site can be glimpsed. Objects of copper alloy were made in some quantity and brooches and dress accessories are often encountered. At Abbey Farm, copper-alloy tweezers, small cosmetic scoops and picks from grooming sets were found among the debris, along with bone needles and pins used for hair decoration and fastenings (Kent Archaeological Society Archives). Rarer items were three copper-alloy pendants, found in the debris filling a well, associated with the early bathhouse at the Abbey Farm Villa. Decorated with fine, punched curvilinear patterns, these were probably the terminal decorations on the leather straps making up a leather 'apron' which hung below the Roman military cross-belts worn by soldiers and Roman officials in the first and early second centuries AD (Tucker 2007b) (*90*).

A Claudian thistle brooch was found in a well associated with the bathhouse, Building 6, at the Minster Villa, and another is recorded, without context, from Sarre. It may be associated with a grave or one of the enclosures recorded in the area. A small copper-alloy model of an athlete's head, with a curious phallic topknot, was found in a backfilled quarry pit at Drapers Mills, associated with the Roman settlement there (Perkins 1981).

The fragmentation of Roman sites through later plough damage has sometimes made it difficult to immediately recognise the complexity of the structures present. Careful analysis of the material reveals the complex network of skills and resources that went into the huge range of objects that were assembled within the buildings.

Of significance to reconstructing the Abbey Farm Villa was the careful consideration of the huge quantity of painted plaster fragments that were found within the building. The painstaking process of sorting these fragments into groups, and then into decorative schemes, has restored some small glimpse of the grandeur of the building when it was in use. The delicate artistry of the wall painters is observed in freehand designs. From the analysis of the range of methods in use, and the wide range of pigments on both basic groundwork and fine freehand work, the roles of different artisans and their assistants can be detected. Rare survivals among the fragments include the remains of an image of a deer, which must be among the first pieces of figurative art known from Kent (TfTA 2006) (*91*). The decoration of the buildings attests to the range of skilled craftsmen who were brought from the rest of the Empire to add their touches to the building.

The economic base of the society was the principal attraction to the Romans. The import of luxury and new cultural forms was funded by the production of the local economy. Although the villas, and their fine objects, indicate some prosperity, it is not clear who was prospering. The buildings may not reflect the state of the indigenous population but the success of the new military and bureaucratic elite. The Romans have traditionally been seen as creating an orderly society, with cultural achievements that are the marks of civilisation, but the system was founded on a disorderly process of continuous revolution, abiding by only a few basic rules: wealth-accumulation and the gaining of power.

Central to the prosperity of the system were the roads and transport networks that allowed the business of trade to be carried out. The main routes across Thanet were part of the economic system. The Stone Gap and Upton sites are linked by the road across the plateau and the millstones found at both sites suggest the transport of grain to powered mills. Other routes are generally suggested in aerial photographs of double ditched trackways, particularly in the area of Birchington. The multiple hollow-way ditches with prehistoric origins at North Foreland and Monkton continued in use in the Roman period (Bennett 1995, 1996). A similar group of deep roadside or hollow-way ditches were excavated at Margate, between the upper ridge of the valley and the site of the Tivoli Villa. These ditches cut through the grain storage pits of an earlier Iron Age settlement and are probably associated with the Tivoli Villa (TfTA Archives). The deep hollow-way at Dumpton was probably associated with the lost building at Dumpton Gap. There is no record of a major metalled road being encountered in Thanet although areas of light metalling with flint pebbles of Late Iron Age date were found at Upton and a possible stretch of pebble road surface was found at Hartsdown (Perkins 1996, 268; 2000c, 378).

An Imperial outpost – the Romans in Thanet

91 A fragment of painted plaster from Abbey Farm depicting the rear end of a deer. © *Trust for Thanet Archaeology*

The road across the central ridge and its counterpart on the plateau were the focus of Roman industrial settlements, possibly making use of the central roads as trade routes. A group of sunken buildings were discovered in excavations along the central ridge near Monkton, north of the multiple ditches of a hollow-way. The buildings were post-built structures, some with subterranean elements cut into the chalk geology, forming sunken cellars, storage areas and tanks. Agricultural tools and querns found within the features suggest that this was a processing area associated with the road network (Bennett 1995). Further east along the ridge, many ironworking waste pits were found near Manston airfield and further examples were identified during excavations for a pipeline in 1971 (Macpherson-Grant 1972). Another sunken structure was found close to this area set within a large enclosure of rectilinear field ditches. A small, fired-clay structure, at the base of a hollow cut feature, excavated at Manston in 2005, may be the base of a bloomery used to smelt iron ore (SWAT Archives).

At Upton, along the route of the track across the central plateau, a series of very large quarry hollows cut into the chalk geology, were sampled. Without other obvious geological deposits in the area, it appears that the chalk was the target of the quarrying. The extraction of chalk might have been for the production of slaked lime for use in construction. However, Charles Roach Smith records in his *Collectanea Antiqua* an inscription by a dealer in British chalk 'who in consequence of having prosperously imported into the low countries … his freight of chalk, discharged his vows to the goddess Nehallennia'. The industrial infrastructure and working zones on Thanet were separated from the luxury houses and their sea views.

John Lewis recorded the discovery of a hoard of Roman silver coins on the central ridge close to the Minster Mills along this ridge route; these do not appear to be associated with any settlement and their deposition may be related to the progress of trade in goods along the road network. Roman cremation and inhumation cemeteries are distributed in small clusters along the two main ridges. A cremation group and an inhumation in a lead coffin are known from the Lord of the Manor area, extending the line of burials toward Ramsgate (Wright 1861).

With Ramsgate's wide bay it would be surprising if there was no evidence in the past of any building or structures of Roman date. Confirmation that a Roman port existed at Ramsgate is provided by Captain Kennet B. Martin, Deputy Harbour Master at Ramsgate in the 1830s:

> In excavating down to the solid chalk to lay the foundations of the Patent Slipway, many coins and relics were found, and at twenty feet below the surface the timbers of an ancient pier were uncovered. Between these timbers Roman brick and fragments of pottery were exhumed together with the small coins of the consulate so well known to the antiquarians by the Wolf and Twins, which I purchased and preserved, and forwarded a drawing of these discoveries to the Antiquarian Society. In the rear of the harbour house a sewer was discovered in digging out a foundation, the material of which was principally the well shaped, hard red Roman brick, a proof by the bye that as to drainage they were so far advanced in civilisation as ourselves. A vessel's bottom was also exhumed, the plank of which was of extraordinary width, and between the timbers was rammed rock sulphur, which remained in a very perfect state. Sicilian vessels often adopt this plan to preserve them from worm, and assist to steady them as ballast.
>
> Martin 1857, 54

An Imperial outpost – the Romans in Thanet

92 Late Iron Age and Roman finds from the Ramsgate area. Hicks 1878

No recent archaeological work has been carried out in the central area of Ramsgate but it is likely that more remains to be discovered of the Roman settlement in this natural harbour. Features of Late Iron Age and Roman date were found during the excavations for a large chalk pit at Ellington in Ramsgate, where a deep well was excavated. A coin hoard deposited in the late third century was found on the upper plateau above Ramsgate (Cullen 1970). Throughout the nineteenth century Roman burials were encountered as the town of Ramsgate expanded onto the surrounding cliff tops, the finds from many of these were illustrated by Robert Hicks in 1878 (*92*).

The cluster of inhumations from the late third and early fourth century, discovered on the West Cliff at Ramsgate, confirms a long series of discoveries in this area that have in most cases not been published in sufficient detail, if at all. Grave goods were present in all the graves. With one was a group of vessels including well-used dishes and a beaker that was imperfectly fired. Although the pottery was somewhat shabby, the woman was buried with copper-alloy bangles and a pair of hobnailed shoes (*93*). This group was of modest status but distinctly Roman in its assemblage of grave goods and personal items (Boast 2007).

In the early to mid third century a new fort was built at Reculver, at around the same time defensive ditches were thrown up round the monument at Richborough. In the late third century, around AD 286, the defences around the monument were

93 The pottery vessels and copper-alloy bangles in situ at the end of late third-century grave at Ramsgate. © Trust for Thanet Archaeology

replaced by the walls of a large stone fortress, part of a system of forts established around the east and south-east of Britain (Johnson 1987). Although these have been seen as a response to an external threat, it is more likely that they were a defence against the resurgent central state, who were trying to restore the periphery of the Empire to central control. This was after a succession of chaotic local regimes beginning with the Gallic Empire between 259 and 273, and the seizure of Britain by Carausius and Allectus between 286 and 296 (de la Bédoyère 2006, 272).

Both the Abbey Farm Villa and the building at Stone Gap went out of use in the late third century, a common pattern in Kent. The study of the pottery from the two sites (Moody 2007, 210) has raised the possibility of military influence on the supply of pottery to the buildings on Thanet in the later third century, for example the arrival of Dorset Black Burnished Ware vessels which would have been supplied to the Roman Army. A military belt buckle was found in the ashes of a hearth in the latest floor of the Stone Road cellar. The end of this phase of the Roman settlement on Thanet coincides with the intense military activity at Richborough and Reculver at this time.

The restoration of the Roman State involved another military intervention, by Constantius (Salway 1991): On his passage to London, to symbolically restore centralised authority, he is very likely to have passed through the Wantsum channel. Few archaeological

An Imperial outpost – the Romans in Thanet

94 The fourth-century malt kiln from Abbey Farm, Minster. © Trust for Thanet Archaeology

features dating to the later Roman period (after the fourth century) have been found on the Isle of Thanet. Other than the coins associated with the wharf timbers at Ramsgate, later Roman coins are recorded on a number of sites. Lewis (1736) mentions coins of Constantine at Dumpton, and coins of a similar period are mentioned by Captain Martin associated with the piling for a Roman wharf. A few Constantinian coins are recorded from the valley at Joss Bay and a large spread of fourth-century coins was discovered at Ebbsfleet (Perkins 1992b, 282). Perhaps the most interesting later Roman feature in this context on Thanet is the malt kiln, set within a post-built barn at the Abbey Farm Villa (KAS Archives) (*94*). This two-chambered structure was formed in a rectangular cut in the natural sandy clay. The sides of the chamber were lined with chalk blocks, originally coated with a surface of clay that had fallen away. A central division created two chambers which were further divided by chalk-block walls, creating a long flue that doubled back on itself, before presumably discharging through vents at either side of the wide sloping stoke chamber at the entrance. A floor suspended above each of the flues would have been warmed by the hot air passing through the structure. The interior of the chamber was filled with fine black soot containing charred grains, and the clay sides of the walls were scorched red by the heat passing through the structure.

It is likely that the warm floors were used to germinate grain, to create malt that was used for brewing. The malt kiln was set in a rectangular timber-framed barn or shed set into cobble-packed postholes. The main villa building had been torn down in the later third century and the barn and malt kiln occupied the centre of the old villa compound. The supply of fresh spring water, diverted through the villa, would have been an important factor in the brewing process, as would the presence of the large tanks of the bathhouse, which might have been used for the later stages of that process. Parts of the outer boundary wall on the north side of the villa compound had been replaced with very similar cobble-packed postholes. It is possible that a timber-framed complex was erected around the useful remains of the original building. Coins, found in a spread over the backfilled structure, dated to the mid fourth century. A villa that could have been the focus for a local person of importance, where he could display his continental tastes and luxury facilities, was replaced by a building with a very practical function in an estate: the supply of malt. This could be used, along with the abundant supply of running water, for brewing. In effect this is the continuity of the Roman industrial activity without the luxury of the buildings.

It appears that at this time there was a shift from the pattern of small settlements located at regular intervals in the valleys. It is likely that the political and military situation in the late third century had some effect on the local society. Perhaps the communities that were direct successors of the Late Iron Age populations were closely associated with Gallic emperors who were in power in Gaul and Britain for long periods in the late third century. On the establishment of a centralised state, again after another military intervention into Britain, these small units may have been reorganised into larger estates, with or without the consent of their owners. No candidate has yet emerged for a fourth-century villa in Thanet that took on the role as the estate centre for the enlarged area, and it is possible that the centre was located on the western side of the Wantsum. The prosperity seen in later villas in Roman Britain may have come at the expense of reducing older and smaller estates into peasant communities under the control of the larger villa, which would collect the tribute of a much greater area.

One of the key agents of the Roman State was the army. Its presence created demand in the economy and this was supplied by a sophisticated procurement system. In the later period, this relied on the direct appropriation of produce from the surrounding countryside in addition to regular payment in coins imported to pay the troops. The coin series discovered in the archaeological excavations at Richborough ends with some of the very latest issues that reached Britain. Small worn copper coins were found in some number and might indicate later exchange. Without the guide of large-scale finds of dated coinage, the events of the last years of the Roman Empire in Britain are hard to trace. It is not entirely clear how the army was finally withdrawn from the Roman province of Britannia but successive attempts to seize control of the Empire were launched by commanders based in Britain. It is likely that the last regular troops were withdrawn by Constantine III, the last of this series of adventuring generals to lead British troops into the continent. The Wantsum ports were of first importance to the Romans and it is very likely that they were the last places in Roman Britain that the field army saw before their march to disaster on the continent. We do not know what arrangements were made for the defence or maintenance of the Roman system in the absence of regular troops (Esmonde Cleary 2000).

Ultimately, in Roman Britain there was no truly urban economy that could be sustained without the surpluses generated from the immense exchanges of product from landed estates. The landed classes delegated the function of markets and theatrical displays of wealth to the locations we know as Roman towns, but industries were based on the agricultural economy and these required strategically located centres such as ports and harbours. In pre-industrial towns and cities, the craftsmen that served them retained connections to a family, an ancestral village or a religious cult, that meant their connections to the agricultural economy were never entirely dissolved (Sjoberg 1960). With the loss of demand for urban services, towns would have melted away and real power was held in the ownership of land. In the absence of evidence to the contrary, we must assume that there was some form of continuity in economy and civilian population into the post-Roman period. This population had to negotiate an identity that did not include some of the most influential structures of the Roman State, such as the regular supply of coins, taxation and extractions based on national and continental demands. The political and intellectual framework that was required to sustain these institutions was also irrelevant and new ways were found to articulate power relationships from which we can begin to trace the development of the Anglo-Saxon period.

10

NEW IDENTITIES – THE FIFTH CENTURY TO THE NORMAN CONQUEST

The events of the last years of Roman Imperial administration in Britain are hard to reconstruct, there is little detail in the documentary sources for this period that explains the practical effects on Romano-British society. It is generally agreed that the last regular Roman troops left from Richborough sometime around AD 410, following another attempt by a British soldier, Constantine III, to make a bid for control of the Empire. The foundation story of Anglo-Saxon England is well known and historians have tried to place some of the earliest events of the sub-Roman occupation of Britain in the east Kent area and on Thanet, on the basis of the few documentary records that exist. The *Anglo-Saxon Chronicle* gives the year of AD 449 as the date of the invitation of the noble men (*Aethelings*) of the Angles to Britain by Vortigern, to assist in fighting the Picts. He settled them somewhere in the south-east of England on condition they assisted the British in their fight against the Picts (Thorpe 1861, vol 11, 11). Throughout Europe, Germanic soldiers were being accommodated on landed estates on the promise of providing military service to the landholders. As our earliest documented testimony, this story has been thoroughly debated and subjected to exhausting critical analysis without resolution (Hawkes 1982). The historical texts do not record sufficient detail of the changes that occurred in post-Roman society. Almost 50 years of sub-Roman Britain passed with a population that continued to grow food and survive before the political effects of the arrival of the Scandinavian Aethelings were played out. A few lines in the *Anglo-Saxon Chronicle* describe the leaders of some of the Scandinavians, Hengest and his brother Horsa, turning on Vortigern in 455 and fighting various battles against the Britons. It is clear that the texts are speaking of aristocratic warriors who were supported in some way by a functioning economy that continued to sustain them over five years of campaigning. There was almost certainly continuity in the system of agricultural production that operated in the last stable period of the Roman administration into the period when the first adventuring groups arrived from the areas of North Germany and Scandinavia which had remained outside the Roman Empire.

We know very little about the late Roman economy of Thanet, however it appears that most, if not all, of the major buildings were lost by the late third century. If the agricultural estates continued producing surpluses of crops and trade goods, they were not consumed locally beyond the subsistence required by the agricultural workers. There may have been a large villa somewhere in the area that administered the tribute from the regional economy; it is also possible that the Roman fort at Richborough took the lands closest to it into direct control, using the food supplied by them to support the garrison and the mobile field army units that passed through the region. It is clear that throughout nearly 1000 years of trading with the continent many ports and havens operated in the Wantsum channel and the bays around the Isle of Thanet. Richborough was not a single port but served as a regulator for the coastal trade and probably operated a system of port tolls as another element of its official system of tribute.

After a century of military settlement at the Saxon Shore fort, an official bureaucracy would have administered the region and it is unlikely that the fort was stripped of the still necessary administrators, clerks and many other functionaries required. It was never intended that the army would not return. Richborough would have continued as an administrative centre, perhaps with additional centres distributed around its lands, to assist in the local collection of tribute, port tolls and duties, and the extractions from the countryside nearby. There may have been a garrison force drawn from the local peasant community, as seems to have become traditional. The garrison of the fort had been supplied for many years by extraction of goods in kind from the rural economy and the troop reductions would have relieved the countryside of a burden. The seaports were still open to trading ships from the continent, and Sarre remained a key interchange in the transport system for produce from Thanet to the fortresses and beyond. The end of Roman towns is no mystery. Pre-industrial towns were patronised by the wealthy of the agricultural economy and these people had been stripped away in the late third century. Administration of the extractions in kind took place in a local context, and the halls of the collectors and administrative officers along with the court of the commandant at Richborough would be the new cultural centres. Without towns and with an active military system drawing heavily on its local community to sustain it, the economy was that of a castle and not a town. On the continent, a regional court administered the surrounding lands of many towns from a walled centre in the contracted urban area.

Across the Isle of Thanet small communities of peasants lived where they always had, in small villages of timber buildings within reach of their pastures and fields, possibly with a small animal enclosure and garden plots close to the houses. It is likely that in the last years of the Roman Empire the forts on the eastern shores would have been protected by some local naval forces, who would have continued to defend the area in the years after the soldiers left. Local men with a long history of seafaring might also have provided the crews of these ships. There was another factor in the post-Roman cultural mix. It is likely that sailing ships had often visited the ports of Thanet from the Scandinavian countries, and that local sailors were familiar with their trade goods and possibly their tendency towards piracy. The Scandinavians' keeled boats were ideally suited to beaching in the bays around the coast, and rather than sailing through the entrance to the official port in the Wantsum, they could land from the seaward side and pull their ships up on the shore when the opportunity arose. The Scandinavian seamen were probably the same pirates with whom the Roman navy had frequently been engaged, their principal crime being coastal raiding and avoiding the port tolls of the official harbours (Jones 1984). Early trading contacts between Scandinavia and Britain cannot have been entirely prevented by Roman policing actions, and the arrival of Scandinavian sailors would not have been uncommon on Thanet. The arrival of adventuring branches of Scandinavian nobility, to assist with the defence of the area in the absence of Imperial authority, would perhaps prove more problematic.

In this context, the appeal by Vortigern for assistance from the Aethelings can be seen as recruitment of military assistance to the local defences that were already structured to supply fighting men who had the means to sustain themselves. The lands that were given over to support them are also likely to have been considerable; the Saxon leaders were not expected to till the soil but just to consume the produce to support their military activity. It is the success of the Angles, when they turned against those who had engaged them, that indicate the continuity of the late Roman agricultural economy. Bede suggested that the first settlers of the Isle of Thanet were Jutes, from the islands off the coast of Denmark, and wherever they took on the defence of an area the earls of the Jutes who settled Kent inherited the power base of the local military supply system (Jones 1984). A man buried with his weapons at Richborough, in the fifth century is the earliest burial known that could be the grave of one of these adventurers. This man may have been an official member of the garrison, or one of the later arrivals from Scandinavia, perhaps it is not an important distinction (Richardson 2004, vol 1, 54).

Events of this early history have been identified with Thanet – particularly the association of Ebbsfleet with the arrival of Hengest – though the lack of firm evidence linking these events to Thanet has been discussed elsewhere. The archaeological record in Thanet does indicate that in the period of the later fifth to seventh centuries there was some cultural influence from Scandinavia. The extent to which this influence indicates a real migration of Scandinavian settlers is a matter that has been tested by excavation in the inhumation cemeteries on Thanet whose origin can be dated to the late fifth century and sixth centuries (*95*).

Although some fifth-century cremations have been found at Woodnesborough near Ash, on the hilltop above the Wantsum channel, the earliest post-Roman cremation burials are rare in Kent and none have been found yet in Thanet (Parfitt *et al* 2007). These post-Roman cemeteries grew over a long period of time, and a number of distinctive forms of spatial distribution and grave types are known, common to many of the cemeteries of the period. In parts of the cemeteries, graves seem to have been added in ordered rows, apparently within defined areas, indicating a phased growth (*96*).

The development of row graves has both continental and late Roman precedents (Brugmann 1997b, 120). The spatial characteristics of the distribution of graves in the cemeteries have not been analysed in depth, although much work has been done on the orientation of graves and the assemblages contained within them. It appears that graves accumulated in several contiguous areas, with overspill and infill elements being visible

New identities – the fifth century to the Norman Conquest

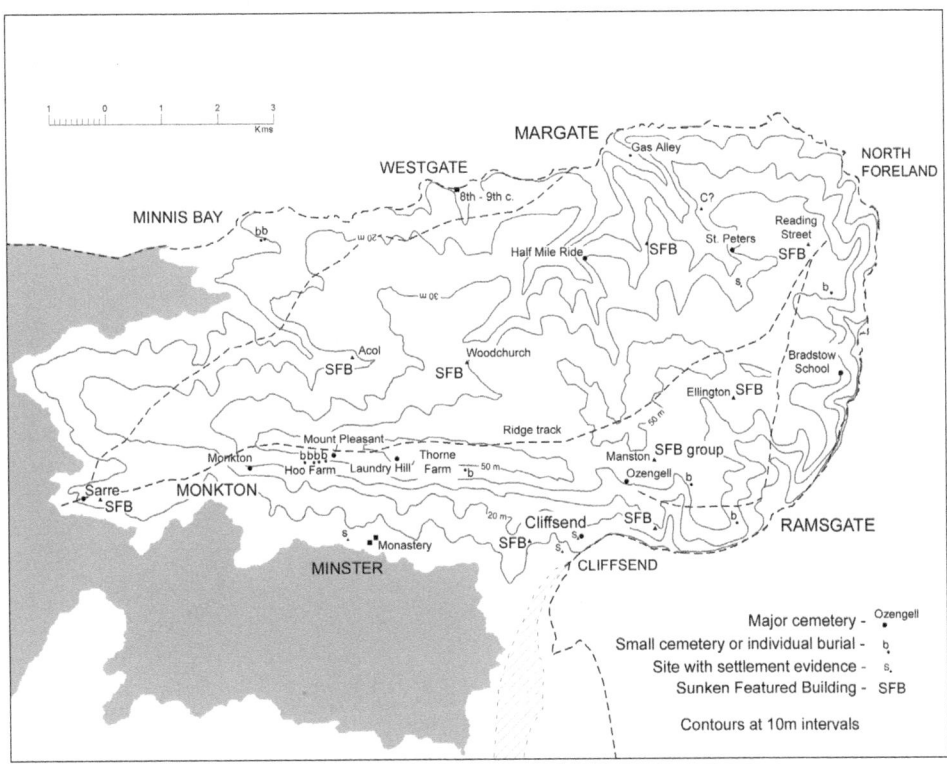

95 Distribution map of Anglo-Saxon sites and finds on Thanet. © *Trust for Thanet Archaeology*

at the fringes of the orderly blocks of graves. In some graves on Thanet dating to the sixth and seventh centuries, various postholes and ledges were added to the upper levels of rectangular grave cuts, suggesting that timber canopies or covers may have been constructed above ground over the burial. These might be compared with the structures that were built in stone and tile over Roman graves and may have been directly influenced by Roman memorial structures. Grave structures in a cemetery at St Peters have been studied in detail and form the basis of a classification system used in other cemeteries (Hogarth 1973). Similar structures have been recognised at several Thanet cemeteries, including Ozengell and Sarre (Richardson 2004, 118; Perkins 1992a, 98) and may have been present on cemeteries that were excavated with less-developed techniques in the nineteenth century or that have been more severely truncated by later ploughing such as at Monkton. At Monkton (Hawkes *et al* 1974), Ozengell (TfTA Archives) and Sarre (Perkins 1992a) some graves also had evidence for a conventional timber coffin.

In the sixth and seventh centuries, inhumations became more elaborately assembled, with the deceased dressed in full costume and accessories; additional objects such as tools, weapons and vessels were added to the layout of the grave. The items within the grave appear to be associated with the person who then remains in possession of them in death. The upper structures of the graves may have been intended to preserve the individual in

The Isle of Thanet – from Prehistory to the Norman Conquest

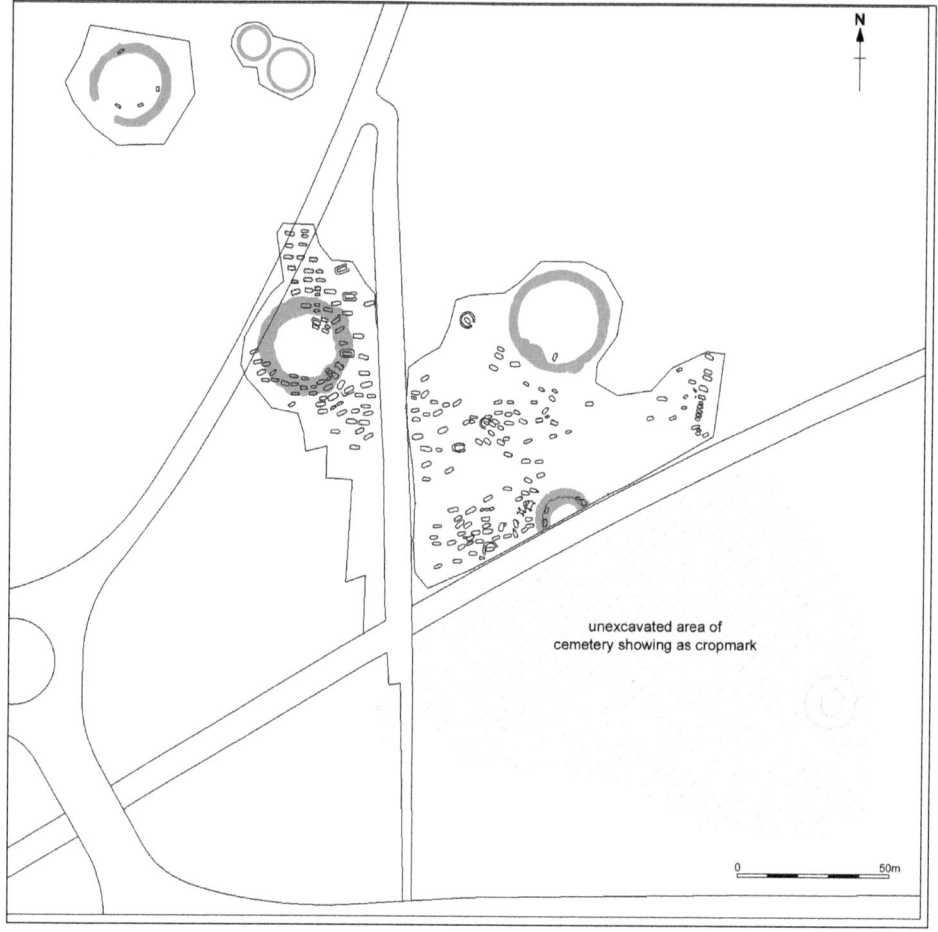

96 Plan of the Anglo-Saxon cemetery at Ozengell 1977-1989. © *Trust for Thanet Archaeology*

a mausoleum below a cover, rather than being immediately covered over with soil. At several cemeteries graves are surrounded by a circular ditch with a small gap in the circuit (97). Often a posthole is located close to, or within, the gap. These graves were probably capped by a small mound. Examples of these structures were found at the cemeteries at St Peters, Ozengell and Bradstow School. There appears to be no correlation between these graves and any particular assemblage of grave goods that might indicate the presence of a person of a particular social significance. The memorial itself indicates a more lasting, and possibly regularly tended, monument to the person within.

While the chronological sequence that could be revealed by the spatial development in cemeteries has not been fully explored, work has been carried out on dating the items found within the graves and the combination of these items accompanying each individual. The cemeteries at Sarre and Ozengell have burials that can be dated to the fifth century (Richardson 2004, vol 1, 65) whilst the earliest dated burial in the cemetery at

New identities — the fifth century to the Norman Conquest

97 Penannular ditch surrounding a grave at St Peters. © *B. Peppiatt*

Monkton, east of Sarre, is early sixth century (Hawkes *et al* 1973; Perkins & Hawkes 1984). A group of 24 graves at Cliffsend were all buried within the sixth century on a hilltop location (WA 2005). A small group of graves excavated at Thorne Farm suggest a late sixth-century beginning for this cemetery, although future discoveries may revise this date (Perkins 1985). At St Peters (Hogarth 1973; Richardson 2004) and Bradstow School, Broadstairs (Hurd 1913; Richardson 2004), the earliest dated burials within the cemeteries are of the late sixth century. The first dateable grave at Half Mile Ride, Margate, is assigned to the seventh century (Perkins 1987) and at Mount Pleasant a group of late seventh- to eighth-century burials were excavated, probably from a larger cemetery (Bennet *et al* 1996; Richardson 2004). Occasionally, single graves have been found probably representing elements of larger groups (e.g. Boulter 1933). There appears to be a general decline in artefacts deposited within graves during the later sixth and seventh centuries, disappearing entirely in the early eighth century. Graves also stopped being added to the large cemeteries in the later seventh and early eighth centuries on Thanet. It would seem likely that the new focus for burial in the periods following were the chapels of ease associated with the newly established monasteries. Some of these were probably the precursors to the present parish churches and later Saxon burials may exist beneath their graveyards.

Although the earliest burials within the cemeteries can be determined by datable grave goods, further work on the sequence of accumulation would explore whether other graves without dateable assemblages would logically fit into an earlier part of the cemetery sequence. These burials originated in the century and a half after the events of the foundation of Britain described in the *Anglo-Saxon Chronicle*, and it might be expected that they would produce evidence of the cultural context of the early post-Roman period. If there had been a general migration of settlers from Scandinavia it might reflect in the array of costumes that can be reconstructed from the finds in the graves. The individual ornaments, dress fittings, tools and weapons that these people were buried with can be reconstructed into typical suites of material that represent changing styles of women's costumes.

The grave assemblages that were first discovered in excavations at Ozengell (Smith 1854) and Sarre (Brent 1863, 1866), in the middle and later nineteenth century, produced stunning evidence of the array of items that were placed in graves of sixth- and seventh-century date. More recent investigations at Sarre and Ozengell have helped to establish the limits of the cemeteries, showing them to be larger than the nineteenth-century excavations indicated. The excavation of the cemetery at St Peters by Hogarth in the late 1960s has provided the most extensive sample of any cemetery on Thanet. Much evidence was revealed of the rich detail of the dress accessories and the array of weaponry buried with these people (*98*). The grave assemblages are a reflection of the self-image of the person, as well as a reflection of how they were perceived by the society in which they lived. An extremely rich grave of a woman at Sarre (grave 4), dating to around the middle of the sixth century, was buried with the following items: six gold bracteates, 135 beads (130 being of amber), two Kentish disc brooches, a glass bell beaker at her head, a weaving baton, a knife with a decorated sheath, two iron keys, shears, a silver spoon with a perforated bowl, a crystal ball mounted in a silver gilt suspension hoop, two square-headed brooches, Roman coins, a bone comb, a buckle and a polished fossil (*99*). Gold braid was found above her right hand suggesting she wore clothes with such trimmings (Brent 1863, 6; Richardson 2004). Items such as the straining spoons indicate that women had a symbolic role in the distribution of the hospitality of the household. The dress styles can be placed in a chronological progression, and it has been suggested that a social hierarchy can also be detected

> In Kent women followed two main types of fashion Anglo-Saxon and Kentish-continental. Whether these fashions expressed identity acquired at birth or allegiance to a certain group is open to discussion ... The Kentish continental group displayed greater wealth than those following Anglo-Saxon fashions
>
> Brugmann 1997a, 116

A Jutish influence is present in the corpus of grave goods in the form of items such as gold bracteates (a bracteate is a disc with a suspension loop), that were actually made in Jutland or are so similar to Jutish types as to suggest that they were made in Kent by Jutish craftsmen. Examples of Jutish-made bracteates occur at Sarre and Ozengell cemeteries. It appears though, that there is no grave assemblage in Kent that can be definitively identified as that of a Scandinavian dressed in national costume or buried with the traditional rites of their homeland (Brugmann 1997a). The deposition of grave goods in increasing numbers and combinations from the sixth century seems to have evolved as an indigenous response to the cultural influences that were reaching Britain from Scandinavia and the Frankish kingdoms of post-Roman Gaul. The earliest burials with grave goods show mixed influences from both the Scandinavian world and from

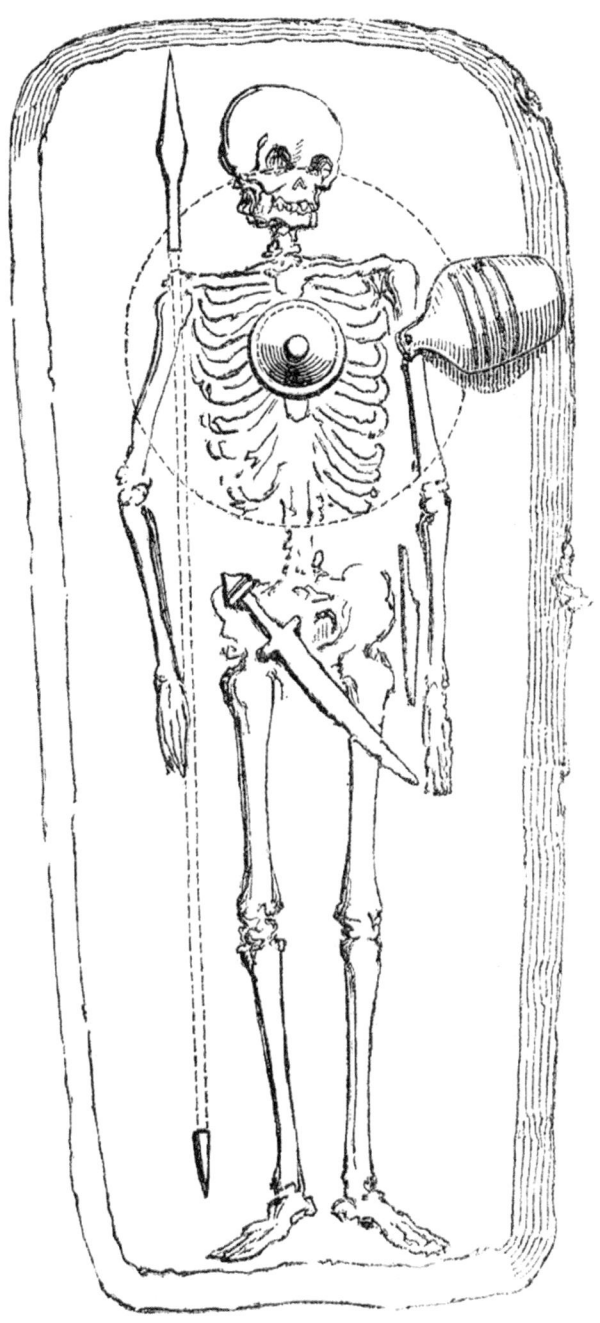

98 A weapon burial from the Ozengell cemetery recorded by C.R. Smith in *Collectanea Antiqua iii*.

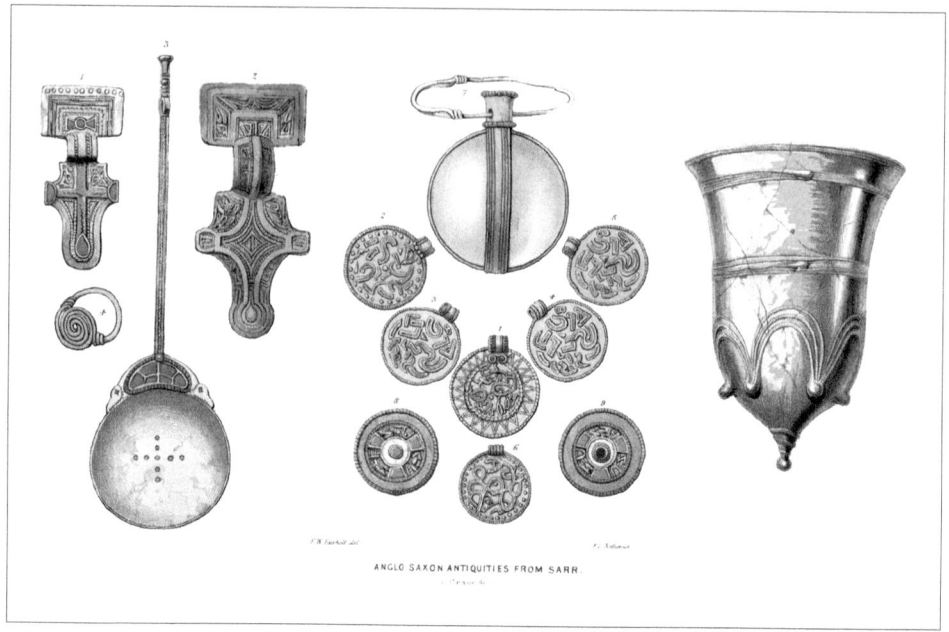

99 A selection of artefacts from Sarre grave 4, after Brent 1863

the Frankish kingdoms, and the accessories they wore were an eclectic mix derived from many different cultures, never used in the same combinations as their cultural sources (Brugmann 1997a).

One specialised form of structure appears in several graves within most of the cemeteries on Thanet. Iron nails and plates (roves), traditionally used to fix the overlapping planks of clinker-built ships have been found in various arrangements in graves, suggesting part of a boat had been used to cover the body. The distribution of these burials around the coastal areas of Kent suggests they were symbolic expressions of the maritime status of the communities where the burials are found (Brookes 2007). It is not clear whether a portion of an existing ship might have been used to cover the body, or whether the coffin structure was built in clinker style in emulation of the traditions of boat-building. Perhaps some other wooden box, such as a private sea chest built using clinker construction, was used for a coffin.

It has been suggested that the original sites of these cemeteries were chosen in direct reference to existing Bronze Age round barrows (Brugmann 2007b). Six round barrows were present within the area covered by the Ozengell cemetery. The group at Cliffsend was located on a small hilltop over one round barrow; the Bradstow School cemetery was located over a complex of four barrows. There was a single round barrow at the northern end of the St Peters site. In most of these cases truncation of both the barrow and the grave were such that an association with a barrow would have to be demonstrated by the distinct spatial arrangement in plan of a group of early graves set over the round barrow. There is a hint of the influence of the underlying barrow in the plan of the St Peters cemetery in that is has distorted the angle of the graves, and graves at Ozengell follow the alignment of the barrow ditches. In most of the cemeteries, orderly arrangements of row graves are present indicating that the influence of the ancient mounds was restricted to the earliest groups; it is not clear whether the grave assemblages support any distinction in the graves. The choice of a cemetery location has implications for interpreting the wider cultural beliefs of the populations buried in the cemeteries. The four cemetery groups in the western part of the island are closely associated with the track that runs up the central ridge. Small groups of Roman burials were also distributed along this track and it appears that the main difference between the Roman and post-Roman cemetery groups is the greater accumulation of inhumations in the later cemeteries. The Ozengell cemetery overlaps a cremation, and an inhumation in a lead coffin of Roman date. Its location is possibly along a continuation of the track across the ridge, although it seems to share another characteristic with the cemeteries in the east of Thanet, being situated on the break of slope on a steep hillside. It is possible these communities shared with their Bronze Age predecessors a preference for locations with impressive visual ranges.

The distinctive patterns of dress and assemblages of grave goods identified in the early graves represent a small proportion of the contemporary population, probably a relatively high-status group with some surplus wealth. Other less well-furnished or unfurnished graves could represent other parts of the population or direct ancestors of the Romano-British population. The grave assemblages are not the artefacts of the Jutish earls themselves, or even their humbler kinsmen, but those of the indigenous population accommodating to the cultural influences of their new lords. There is a political context to the development of the cultural identity of early Anglo-Saxon Kent, not an ethnic one.

The Kingdom of Kent was established in a process that involved the personal charisma and authority of warrior aristocrats of Scandinavian origin, working with the established system of redistribution of the produce of the land to the various unproductive classes. The Kentish style emerged in parallel with the creation of a new political and social framework in the region, as interchange with the Frankish kingdoms over the English Channel increased. The Franks preserved much of the culture of Roman Gaul, operating in parallel with a Roman administration system that still functioned and adopting much of the Roman State apparatus. Many of the industries of the Roman period survived in Gaul and the importation of large quantities of wheel-turned pottery is demonstrated in the grave assemblages in the cemeteries on Thanet (*100*). Frankish goods were brought to Kent through the ancient trading relationships with the continent. Some diplomatic gifts may have been exchanged and some goods were possibly obtained through a degree of piracy (Brugmann 1997b, 123).

The power of the Frankish kings was determined partly by their usurpation of the Roman administration system and partly by their cultural heritage. They claimed similar mythological lines of descent from Woden to enhance their power, as did many of the early Lords of the Angles (Wallace-Hadrill 1982). They had forged a Franko-Roman culture whose influence spread to alliances with British leaders such as the Kentish King Aethelbert, who married a Frankish woman of the Royal family (Hawkes

The Isle of Thanet – from Prehistory to the Norman Conquest

100 Wheel-turned bottle vase from Sarre, grave 277. © *Trust for Thanet Archaeology*

1982). Another influence on the culture of the emerging Kentish kingdom was Christianity. King Aethelbert's wife Bertha was a Christian and brought her own bishop with her to Kent (Sellar 1907). At the invitation of Aethelbert a mission lead by Augustine was sent by the Roman Church to negotiate the conversion of the Kentish kingdom to Christianity. The mission was requested by Aethelbert and was a key element in creating an identity for his kingdom. Aethelbert may have been motivated to emulate the Frankish Kings for whom Christianity restored a connection to the legitimacy of Imperial Rome. If it is wise to be cautious about the presence of a major Scandinavian element in the population, it is equally important to consider what the nature of the paganism of pre-Christian communities was. Rather than worshipping the gods of German mythology, it is likely that the religion of the population was more a simple animism, inherited from the Iron Age and Roman past, where springs, trees and other natural phenomena were given spiritual significance.

As the Kentish kingdom fervently embraced Christianity in the late sixth century, a woman was being brought up in the royal household who would be significant to Thanet's history. Aefa (known more familiarly as Saint Domneva from her title, *Domne Aefa* (Lady Eva), had an impressive heritage: her grandfather was King Aethelbert and her father, Eormenred, was the brother of Eorcenbehrt, king from AD 640-664. In the middle of the seventh century, while Aefa was living in Herefordshire with her husband Merewalh, King of the Magonsaete, her two young brothers were murdered in a dynastic intrigue, probably at Eastry. She was called back to Kent by her cousin King Egbert (664-73) to receive due compensation for the princes according to Aethelbert's laws, and in 670 Aefa was given land in Thanet to found a monastery; members of her extended family had already founded monastic houses at Sheppey and Lyminge. The original land grant appears to have been an estate called North Minster, nearer the uplands of the central ridge (Brooks 1991). A tradition associated with the foundation of the abbey is that Aefa asked for all the land that her pet deer could run around. According to the legend, the deer crossed the island in an irregular line from south to north, the stations of the route later described as the run of the hind (*cursus cervi*) on Thomas of Elmham's map of Thanet. It has been demonstrated that the Abbey at Minster accumulated land over a period of time and only established the boundary of the course of the hind through a series of land exchanges in the later medieval period (Scott-Robertson 1878, 344). The tradition of the hind may have been invented to support the claim over this irregular land holding.

Charters record that the monastery only moved closer to the Wantsum channel in the eighth century under the third Abbess Edburga. Lewis (1736, 46) suggested that rights over the tolls at Sarre were given to the Abbey at Minster in 726 but there is no other corroboration of this information. Historical sources suggest that Sarre may have been a trading port, possibly seasonal, in the mid eighth century (Perkins 2001b; Riddler 2004, 28). Five ship toll charters exist for Minster from the 730s to the 760s, demonstrating that the monasteries had an interest in maritime trade from the Wantsum. Some elements of the first buildings at the waterside in Minster survive near the modern village and the Parish Church of St Mary appears to preserve remnants of earlier buildings within a very complicated structure. Ancient foundations were observed between the vicarage and the parish church at Minster and described as being 5ft thick; it was thought these could have been associated with a harbour belonging to the earliest monastery, although they could be of Roman date associated with the Abbey Farm Villa nearby (Bubb 1862). The first monastery accommodated both monks and nuns under the rule of an abbess, who would have carried out practical work on the estates including managing the port and possibly boat-building. Land in Thanet was granted to the Abbott Berhwald of Reculver Abbey in 679, possibly that of Downbarton near St Nicholas. The grants to Reculver formed the basis of the landholdings of the See of Canterbury in Thanet (Quested 2001).

The Kentish kings hedged their bets with the establishment of the early monastic estates, delegating the land to junior members of their own families or widowed aunts, and the monastic estates were still obliged to render hospitality to the king's household on its circuit.

What is missing from the cemeteries and the records of the early church is evidence for the ordinary lives of the peasant farmers, stockmen and fishermen whose produce sustained a system of food rents consumed by the king's household (Quested 2001, 14). Archaeological features related to settlement in the early Anglo-Saxon period on Thanet are limited, but it is possible to construct some idea of the economy using archaeological and place name evidence. Thirteen sunken-featured buildings have been excavated on Thanet, most as single isolated examples on multi-period sites. It has generally not been possible to carry out further exploration of these sites to determine whether widely dispersed groups are present or whether they are genuinely isolated. A group of five structures at Manston might indicate nucleation in a village, possibly associated with the Ozengell cemetery nearby (Hutcheson *et al* 1998). The other sunken-featured buildings have been located on the central plateau, or on the slopes on the southern side of the central ridge. The majority excavated on Thanet have conformed to a similar plan with two posts at either end of the long axis (*101*).

Sunken-featured building is a term used to describe a small timber building constructed on a cellar-like pit. These structures appear to have many uses and tend to be associated with storage or semi-industrial uses such as loom sheds, rather than dwellings. Other forms of structure probably remain to be discovered to complete the layout of an early Saxon settlement on Thanet, although contemporary post-built structures of Anglo-Saxon date have been excavated elsewhere, such as at Mucking, Essex (Hamerow 2003). The dating evidence from the backfilling of these features, after they had been abandoned, suggests they were of sixth- to seventh-century date, contemporary with the main cemeteries on Thanet. Pits containing large dumps of shellfish remains have been found close to the shore at Cliffsend (WA 2005) and at St Mildred's Bay (Boast *et al* 2006c), and the remains of a large cod have been found in a pit at Cottington Hill (Perkins 1998c). The pits at Cliffsend were thought to be contemporary with the nearby cemetery; those at St Mildred's Bay and Cottington Hill are later, dating to the eighth and ninth centuries. These remains indicate that produce from fisheries and the foreshore would have been important in the economy. Salt-working remained of vital importance in this period too as much of the food delivered to the royal household, wherever it was based, would have been preserved for long-term storage.

New identities – the fifth century to the Norman Conquest

101 Sunken-featured building excavated at Sarre. © *Trust for Thanet Archaeology*

We should expect that the villages and farmsteads of Thanet were located on the ancient trackways that had been used for thousands of years. Place names with the element *street* indicate routes persisting from the Roman period and still utilised by the Anglo-Saxons (Everitt 1986). The place names of Thanet villages recorded on early maps originate in the system of production and exchange that developed. Place names ending in *-ton* indicate enclosed farmsteads named in the Anglo-Saxon period. The two main harbours may have had their *-gat* suffixes added in this period; Margate is from *Mere-gat* meaning broadly 'way through the meres' and Ramsgate, more controversially *Rhuim-gat*, after an ancient British name for the Isle of Thanet (Lewis 1736; Rivet & Smith 1979). There is an early tradition for the origin of Ramsgate as 'Rome's Gat', dismissed by Lewis and revived with enthusiasm by Captain Kennet Martin (Martin 1857). The entire island can be traversed through locations with these place name elements (*102*) using the First Edition one inch Ordnance Survey map (1820); from Birchington through Street (near Westgate) to Margate; from Salmestone on the north side of Thanet to Ramsgate. On the east and south sides of Thanet they can be traced from the port of Sarre following ancient Dun Street through Monkton, Manston, Newington and Ellington, to Ramsgate; from Ramsgate along the straight road of Sowell Street through Hereson (*Herestun*), Dumpton, Bromston and Upton to Reading Street and the north-east coast. Many of the locations are familiar from the study of the Iron Age and Roman economy and can be traced in a line along the ancient trackway across the ridge and plateau and up the hollow-ways from the ports. On the central plateau there are names indicating the preservation or regeneration of some woodland resources. The villages of Westwood,

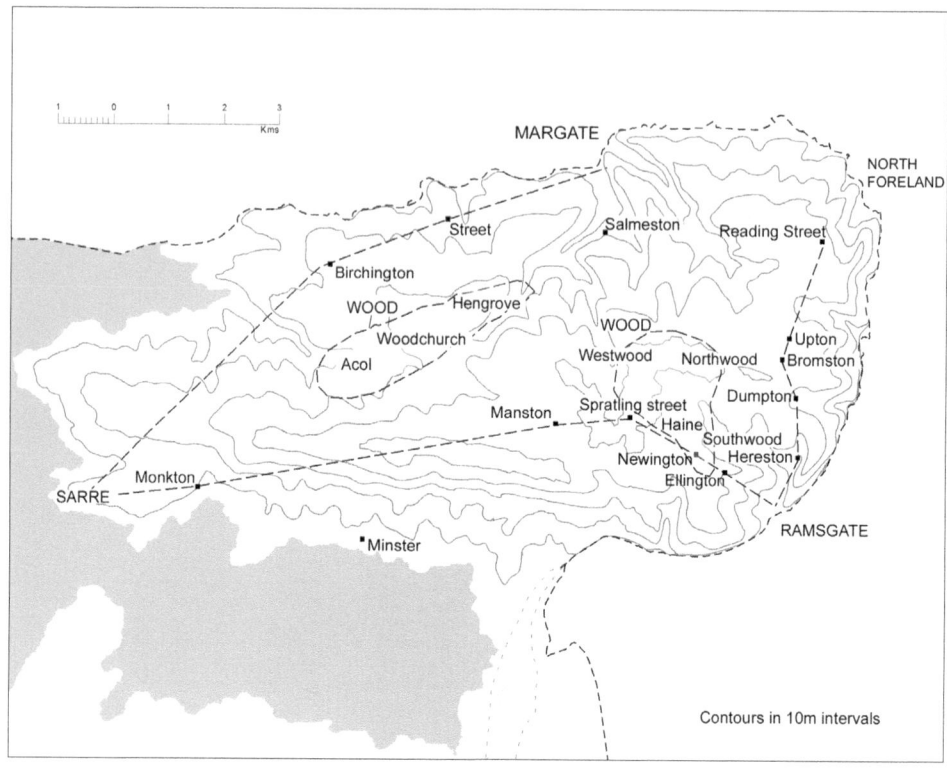

102 Distribution map of place names relating to the Saxon agricultural distribution system

Northwood, Southwood, Haine (?*Hagen*) and Coles Wood enclose the highest point of the central plateau. Acol (*Ac-Holt*, 'Oak wood') and Woodchurch (i.e. 'church in a wood') indicate woodland on the north-west side of the island (Everitt 1986).

The later history of Anglo-Saxon Thanet is dominated by further contacts from Scandinavia. Around AD 830, Viking sea-raiders from Denmark began to attack coastal areas in Britain including Kent. Small annual raiding seasons between spring and autumn gradually became sustained campaigns persisting over more than a single year. These forces would have frequently used the passage through the Wantsum channel, and the agricultural system that produced and stored food for consumption by the royal households was an attractive target for these men. A group of raiders spent the winter of AD 850 on the islands of Thanet and Sheppey (Jones 1984). The early raids by small groups were a prelude to major incursions in the late ninth century, culminating in permanent settlement by groups of Danes in areas of the north of England. An attack launched by Danes from northern France almost certainly used the Wantsum to reach the Medway estuary where they laid siege to Rochester in 884. King Alfred (king from AD 871-899) battled the Danes at Stourmouth in the Wantsum channel. To date there has been no corroborating archaeological evidence excavated on Thanet of these attacks or the periods of settlement recorded.

New identities – the fifth century to the Norman Conquest

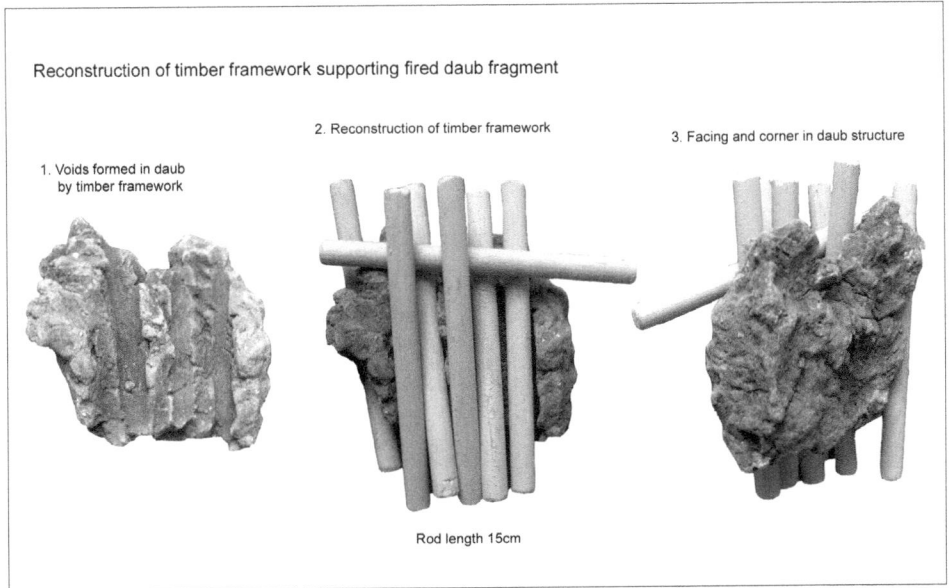

103 Reconstruction of fragments of fired clay from a ninth century pit at Westgate. © *Trust for Thanet Archaeology*

A site on the coastline at Westgate has produced rare evidence of settlement on Thanet's northern coast in the later Anglo-Saxon period. A group of rectangular pits, possibly cut as wells or ditches for household waste were dated by pottery to the eighth century. Later two linear gullies filled with marine shells were cut through the backfilled pits. Another pit was cut through the gullies and packed with fragments from a fired-clay structure, preserving the impressions of the timber framework that had supported it (*103*).

In a small patch of burnt clay, in a hollow over one of the pits, an iron lock mechanism was found. This would have been attached to a large household chest; a very similar lock was found in grave 16 at Ozengell. Keys on chatelaine rings are often found in the graves of the sixth- and seventh-century cemeteries, some are undoubtedly ornamental but some may have fitted the locks of private chests where household valuables were kept. The fired clay packed into the latest pit was dated by pottery to the ninth century (Boast *et al* 2006c).

Over the following century Viking kingdoms were established in the north of England. Danish raiders again attacked Thanet in 980 and regular raids were carried out in the next three decades until the final victory and coronation of the Dane Cnut as king in 1017. Due to the prosperous sea trade, the land settled by the early monastic houses had been some of the most profitable in Kent. This location so close to the open sea had made them vulnerable to attack from the latest of generations of Scandinavian sea raiders. The original monastery at Minster seems to have succumbed to the pressure of the raiders and disappears from the records in the ninth century, possibly burned to

173

the ground by the raiders (Quested 2001, 13). Thomas of Elmham's chronicle indicates that Cnut granted the lands that had formerly belonged to Minster Abbey to the monks of St Augustine's Abbey at their request in 1027, although this may have been a later embellishment to strengthen the Abbey's hold over the lands. The later history of the landholdings and charters of the Isle of Thanet becomes complex and it is sufficient to say that the rich farmlands of Thanet passed into the possession of the three largest regional institutions of the Church, the See of Canterbury, the Abbey of St Augustine and the Priory of Christ Church, Canterbury (Quested 2001, 15). The period when the older monastic houses fail is a watershed in the Saxon settlement of Thanet. The first phase of monastic settlement ended and the institutions at Canterbury held the lands as agricultural estates rather than religious communities.

William of Normandy's invasion of England in 1066 avoided the traditional landing place of previous invaders in Kent, instead choosing Pevensey in Sussex, only later entering into east Kent. The Abbott of St Augustine may have been involved in resistance to William's invasion and in consequence Williams' soldiers ravaged the lands of the Abbey at Minster. In 1086, the Domesday Book listed William's assets in the Isle of Thanet as the two Manors of Minster and Monkton. For the first time in Thanet's long history we catch a glimpse of the families living and working on Isle of Thanet. In a few lines the Domesday Book listed more information on the people of Thanet in the 1080s than we hold for the hundreds of previous generations. The Manor of Monkton answered for 89 villagers and 21 smallholders, with a mill and two churches at Monkton and St Giles at Sarre. There was a new fishery, and a salt house and woodland, with pigs, all in the lordship of Christ Church, Canterbury. At Minster, recovering well from its devastation a decade or two before, were 150 villagers and 50 smallholders with a church and a priest, a salt house, two fisheries and a mill in the lordship of the Abbey of St Augustine, Canterbury. Three 'men at arms' held some of Minster villagers' land (Quested 2001). A few monks tended to the abbot's residence at the Manor house in Minster (Hills 1970). As the abbot visited his Minster grange he may have looked out on the marshy fringes of the Wantsum channel and made plans for embankments that could turn the land to some profit. The industry of the monks of the later medieval period would succeed in making pasture and farmland from the channel that once brought profit from its ports and ships.

A FINAL PASSAGE FROM THANET

Although a great deal is known about the archaeological discoveries on the Isle of Thanet, how much of this information is really understood? In a seminal essay on 'Bridging the two cultures' of commercial archaeology and academic research the noted British prehistorian, Richard Bradley, noted that in Britain:

> ... the amount of fieldwork has increased so fast over the last two decades that it is no longer a question of waiting for the results of major projects to be published in a journal or a monograph; it is difficult to know which are major projects, let alone to discover what they have achieved ... In this sense field archaeology has drifted out of control, although this is simply part of an information explosion that characterises our modern society. More is published, more is spoken, more is circulated on the internet ... we cannot hope to assimilate it all.

> ... it is quite obvious now that no existing synthesis of British or Irish prehistory reflects the current state of play. We are finally able to break free from a dependence on the prehistory of central southern England as a source of classic sites. When we do so, we gain the uneasy suspicion that it is the archaeological sequence in other regions – especially along the north sea coast – that may provide a more acceptable general framework, if any is to be found
>
> Bradley 2006

To follow the long span of human society on Thanet, the primary source of evidence is the distribution of archaeological sites and artefacts over the landscape. Thanet possesses a unique resource in a having a local repository of archaeological data covering the earliest explorations up to the present day. In the research for this book the information explosion referred to by Bradley – the so-called archaeological 'grey' literature – has been used extensively to construct a local narrative framework.

A narrative form of description taking a story from beginning to end is not always compatible with the nature of archaeological evidence. For any period of time, the artefacts and structures that are most clearly defined and coherently associated in the archaeological record shape the content of archaeological narratives. Cultural changes are recognised by the appearance or loss of some defining feature or artefact in the site sequence. Only rarely do we consider how one cultural form merged into another. To produce a continuous narrative for an area through several changes in cultural form, the transitions must be explained in some way. The traditional divisions between archaeological periods do not always provide satisfactory accounts and it is rare that there is tangible evidence of the change between two distinct cultural forms.

While archaeological excavation and research adds continually to our knowledge, some of the things we would like to know about the societies of the past will remain obscure and will always be beyond our grasp. It is too easy for archaeological features that preserve events in history in their own right to become exemplars of theoretical cultural forms; behind each class of monument is a society for whom these structures were part of everyday life. The issue of scale in the study of past society is significant. It is hard to trace great events in the past from the evidence contained in a small area, but equally, significant local events can be lost in debates over cultural process. If great events cannot be read on the small scale, how can they be measured at all? This study is concerned with the changing evidence for human occupation over the area of Thanet rather than a process of selection of sites and artefacts to illustrate conventional narratives of social development.

Where the archaeological story runs out, some other language has to be used to continue the narrative, and sometimes geography has to replace the archaeological sequence. In this study of the Isle of Thanet, the shape and physical form of the landscape has been used to continue the narrative; as society changed, the landscape endured as an independent material condition. Tracing the changing landscape provides a narrative continuity in periods for which there is little evidence for human stories that might have unfolded. The landscape followed its own grand scale of change oblivious to the minor changes that humans made to its surface. Under the influence of the sea, the geography of Thanet has undergone continuous change since the end of the last Ice Age. This chalk outcrop has suffered continuous erosion and reduction and each generation experiences the loss of familiar landmarks. Understanding the landscape of Thanet's past requires an understanding of the scale of the loss of landmass and the steady rise of the sea. It also requires careful reconstruction of the changing experience of Thanet's landscape by those living within it. The sea grew into the consciousness of the occupants of Thanet as it encroached daily on their lives and progressively supplemented the land as a resource in the daily struggle for survival. Always a resourceful adaptor, man developed tools and equipment to negotiate the rising water and maintain relationships with the societies across the Channel and the North Sea; the sea provided an interface with new ideas and social forms rather than a barrier.

Thanet remained relatively isolated by marsh and windswept downland until the early nineteenth century and the coming of the railways. In the modern era it is striking to read the language of bleak isolation with which it is described by observers as late as the early twentieth century. Even today 'Planet Thanet' is still seen as a place apart even though it is firmly linked to the rest of Kent by modern transport links. Thanet's maritime tradition spanned the period from the Bronze Age to the later twentieth century, but now, other than a few fishing boats and leisure craft, the tradition is almost gone. Few people have the experience of regularly crossing the channel through their own navigational skills and seacraft. It becomes necessary to recreate the experience from other people's descriptions and memories and to use these to animate the material remains in the archaeological record.

In the early twenty-first century it has become difficult to farm Thanet's fertile land profitably and new uses are found for the rolling landscape, from golf courses to new housing estates. The visual amenity of the coastal landscape is an enduring attraction and it is not hard to imagine why some of the most impressive views appealed to our ancestors. Thanet has had continuous contact with the continent for thousands of years and our relationship with our nearest neighbours continues to be negotiated through a strong sense of local identity. In the present day the sea is more often seen as a powerful spectacle than a force to be contended with for survival. In a society increasingly isolated from nature where we fear change in the natural environment, it is difficult to envisage the continuous effects of the 'rage of the sea' as a permanent fixture in our lives.

Each period in this work is a sketched narrative based on real data. Some aspects of our past can never be reconstructed by our present methods of study but should nevertheless be explored for the sake of completeness in understanding past societies. There is a degree of impressionistic narrative in the text based on intuition rather than information where I have wanted to set out a context in terms of the landscape or social conditions. There is an element of history and some 'wishtory' where I wish we knew more about some aspects of the periods in question, but many of my interpretations can be demonstrated in a level of detail for which space simply did not allow. The preceding pages of this book are my attempt to bring a small part of the 'information explosion' into some form of coherent story and I hope that from the building blocks of local studies such as this, a more consistent narrative for the whole Kent region may be constructed.

BIBLIOGRAPHY

Allen, T.L. and Green, C. 2003, *An Assessment of Archaeological Works on Land North-West of the 'Loop', Manston, The Isle of Thanet, Kent*. Unpubl. Canterbury Archaeological Trust Client Report

Allen, M.J. 2005, Beaker Settlement and Environment on the Chalk Downs of Southern England. *Proceedings of the Prehistoric Society* 71, 219-245

Anon 1860, Obituary for W. Rolfe of Sandwich. *Gentlemans Magazine* 208, 84. Preserved online by Google Books at http://books.google.com/

Ashbee, P. and Dunning, G. 1960, The roundbarrows of East Kent. *Archaeologia Cantiana* 74, 43-57

Ashbee, P. 2001, William Stukeley's Kentish studies of Roman and Other Remains. *Archaeologia Cantiana* 121, 61-102

Ashbee, P. 2005, *Kent in Prehistoric Times*. Gloucestershire, Tempus

Baker, C.A. 2005, *Cave Site, Spratling Court Farm, Ramsgate*, Unpubl. report

Barber, M. 2003, *Bronze and the Bronze Age*. Gloucestershire, Tempus

Barrett, J.P. 1893, *A History of the Ville of Birchington* (2nd ed.), Birchington, reprinted 2005 by Michaels Bookshop, Ramsgate

Bennett, P. 1995, Monkton, www.canterburytrust.co.uk/schools/keysites/monk.htm, last accessed January 1st 2008

Bennett, P. (ed.) 2004, *Canterbury Archaeological Trust Annual Report 2003-2004*, Norfolk, Heritage Marketing and Publications Ltd

Bennett, P. et al 1996, Interim report on excavations in advance of the dualling of the A253 between Monkton and Mount Pleasant, Thanet. *Archaeologia Cantiana* 117, 305-310

Bersu, G. 1940, Excavations at Little Woodbury, Wiltshire, Part I, The settlement as revealed by excavation. *Proceedings of the Prehistoric Society* 6, 30-111

Biggs, H. 1972, Belgic and Roman Discoveries at Lanthorne Road, Broadstairs, An Interim Report. *Kent Archaeological Review* 29, 273

Birch, D., Boakes, P., Elworthy, S., Hollins, C. and Perkins D.R.J. 1987, *The Gateway Island - Archaeological Discoveries in Thanet 1630-1987*. Thanet, Thanet Archaeological Unit

Boast, E.J. 2000, *An Archaeological Evaluation carried out on land adjacent to Nash Road and Salmestone Grange, St Johns Parish, Margate, Kent*. Unpubl. Trust for Thanet Archaeology Client Report

Boast, E.J. 2001, *Land to the rear of 23-25 Anne Close, Birchington, Kent. Archaeological Evaluation Report*. Unpubl. Trust for Thanet Archaeology Client Report

Boast, E.J. 2002, *Queensdown Riding and Livery Centre, Castlemayne Avenue, Woodchurch, Thanet, Kent. Evaluation Assessment Report*. Unpubl. Trust for Thanet Archaeology Client Report

Boast, E.J. 2003, *Minster Wheels Park, Minster Recreation Ground, King George's Field, Molineaux Road, Minster, Thanet, Kent. Archaeological Evaluation*. Unpubl. Trust for Thanet Archaeology Client Report

Boast, E.J. 2004a, *Seapoint, The Parade, Birchington, Kent*. Unpubl. Trust for Thanet Archaeology Client Report

Boast, E.J. 2004b, *Construction of a Garage, 12 North Foreland Road, North Foreland, Broadstairs, Kent*. Unpubl. Trust for Thanet Archaeology Client Report

Boast, E.J. 2006, *South Side of Clifton Place, Margate, Kent, Archaeological Watching Brief.* Unpubl. Trust for Thanet Archaeology Client Report

Boast, E.J. 2007a, Multi-period features: Spratling Street, Manston. *Archaeologia Cantiana* 127, 421-422

Boast, E.J. 2007b, Bronze and Iron Age Occupation: Hartsdown Road, Margate. *Archaeologia Cantiana* 127, 429

Boast, E.J. 2007c, *Former Sticky Fingers Nursery, Grange Road, Ramsgate, Archaeological Assessment Report*. Unpubl. Trust for Thanet Archaeology Client Report

Boast, E.J. and Gardner, O.W. 2006, *1 Seacroft Road, Broadstairs, Kent. Archaeological Report*. Unpubl. Trust for Thanet Archaeology Client Report

Boast, E.J. and Gibson, A. 2000, Neolithic, Beaker and Anglo-Saxon remains, Minster in Thanet. *Archaeologia Cantiana* 120, 359-372

Boast, E.J., Gardner, O.W. and Moody, G.A. 2006a, *Excavations at St Stephen's College, North Foreland, Broadstairs, Kent. Archaeological Excavation Report*, Unpubl. Trust for Thanet Archaeology Client Report

Boast, E.J., Gardner, O.W. and Moody, G.A. 2006b, *East Kent Community NHS Health Trust Medical Centre, Manston Road, Ramsgate, Archaeological Report*. Unpubl. Trust for Thanet Archaeology report

Boast, E.J., Gardner, O.W. and Moody, G.A. 2006c, *Sea Tower, Sussex Gardens, Westgate on Sea, Archaeological Report*. Unpubl. Trust for Thanet Archaeology Client Report

Boast, E.J. and Moody, G.A. 2003, *Former Bon Secours Nursing Home, Junction of London Road and Pegwell Road, Ramsgate, Kent, Archaeological Assessment Report*. Unpubl. Trust for Thanet Archaeology Client Report

Boast, E.J. and Perkins, D.R.J. 2001, *London Manston Airport, Manston, Thanet, Kent. Archaeological evaluations and investigations of Passenger and Cargo side taxiways and aprons*. Unpubl. Trust for Thanet Archaeology Client Report

Boulter, H.E. 1933, Anglo-Saxon remains found at Ramsgate. *Archaeologia Cantiana* 45, 283-4

Bradley, R.J. 1984, *The social foundations of prehistoric Britain*. London, Longman

Brayley, E.W. 1817, *Delineations Historical and Topographical of the Isle of Thanet and the Cinque Ports, 1*. Reprinted 2005 by Michaels Bookshop, Ramsgate

Brent, J. 1863, Account of the Society's Researches in the Saxon Cemetery at Sarr, Part 1. *Archaeologia Cantiana* 5, 305-22

Brent, J. 1866, Account of the Society's Researches in the Saxon Cemetery at Sarr, Part 2. *Archaeologia Cantiana* 6, 157-85

Brookes, S. 2007, Boat rivets in Graves in pre-Viking Kent: Reassessing Anglo-Saxon Boat-burial traditions. *Medieval Archaeology* 51, 1-18

Brooks, B. 1991, *Saint Domneva and the foundation of Minster-in-Thanet*. Thanet, Thanet District Council

Brugmann, B. 1997b, Mill Hill: A Typical 6th-Century East Kent Cemetery? In K. Parfitt *et al*, *The Anglo-Saxon Cemetery on Mill Hill, Deal, Kent*. The Society for Medieval Archaeology Monograph Series 14, Ch 6

Brugmann, B. 1997a, Britons, Angles, Saxons, Jutes and Franks. In K. Parfitt *et al*, *The Anglo-Saxon Cemetery on Mill Hill, Deal, Kent*. The Society for Medieval Archaeology Monograph Series 14, Ch 5

Burgess, C. and Coombs, D. 1979, *Bronze Age Hoards*. Oxford, British Archaeological Reports Series 67

Bubb, R.B. 1862, Minster, Thanet. *Gentlemans Magazine* 13, 82-84. Preserved online by Google Books at http://books.google.com

Carder, D. 2004, Anglo-Saxon Churches. In T. Lawson (ed.) *et al, An Historical Atlas of Kent*. Chichester, Philmore & Co., 31

Champion, T. 2007, Prehistoric Kent. In J.H. Williams (ed.), *The Archaeology of Kent to AD 800.* East Lothian, The Boydell Press, Ch. 3
Chandler, J.H. (ed.) 1998, *John Leland's Itinerary: Travels in Tudor England.* Gloucestershire, Sutton
Clarke, D.L. 1970, *Beaker pottery of Great Britain and Ireland.* Cambridge, Cambridge University Press
Clark, P. (ed.) 2004, *The Dover Bronze Age Boat.* Swindon, English Heritage
Clark, P. (ed.) 2005, *The Dover Bronze Age Boat in Context.* Swindon, English Heritage
Clinch, G. 1901, Palaeolithic Implement from the Isle of Thanet. *Reliq. and Illust. Archaeologist.*, January edition
Coles, B.J. 1998, Doggerland: a Speculative Survey. *Proceedings of the Prehistoric Society* 64, 45-81
Cook, G. and Naysmith, P. 1995, Appendix 1 - Radiocarbon Dating. In C. Hearne *et al*, *Archaeologia Cantiana* 115, 345
Corcoran, J. 2003, *Residential Development: Land North of the River Stour, Ramsgate Road, Sandwich, Kent. A Geographical Assesssment Report.* Unpubl. Museum of London Archaeology Service Report
Cotton, J. and Field, D. (ed.) 2004, *Towards a New Stone Age. Aspects of the Neolithic in south-east England.* York, CBA Research Report 137
Coy, J. 1965, News from the Groups: Thanet Group. *Kent Archaeological Review* 2, 33-35
Cullen, P. 1970, Roman Coin-Hoard at Ramsgate. *Kent Archaeological Review* 19, 23
Cullen, P. 1971, Anglo-Saxon Cemetery at Broadstairs. *Kent Archaeological Review* 24, 112
Cullen, P. 1983, A Roman Site at Pysons Road, Ramsgate. *Kent Archaeological Review* 71, 2-3
Cunliffe, B.W. (ed.) 1968, Fifth Report on the Excavations of the Roman Fort at Richborough, Kent. *Reports of the Research Committee of the Society of Antiquaries of London* 23, Oxford
Cunliffe, B.W. 1991, *Iron Age Communities in Britain.* London, Routledge (3rd ed.)
Darvill, T. 1987, *Prehistoric Britain.* London, Routledge
de Jersey, P. 1996, *Celtic Coinage in Britain.* Buckinghamshire, Shire
de la Bédoyère, G. 2006, *Roman Britain. A new History.* London, Thames and Hudson
Detsicas, A. (ed.) 1981, *Collectanea Historica.* Gloucester, Alan Sutton
Detsicas, A. 1987, *The Cantiaci.* Gloucester, Alan Sutton
Devoy, R.J.N. 1979, Flandrian Sea-level changes and vegetation history of the lower Thames Estuary. *Philosophical Transactions of the Royal Society of London* B285, 355-407
Dowker, G. 1897, On the Landing Place of St. Augustine. *Archaeologia Cantiana* 22, 123-143
Dowker, G. 1872, Account of the Society's researches in the Roman Castrum at Richborough. *Archaeologia Cantiana* 8, 1-17
Dunning, G.C. 1966, Neolithic occupation sites in East Kent. *Antiquaries Journal* 46, 1-25
Esmonde Cleary, A.S. 2000, *The Ending of Roman Britain.* Routledge
Everitt, A. 1986, *Continuity and Colonization. The evolution of Kentish settlement.* Bath, Leicester University Press
Evans, J. 1864, *The Coins of the Ancient Britons.* London, J.R. Smith. Preserved online by Google Books at http://books.google.com
Fairholme, G. 1837, *New and conclusive physical demonstrations both of the fact and period of the Mosaic Deluge.* T. Ridgeway and Sons. Preserved by Google Books at http://books.google.com
Fisher, T. 1779, *The Kentish Travellers Companion.* (2nd ed.) Canterbury, T. Fisher, reprinted 2005 by Michaels Bookshop, Ramsgate
Fisk, P.M. 2003, *An examination of the excavated ring ditch enclosures on the Isle of Thanet.* Unpubl. University of Kent at Canterbury undergraduate thesis
Gardner, O.W. 2004, *East Kent Community NHS Heath Trust Medical Centre, Land Adjacent Tesco Store, Manston Road, Ramsgate. Archaeological Assessment Report, Volume 1 & 2.* Unpubl. Trust for Thanet Archaeology Client Report
Gardner, O.W. and Moody, G.A. 2005, *Queen Elizabeth the Queen Mother Hospital, St. Peter's Road, Margate, Archaeological Excavation Report.* Unpubl. Trust for Thanet Archaeology Client Report
Gardner, O.W. and Moody, G.A. 2006a, *Excavations at Drapers Mills County Primary School, Margate, Kent, Archaeologial Report.* Unpubl. Trust for Thanet Archaeology Client Report

Gardner, O.W. and Moody, G.A. 2006b, *East Kent Community NHS Health Trust Medical Centre, Manston Road, Ramsgate, Kent, Archaeological Report*. Unpubl. Trust for Thanet Archaeology Client Report

Gibson, A. 2002, *Prehistoric pottery in Britain and Ireland*. Gloucestershire, Tempus

Gollop, A. 2004, *Detailed Archaeological Investigations on land at Westwood Cross, Broadstairs, Thanet (Draft)*. Unpubl. Canterbury Archaeological Trust Client Report

Gollop, A. 2004, Westwood Cross, Broadstairs. *Canterbury's Archaeology 2003-2004* 28, 18-19

Gollop, A. and Mason, S. 2005, Tothill Street, Minster, *Canterbury's Archaeology 2004-2005* 29, 24-25

Grainge, G. 2006, Double tides in the Wantsum - Fact or Fiction? *Archaeologia Cantiana* 126, 381-391

Greatorex, R. 2005, Cliffs End Conundrum. *Kent Archaeological Society Newsletter* 64, 1-2

Green, S.H. 1980, *The flint arrowheads of the British Isles*. British Archaeological Report British Series 75

Grimes, W.F. 1960, *Excavations on Defence Sites 1939-45, Volume 1*. London, HMSO

Gupta, S., Collier, J.S., Palmer-Felgate, A. and Potter, J. 2007, Catastrophic Flooding Origin of the Shelf Valley Systems in the English Channel. *Nature* 448, 342-345

Halliwell, G. and Parfitt, K. 1983, A Mesolithic site at Finglesham. *Kent Archaeological Review* 72, 29-32

Hamerow, H. 2003, *Excavations at Mucking. Volume 2: The Anglo-Saxon Settlement*. Swindon, English Heritage Archaeological Report 21

Hammond, J. 2007, How Kent's recently discovered Causewayed Enclosures impact on our understanding and interpretation of the Early Neolithic in the region. *Archaeologia Cantiana* 127, 357-382

Harding, J. 2003, *Henge monuments of the British Isles*. Gloucestershire, Tempus

Hardman, F.W. and Stebbing, W.P.D. 1940, Stonar and The Wantsum Channel - Part I – Physiographical. *Archaeologia Cantiana* 55, 62-80

Hardman, F.W. and Stebbing, W.P.D. 1941, Stonar and The Wantsum Channel - Part II – Historical. *Archaeologia Cantiana* 56, 41-55

Hardman, F.W. and Stebbing, W.P.D. 1942, Stonar and The Wantsum Channel - Part III - (Conclusion) The site of the Town of Stonar. *Archaeologia Cantiana* 57, 37-49

Hart, P.C. 2004, *Land to the rear of 16-18 Dane Hill, Margate, Kent*. Unpubl. Trust for Thanet Archaeology Client Report

Hart, P.C. 2005, *'Beauforts', North Foreland Avenue, Broadstairs, Kent, Archaeological Report*. Unpubl. Trust for Thanet Archaeology Client Report

Hart, D. 2006, Excavations at Bradstow School, Broadstairs. *Kent Archaeological Society Newsletter* 69, 14-15

Hart, P.C. and Moody G.A. 2005, *All Saints Avenue, Margate, Kent. Trust for Thanet Archaeology Assessment Report*. Unpublished Trust for Thanet Archaeology Client Report

Hart, P.C. and Moody, G.A. forthcoming, Two Beaker burials recently discovered on the Isle of Thanet. *Archaeologia Cantiana*

Hasted, E. 1800, *The History and Topographical Survey of the County of Kent*. (2nd ed.) Canterbury, W. Bristow

Hawkes, C.F.C. 1942, The Deverel Urn and the Picardy Pin: A Phase of Bronze Age Settlement in Kent. *Proceedings of the Prehistoric Society* 8, 26-47

Hawkes, S.C. 1968, Richborough - The Physical Geography. In B.W. Cunliffe (ed.), *Fifth Report on the Excavations of the Roman Fort at Richborough, Kent*. Reports of the Research Committee of the Society of Antiquaries of London 23

Hawkes, S.C. 1982, Anglo-Saxon Kent c 425-725. In P.E. Leach (ed.), *Archaeology in Kent to AD 1500*. Council for British Archaeology Research Report 48, 64-78

Hawkes, S.C. 1984, The Amherst Brooch. *Archaeologia Cantiana* 100, 129-151

Hawkes, S.C. and Grainger, G. 2006, *The Anglo-Saxon Cemetery at Finglesham, Kent*. Oxford University School of Archaeology Monograph 64

Hawkes, S.C., Hogarth, A.C. and Denston, C.B. 1974, The Anglo-Saxon cemetery at Monkton, Thanet. *Archaeologia Cantiana* 89, 49-90

Healey, E. 1994, The lithic artefacts. In Perkins *et al.*, Monkton Court Farm Evaluation 1992, *Archaeologia Cantiana* 114, 297-304

Hearne, C., Perkins, D.R.J. and Andrews, P. 1995, The Sandwich Bay Wastewater Treatment Scheme Archaeological Project 1992-1994. *Archaeologia Cantiana* 115, 239-354

Hicks, R. 1878, Roman Remains from Ramsgate. *Archaeologia Cantiana* 12, 14-18

Hills, D. and Cowie, R. (ed.) 2001, *Wics: The Early Medieval Trading Centres of Northern Europe*. Sheffield, Sheffield Academic Press

Hills, P.J. 1970, *The Parish Church of St. Peter-in-Thanet*. Lincolnshire, G.W. Belton Ltd

Hind, J.G.F. 1989, *The Invasion of Britain in AD 43 - an alternative strategy for Aulus Plautius*, Britannia 20, 1-21

Hodges, R. (ed.) 1982, *Dark Age Economics* (2nd ed.). London, Duckworth

Hogarth, C. 1972, Anglo-Saxon Cemetery, St Peters, Thanet. *Kent Archaeological Review* 28, 234

Hogarth, C. 1973, Structural Features in Anglo-Saxon graves. *The Archaeological Journal* 130, 104-19

Hogwood, P. 1995, Investigations at North Foreland Hill. *Archaeologia Cantiana* 115, 475

Holman, D. 2005a, Iron Age Coinage and Settlement in East Kent. *Britannia* 36, 1-54

Holman, D.J. and Parfitt, K. 2005b, The Roman Villa at Minster-in-Thanet. Part 2: The Iron Age, Roman and Later Coinage. *Archaeologia Cantiana* 124, 203-228

Hurd, H. 1909, On a Late-Celtic Village near Dumpton Gap, Broadstairs. *Archaeologia* 61, 427-38

Hurd, H. 1913, *Some notes on recent archaeological discoveries at Broadstairs*. Broadstairs, Broadstairs and St Peter's Archaeological Society

Hurd, H. 1913, Proceedings of the Society of Antiquaries of London XXV, 21st November 1912 to 26th June 1913, 89-90

Hurd, H. 1914, Late Celtic Discoveries at Broadstairs. *Archaeologia Cantiana* 30, 309-312

Hutcheson, A. and Andrews, P. 1998, *Excavations on a Late Bronze Age, Anglo-Saxon and Medieval Settlement Site at Manston Road, Ramsgate 1995-7*. Wessex Archaeology draft report ref. 39171a

Jay, L. 1990, Trust for Thanet Archaeology: Excavation and Evaluations 1989-1990. *Archaeologia Cantiana* 108, 237

Jay, L. 1993, Barrow reconstruction. *Archaeologia Cantiana* 112, 420-21

Jay, L. 1995, *Thanet Beakers*. Broadstairs, Trust for Thanet Archaeology

Jenkins, F. 1981, The Church of All Saints, Shuart in the Isle of Thanet. In A. Detsicas (ed.), *Collectanea Historica*. Gloucester, Alan Sutton, Ch. 18

Jessop, F.W. 1957, The Origin and first Hundred Years of the Society. *Archaeologia Cantiana* 70, 1-43

Jones, B. 1984, *Past Imperfect, The Story of Rescue Archaeology*. London, Heinemann

Jones, G. 1984, *A History of the Vikings* (rev. ed.). Oxford, Oxford University Press

Johnson, J.S. 1987, *Richborough and Reculver*. Swindon, English Heritage

Lambard, W. 1585, Map of the Beacon Network of Kent. The British Library. Shelfmark: Royal MS. 18. DIII, f.22. www.collectbritain.co.uk/personalisation/object.cfm?uid=001R0Y000018D03U00022000

Lane Fox, A. 1869, On some flint implements found associated with Roman remains in Oxfordshire and the Isle of Thanet. *The Journal of the Ethnological Society of London*, March 1869, 1-12

Lanting, J.N. and Van der Waals J.D. 1972, British Beakers as seen from the Continent. *Helinium* 12, 20-46

Lawson, T. 2004, The Viking Incursions. In Lawson (ed.) *et al*, *An Historical Atlas of Kent*. Chichester Phillimore & Co., 32

Lawson, T. & Killingray, D. (eds) 2004, *An Historical Atlas of Kent*. Chichester, Phillimore & Co.

Leach, P.E. (ed.) 1982, *Archaeology in Kent to AD 1500*. Council for British Archaeology Research Report 48

Lewis, J. 1736, *The History and Antiquities, as well Ecclesiatical as Civil, of the Isle of Tenet, in Kent* (2nd ed.). Reprinted in a third edition in 2005 by Michael's Bookshop, Ramsgate

Long, A.J. 1992, Coastal responses to changes in sea-level in the East Kent Fens and southeast England, UK over the last 7,500 years. *Proceedings of the Geologists Association* 103, 187-199

Lynch, F. 1997, *Megalithic Tombs and Long Barrows in Britain*. Buckinghamshire, Shire

Lyne, M. 2003, Some New Coin Types of Carausius and Allectus and the History of the British Provinces AD 286-296. *The Numismatic Chronicle*, 147-168

Lyne, M. 2006, *The Pottery from the abbey Farm, Minster Roman Villa*. Archive report commissioned by Kent Archaeological Society

Macready, S. and Thompson, F.H. (eds) 1984, *Cross Channel Trade between Gaul and Britain in the Pre-Roman Iron Age*. Bath, The Society of Antiquaries Occasional Paper (New Series) IV

Malone, C. 2001, *Neolithic Britain and Ireland*. Gloucestershire, Tempus

Macpherson-Grant, N. 1968, A Beaker from Cliffsend, Ramsgate. *Archaeologia Cantiana* 83, 269-271

Macpherson-Grant, N. 1969, Two Neolithic Bowls from Birchington, Thanet. *Archaeologia Cantiana* 84, 249-50

Macpherson-Grant, N. 1971a, Site 127 and 128 in Group Emergency Report. *Kent Archaeological Review* 24, 113

Macpherson-Grant, N. 1971b, An Iron Age Site at Northdown School, Margate. *Kent Archaeological Review* 25, Autumn 1971, 156

Macpherson-Grant, N. 1972, Operation Gas Pipe, Thanet section. *Kent Archaeological Review* 30, 298

Macpherson-Grant, N. 1977, *Excavation of a Neolithic/Bronze Age Site at Lord of the Manor, Haine Road, Ramsgate*. Broadstairs, Isle of Thanet Archaeological Unit, Publication No. 1

Macpherson-Grant, N. 1992, A Review of Late Bronze Age pottery in East Kent. *Canterbury's Archaeology 1991-1992*, 55-63

Macpherson-Grant, N. 1994, The Pottery. In D.R.J. Perkins *et al*, Monkton Court Farm Evaluation, *Archaeologia Cantiana* 114, 248-288

Martin, K.B. 1857, Oral Traditions of the Cinque Ports, Part III. *Hunts Yachting Magazine* 6, 79-87. Preserved by Google Books at http://books.google.com

Mattingly, D. 2006, *An Imperial Possession. Britain in the Roman Empire*. London, Penguin

Merrifield, R. 1970, The Ramsgate Coin Hoard. *Kent Archaeological Review* 21, 2

Millett, M. 2007, Roman Kent. In J.H. Williams (ed.), *The Archaeology of Kent to AD 800*. East Lothian, The Boydell Press, Ch. 4

Milner, N. 2007, Fading Star. *British Archaeology* September/October 2007, 11-14, Council for British Archaeology

Minter, K.S. and Herbert, E.F. 1973, *Archaeological Discoveries in Broadstairs and St. Peter's up to 1972*. Broadstairs, Broadstairs and St Peters Archaeological Society

Moody, G.A. 2004, *Land Adjacent to Preston Park Caravan Site, Spratling Street, Manston, Kent. Archaeological Evaluation Report*. Unpubl. Trust for Thanet Archaeology Client Report

Moody, G.A. 2005, *Land to the rear of 103 Stone Road, Broadstairs, Kent, Archaeological Report*. Unpubl. Trust for Thanet Archaeology Client Report

Moody, G.A. 2007a, Iron Age and Romano-British Settlement at Bishop's Avenue, Broadstairs. *Archaeologia Cantiana* 127, 197-212

Moody, G.A. 2007b, *Court Stairs Lodge, Pegwell Road, Ramsgate, Interim Excavation Report*. Unpubl. Trust for Thanet Archaeology Client Report

Moody, G.A. 2007c, *Proposed Residential Development, Land at Upton House, Vale Road, Broadstairs. Archaeological Report*. Unpubl. Trust for Thanet Archaeology Client Report

Moody, G.A. and Boast, E.J. 2003, *Former Bon Secours Nursing Home, 34 London Road, Ramsgate, Kent*. Unpubl. Trust for Thanet Archaeology Client Report

Murton, J.B. *et al* 2003, The Devensian Periglacial Record on Thanet, Kent, UK. *Permafrost and Periglacial Processes* 14, 217-246

Ocock, M.A. 1969a, Regional Archaeological Surveys Part 1 - A guide to procedure. *Kent Archaeological Review* 17, 10

Ocock, M.A. 1969b, Regional Arcaeological Surveys Part 2 - Further Investigation and Detailed Survey. *Kent Archaeological Review* 18, 22

Ogilvie, J.D. 1983, A Mesolithic Adze from Sandwich. *Kent Archaeological Review* 71, 14

Ocock, M. 1971, Regional Surveys in Action. *Kent Archaeological Review* 22, 49

O'Neil, B.H. St. J. 1948, War and Archaeology in Britain. *Antiquaries Journal* 28, 20-44

Osborne White, H.J. 1928, *The Geology of the Country near Ramsgate and Dover*, London, HMSO, 66

Oswald, A., Dyer, C. and Barber, M. 2001, *The Creation of Monuments*. Swindon, English Heritage

Parfitt, K. 2000, A Roman site at Dickson's Corner, Worth. *Archaeologia Cantiana* 120, 107-148

Parfitt, K. 2001, An early excavation plan of Stonar Church, Near Sandwich. *Kent Archaeological Review* 145, 95

Parfitt, K. 2004, Early settlement at Sandwich, Part 2: The Prehistoric Background. *Canterbury Archaeological Trust Sandwich Survey Report* no. 2

Parfitt, K. 2005, *Report on Evaluation Trenching (Phase 1) at the Royal Sea Bathing Hospital, Margate*. Unpubl. Canterbury Archaeological Trust Client Report

Parfitt, K. 2006, The Roman Villa at Minster-in-Thanet. Part 3: The Corridor House, Building 4. *Archaeologia Cantiana* 126, 115-133

Parfitt, K. 2007, The Roman Villa at Minster in Thanet. Part 4: The South-West buildings, 6A and 6B. *Archaeologia Cantiana* 127, 261-296

Parfitt, K. and Brugman, B. 1997, *The Anglo-Saxon Cemetery on Mill Hill, Deal, Kent*. Society for Medieval for Medieval Archaeology Monograph Series 14, London

Parfitt, K. and Needham, S. 2007, Excavations at Ringlemere Farm, Woodensborough, 2002-2006. *Archaeologia Cantiana* 127, 39-55

Parker Pearson, M. 1993, *Bronze Age Britain*. London, Batsford

Parsons, F.G. 1913, On some Bronze Age and Jutish bones from Broadstairs. With type contours of all the Bronze Age skulls in the Royal College of Surgeons Museum. *The Journal of the Royal Anthropological Institute of Great Britain and Ireland* 43, 550-592

Payne, G. 1895, Researches and discoveries in Kent. *Archaeologia Cantiana* 21, xlvii-lvi

Pearce, B.W. 1939, Stonar, Miscellaneous Notes. *Archaeologia Cantiana* 50, 166

Penn, W.S. 1965, Letters from the Chairman. *Kent Archaeological Review* 1, 2

Percival, A. 1969, Local Archaeology in the 1970's. *Kent Archaeological Review* 15, 13-17

Perkins, D.R.J. 1980a, Site 3 - Lord of the Manor (Ozengell) Ramsgate. In, Isle of Thanet Archaeological Unit, *1980 Interim excavation reports 1977-80*, 13-17

Perkins, D.R.J. 1980b, Site 4 - Lord of the Manor (Ozengell) Ramsgate. In, Isle of Thanet Archaeological Unit, *Interim Excavation Reports 1977-1980*, 18-20

Perkins, D.R.J. 1980c, A ditched enclosure at Shuart Farm, St. Nicholas at Wade. In, Isle of Thanet Archaeological Unit, *Interim Excavation Reports 1977-1980*, 25-29

Perkins, D.R.J. 1981, A Roman Bronze Head from Margate. *Archaeologia Cantiana* 97, 307-311

Perkins, D.R.J. 1982, The Isle of Thanet Archaeological Unit, Recent Activities. *Archaeologia Cantiana* 98, 242

Perkins, D.R.J. 1983, The Isle of Thanet Archaeological Unit: Nethercourt Estate, Ramsgate. *Archaeologia Cantiana* 99, 272

Perkins, D.R.J. 1985, The Monkton Gas Pipeline: phases III and IV, 1983-84. *Archaeologia Cantiana* 102, 43-69

Perkins, D.R.J. 1987, The Jutish Cemetery at Half Mile Ride, Margate: A reappraisal. *Archaeologia Cantiana* 104, 219-236

Perkins, D.R.J. 1988a, A Middle Bronze Age Hoard from a Prehistoric settlement at St. Mildred's Bay, Westgate-on-Sea. *Archaeologia Cantiana* 105, 243-249

Perkins, D.R.J. 1988b, The site of the Church of St. Giles, Sarre. *Archaeologia Cantiana* 105, 291-297

Perkins, D.R.J. 1988c, A Late Bronze Age Hoard from Shuart, Thane. *Archaeologia Cantiana* 106, 201-204

Perkins, D.R.J. 1989a, The Selling to Thanet trunk water-main, Phase II, 1987: An Interim report. *Archaeologia Cantiana* 107, 267-279

Perkins, D.R.J. 1989b, *Rescue excavations at Ozengell/Lord of the Manor, Ramsgate*. Unpubl. Trust for Thanet Archaeology Report

Perkins, D.R.J. 1991a, The Jutish cemetery at Sarre revisited: A rescue evaluation. *Archaeologia Cantiana* 109, 139-166

Perkins, D.R.J. 1991b, A Late Bronze Age Hoard found at Monkton Court Farm, Thanet. *Archaeologia Cantiana* 109, 247-264

Perkins, D.R.J. 1992a, The Jutish cemetery at Sarre revisted: Part II. *Archaeologia Cantiana* 110, 83-120

Perkins, D.R.J. 1992b. Archaeological Evaluations at Ebbsfleet in the Isle of Thanet. *Archaeologia Cantiana* 110, 269-311

Perkins, D.R.J. 1993, North Foreland Avenue, Broadstairs. *Archaeologia Cantiana* 112, 411-413

Perkins, D.R.J. 1995a, Report on work by the Thames [Thanet] Trust for Archaeology. *Archaeologia Cantiana* 115, 468-474

Perkins, D.R.J. 1995b. *Assessment/Research Design; South Dumpton Down, Broadstairs, 1994.* Unpubl. Trust for Thanet Archaeology Client Report

Perkins, D.R.J. 1996, The Trust for Thanet Archaeology; Evaluation work carried out in 1995, Hartsdown Community Woodland Scheme, Margate. *Archaeologia Cantiana* 116, 265-281

Perkins, D.R.J. 1997a, Researches and discoveries: A report on work by the Trust for Thanet Archaeology. *Archaeologia Cantiana* 117, 227-237

Perkins, D.R.J. 1997b, A polished flint axe from Netherhale, Thanet. *Archaeologia Cantiana* 117, 230-232

Perkins, D.R.J. 1998a, *ASDA Superstore Westwood: The Archaeological Implications.* Unpubl. Trust for Thanet Archaeology Client Report

Perkins D.R.J. 1998b, A report on work by the Trust for Thanet Archaeology 1997-1998. *Archaeologia Cantiana* 118, 365-371

Perkins, D.R.J. 1998c, *Oaklands Nursery Site, Cliffsend, Ramsgate: Archaeological Evaluation.* Unpubl. Trust for Thanet Archaeology Client Report

Perkins, D.R.J. 1998d, *Archaeological Excavations at Fort Hill, Margate; an Assessment Report.* Unpubl. Trust for Thanet Archaeology Client Report

Perkins, D.R.J. 1999a, Acheulian and Later Prehistoric finds: Broadstairs. *Archaeologia Cantiana* 119, 369-373

Perkins, D.R.J. 1999b, *A Gateway Island.* Unpubl. Ph.D thesis, University College London

Perkins, D.R.J. 2000a, Jutish glass production in Kent: and the problem of the Base cups. *Archaeologia Cantiana* 120, 297-310

Perkins, D.R.J. 2000b, Acheulian Hand-Axe: Westwood, Broadstairs. *Archaeologia Cantiana* 120, 373

Perkins, D.R.J. 2000c, Roman Road Metalling and Prehistoric Sherds: Hartsdown, Margate. *Archaeologia Cantiana* 120, 378-79

Perkins, D.R.J. 2001a, The Roman Archaeology of the Isle of Thanet. *Archaeologia Cantiana* 121, 43-60

Perkins, D.R.J. 2001b, Sarre, Isle of Thanet, Kent. In D. Hills *et al.* (eds), *Wics: The Early Medieval Trading Centres of Northern Europe.* Sheffield Academic Press, 102

Perkins, D.R.J. 2004, Oval barrows in Thanet. In J. Cotton *et al, Towards a New Stone Age. Aspects of the Neolithic in south-east England.* CBA Research Report 137, 76-81

Perkins, D.R.J. 2006, Prehistoric Maritime traffic in the Dover Strait and Wantsum: Some thoughts as to the Vessels and their crews. *Archaeologia Cantiana* 126, 279-293

Perkins, D.R.J. 2007, The long demise of the Wantsum Sea Channel: a recapitulation based on the data. *Archaeologia Cantiana* 127, 249-259

Perkins, D.R.J. and Hawkes, S.C., 1984, The Thanet Gas Pipeline Phases I and III (Monkton Parish), 1982. *Archaeologia Cantiana* 101, 83-114

Perkins, D.R.J. and Gibson, A.M. 1990, A Beaker burial from Manston near Ramsgate. *Archaeologia Cantiana* 108, 11-27

Perkins, D.R.J., Macpherson-Grant, N. and Healey, E. 1994, Monkton Court Farm Evaluation, 1992. *Archaeologia Cantiana* 114, 237-316

Perkins, D.R.J., Boast, E.J., Wilson, T. and Macpherson-Grant, N. 1997, *Kent International Business Park, Manston, Excavations and Evaluations 1994-1997.* Unpubl. Trust for Thanet Archaeology Archive Report

Perkins, D.R.J., Austin, R. and Cross. R.P. 1998, *St. Stephens College, North Foreland, Broadstairs, Architectural and Archaeological Study.* Unpubl. Trust for Thanet Archaeology Client Report

Perkins, D.R.J. and Parfitt, K. 2004, The Roman Villa at Minster-in-Thanet. Part 1: Introduction and Report on the Bath-House. *Archaeologia Cantiana* 124, 25-49

Philp, B. 1971, All hands to the Rescue. *Kent Archaeological Review* 24, 111

Philp, B. 2002, Richborough and the Claudian Invasion Base, New ideas on the Erosion and Layout. *Kent Archaeological Review* 148, 165-169

Philp, B. 2005, *The Excavation of the Roman Fort at Reculver, Kent*. Dover, Kent Archaeological Rescue Unit

Philp, B. and Philp, E. 1975, *Rescue excavations in Kent 1972-74*. Dover, Kent Archaeological Rescue Unit

Philp, B. and Chenery M. 2002, *Prehistoric sites at Dumpton, Ramsgate, Kent*. Kent Archaeological Rescue Unit; Kent Minor Sites Series no. 17

Pollard, R.J. 1988, *The Roman Pottery of Kent*. Monograph series of the Kent Archaeological Society 5

Powell-Cotton, P.H.G. and Crawford, O.G.S. 1924, The Birchington Hoard. *The Antiquaries Journal* 4, 220-226

Powell-Cotton, P.H.G. and Pinfold G.F. 1939, The Beck Find Prehistoric and Roman Site on the Foreshore at Minnis Bay. *Archaeologia Cantiana* 51, 191-194

Quested, R.K.I. 2001, *The Isle of Thanet Farming Community* (2nd ed.). London, Intype

Rahtz, P. 1989, *Little Ouseburn Barrow 1958*. York University Archaeological Publications 7

RCHME 1989, *The classification of cropmarks in Kent, A report for the Monuments Protection Programme, Air Photography Unit*. Royal Commission on the Historical Monuments of England

Richardson, A. 2005, *The Anglo Saxon Cemeteries of Kent*. Oxford, British Archaeological Reports British Series 391, Volumes 1 and 2

Riddler, I. 2004, Anglo-Saxon Kent: Early Development c.450 - c.800. In T. Lawson et al (eds), *An Historical Atlas of Kent*. Chichester, Phillimore & Co., 25-28

Rivet, A.L.F. and Smith, C. 1979, *The Placenames of Roman Britain*. London, Batsford

Robinson, A.H.W. and Cloet R.L. 1953, Coastal Evolution in Sandwich Bay. *Proceedings of the Geologists Association* 64, Part 2

Rowe, A. 1924, Our Roman House. *Isle of Thanet Gazette* 24th June 1924

Rowe, A. 1925, Notes: Early British Pottery. *The Antiquaries Journal* 5, 164-165

Salway, P. 1991, *Roman Britain. The Oxford History of Britain*. Oxford, Oxford University Press

Scott, B. 2004, Kentish evidence of the Palaeolithic and Mesolithic periods. In T. Lawson et al (ed), *An Historical Atlas of Kent*. Chichester, Phillimore & Co.

Scott Robertson, W.A. 1878, Archaeological Notes on Thanet by the Editor. *Archaeologia Cantiana* 12, 331-419

Shand, G. 2002, *Excavations at Chalk Hill, near Ramsgate, Kent 1997-8, Integrated assessment and updated research design*. Unpubl. Canterbury Archaeological Trust Client Report

Sjoberg, G. 1960, *The Preindustrial City*. USA, The Free Press

Smith, C.R. 1850, *The Antiquities of Richborough, Reculver and Lymne in Kent*. London, John Russell Smith

Smith, C.R. 1854, *Collectanea Antiqua 3*. C.R. Smith

Smith, C.R. 1860, On Anglo-Saxon remain discovered recently in various places in Kent. *Archaeologia Cantiana* 3, 36-39

Smith, G.H. 1987, A Beaker (?) Burial Monument and a Late Bronze Age assemblage from East Northdown, Margate. *Archaeologia Cantiana* 104, 237-85

Smythe, J. 2006, An Early Bronze Age wristguard from Kent. *Kent Archaeological Society Newsletter* 69, 16

So, C.L. 1964, Coastal Platforms of the Isle of Thanet, Kent. *Transactions of the Institute of British Geographers* 37, 147-156

So, C.L. 1971, Early Coast Recession around Reculver, Kent. *Archaeologia Cantiana* 86, 93-97

Stoertz, C. 1997, *Ancient Landscapes of the Yorkshire Wolds*. Swindon, Royal Commission on the Historical Monuments of England

Southworth, E. (ed.) 1990, *Anglo-Saxon Cemeteries A Reappraisal*. Gloucestershire, Sutton

Suttie, J.M. and Reynolds, S.G. (eds) 2003, *Transhumant grazing systems in Temperate Asia. Plant and Production Series. 31 (Rev 1)*. Food and Agriculture Organization of the United Nations, Rome

Thanet Archaeological Unit 1981, *Interim excavation reports 1977-1980*. Broadstairs, Thanet Archaeological Unit

Thanet Archaeological Unit 1986, *Eroding History. The Archaeology of the Thanet Cliffs*. Survey and report by Manpower Services Commissions's Community Programme sponsored by Thanet District Council and Thanet Archaeological Unit

Thorpe, B. (ed.) 1861, *The Anglo-Saxon Chronicle*, vol. I and II. London, Longman, Green, Longman and Roberts

The University of Sheffield 2007, www.shef.ac.uk/archaeology/research/beaker-isotope, last accessed January 1st 2008

Trust for Thanet Archaeology 2006, *The Abbey Farm Painted Plaster Project*. www.thanetarch.co.uk/Virtual%20Museum/3_Displays/G13%20Special%20Display%202/web%20page/introduction_page.html, last accessed January 1st 2008

Tucker, C. 2007a, *Transcriptions of an account of excavations carried out by G. Dowker read to Kent Archaeological Soicety in 1877 from notes in the library of Kent Archaeological Society, Maidstone*. Unpubl. archive notes

Tucker, C. 2007b, *Three Pendants from Abbey Farm, Minster in Thanet*. Unpublished report

Villette, J. and Williams, J. 1983, A Bronze Axe from Margate. *Kent Archaeological Review* 73, 50

Wallace-Hadrill, J.M. 1962, *The Long-haired Kings and Other Studies of Frankish History*. London, Methuen & Co. Ltd

Weir, A.H., Catt, J.A. and Madgett, P.A. 1971, Postglacial soil formation in the loess at Pegwell Bay, Kent. *Geoderma* 5, 131-149

Welch, M. 2007, Anglo-Saxon Kent to AD 800. In J.H. Williams (ed.), *The Archaeology of Kent to AD 800*. The Boydell Press, Ch. 5

Wenban-Smith, F. 2007, The Palaeolithic archaeology of Kent. In J.H. Williams (ed.), *The Archaeology of Kent to AD 800*. The Boydell Press, Ch. 2

Wessex Archaeology 2005, *Cliffsend Farm, Ramsgate, Kent. Archaeological Assessment Report*. Unpubl. Wessex Archaeology Client Report ref. 56950, 04

Wessex Archaeology 2006, *Margate and Broadstairs Urban Wastewater Treatment Scheme, Kent. Archaeological Assessment Report and UPD for Analysis and Publication*. Unpubl. Wessex Archaeology Client Report ref. 59481, 02

Wheeler, R.E.M. 1943, *Maiden Castle, Dorset*. Research Report of the Society of Antiquaries of London 12, London

Whiting, W. 1923, Further Roman finds in Kent. *Antiquaries Journal* 4, 22-25

Whittle, A. 2007, quoted in: The new radio-carbon dating revolution. *Current Archaeology* 209, 9-20

Williams, J. and King, M. 1974, Book Reviews. *Kent Archaeological Review* 35, 140-141

Williams, J.H. (ed.) 2007, *The Archaeology of Kent to AD 800*. Suffolk, The Boydell Press

Willson, J. 1983, A Romano-British Site at Broadstairs, Kent. *Kent Archaeological Review* 72, 34-41

Worsfold, F.H. 1943, A Report on the Late Bronze Age Site excavated at Minnis Bay, Birchington, Kent 1938-40. *Proceedings of the Prehistoric Society* 9, 28-47

Wright, T. 1854, *Wanderings of an Antiquary*. London, Nichols and Son, preserved by Google Books at http://books.google.com

Wright, T. 1861, *The Celt, The Roman, The Saxon* (2nd ed.). London, preserved by Google books at http://books.google.com/

Wymer, J.J. 1977, *A Gazetteer of Mesolithic and Upper Palaeolithic Sites in England and Wales*. York, CBA Research Report 20

INDEX

A253, Thanet Way excavations 25
Abbey Farm Villa, Minster 24,
    135, 143-50, 147, 149-50, 154,
    155
    painted plaster from 150
Abbot's Wall 36
Acol 60, 172
Aefa 169
aerial photography
    Claudian sites 141
    Late Iron Age sites 134-5
    Roman buildings 148
    round barrows 93-4
Aethelbert 167, 169
agriculture
    Anglo-Saxon 159, 172
    Bronze Age 93, 98-9, 108
    Iron Age 118, 120, 121, 123,
        128, 137
    Neolithic 61, 62, 63
    Roman 152, 155, 158-9
Alfred 172
All Saints Shuart, Church of 24
Angles 158, 160, 167
Anglo-Saxon
    animism 169
    dress 164-6
    grave structures 161-2, 166
    paganism 169
    place names 171-2
    settlement sites 170-1
    weapon burial at Richborough
        160
Anglo-Saxon cemeteries
    association with round barrows
        166-7
    association with trackways 167
    Cliffsend 163

dating of grave assemblages
    162-3
development of 160-2
Grave assemblages 164-6
Half Mile Ride 163
Monkton 163
Monkton, Mount Pleasant
    163
Ozengell 162
Sarre 162
St Peters 163
sunken featured buildings 170
Thorne Farm 163
Anglo-Saxon Chronicle 158
Archaeological Groups, formation
    of in 1960s 22
Archaeological Implications
    Report, Thanet 24
Archaeology, publication of
    fieldwork 175
Archer's Low, Sandwich 139
arrowheads
    barbed and tanged 84, 98
    leaf-shaped 68
Ash, nr Canterbury 30
Augustine 40, 42
axes
    flanged axes 98
    handaxes 54
    palstave hoards 99-101
    polished flint and stone 70

Baldwin, C.E. 20
Bartrum, Miss 19
Battely, J. 37
Beakers 79
    as grave goods 81-2
    bone isotope analysis 91

coffin structures, associated
    with 84
dating of Thanet Beakers 82,
    83
decoration 79
enclosure at Minster 82
flat graves 85, 87
forms of burial 88-90
grave goods associated with 84
hengiform enclosures,
    association with 79
human remains associated with
    88-90
Margate 82
North Foreland 81
round barrows, association with
    85-8
social function 82
Beck, J. 21
    Beck find bronze hoard 22
Bede 35-36, 160
Behrwald, Abbott 170
Belgic 132
Bertha 169
Bexley 54
Birchington 16, 18, 19, 21, 93, 101,
    116, 122, 132, 134, 150, 171
Boast, E.J. 24
Boulogne, France 139
Boxlees Hill 22, 26, 42, 43, 149
Bradstow School, Broadstairs 19,
    74, 88, 95, 162, 163, 166
    discoveries at 19
Brent, J. 15-16
Brickearth 61
    archaeological discoveries made
        while quarrying 19
Britannia 142, 145, 156

Index

British Archaeological Association 13
Broadstairs 9, 10, 16, 19, 108, 147
Broadstairs and St Peters Archaeological Society 19, 23
Bromstone 171
Bronze Age 99, 110
   axes 98-102, 106
   bronze hoards 10, 12-13, 99-104
   bronze personal ornaments 108
   bronze tools 102, 104
   burials 87, 96-97 98
   coastal trade 107
   Dover boat 104
   field systems 98-9
   flat axes 98
   Hackemdown Banks 11
   landscape 92-3
   Middle Bronze Age cremation cemeteries 108
   organic deposits 21, 101
   pottery 49, 98, 101, 108
   weapons and conflict 114-15
Brooksend 60, 116
Burchell, J.P.T. 22

Calais, France 29
Calkin, J.B. 22
Canterbury 30, 54
Canterbury Archaeological Trust 25
causewayed enclosures 64-8, 69
   Chalk Hill, Ramsgate 61, 64, 69-70
   Court Stairs, Ramsgate 61, 64-68, 69, 70
Chalk Hill 59, 72, 84, 85, 99
Champion, T. 23
chapels of ease 163
Chatham House School, Ramsgate 23
Chessboard estate 18, 22
Chislet 30
Christ Church Priory, Canterbury 36, 174
Christianity 169
Claudian invasion 139-41
Cliffsend 22, 26, 41, 42, 45, 48, 57, 85, 92, 113, 115, 163, 166, 170
Clifton, J. 24
Cliftonville, Margate 70
Cnut 36, 173, 174
coastal erosion 31-3
coins 126
   British 9
   Iron Age 126
   Late Iron Age named issues 134
   Potin hoard at Birchington 127
   Potin 126
   Roman 148
   Roman hoard at Ramsgate 153
Coles Wood 172
Conyngham, Marquess of 15
Cottington Hill 127, 147, 170
Council for Kentish Archaeology (CKA) 23
Court Stairs 61
Coxon's Hill 26
Coy, J. 22
cremations
   Anglo-Saxon 160
   Bronze Age 108
   Iron Age 136
cursus 71, 72

Dandelion, Birchington 16
Danebury 118
Darnley, Earl of 16
Deal 29, 41, 45, 48, 53, 92, 108, 139, 140
deforestation
   Neolithic 69
Denmark 160, 172
Dickson's Corner 49
Docker Hill 26
Doggerland 28
Domesday Book 174
Domneva, Saint, *see* Aefa
Dover 23, 29, 53, 139
   harbour 42, 43
Dover Bronze Age boat 104-5, 107, 108
Dover Strait 39
Dowker, G. 16-17
   excavations at North Foreland 17
Downbarton, St Nicholas at Wade 170
Drapers Mills, Margate 22, 150
Dumpton 23, 24, 75, 91, 93, 108, 116, 120, 133, 147, 150, 155, 171
Dumpton Gap 19, 64, 108, 120, 134, 135-136, 147, 150
Dun Street 171
Durlock 59, 116, 140
Durlock Stream 59

East Cliff, Ramsgate 33
East Northdown 79, 108, 117
Eastry 69, 169
Ebbsfleet Farm bronze hoard 18
Ebbsfleet (Thanet) 36, 39, 40, 43, 44, 48, 57, 58, 70, 82, 92, 113, 116, 117, 131, 140, 155
Anglo-Saxon Chronicle 39
landing place of Hengest 160
landing place of St Augustine 40
peninsular 26, 36, 37, 40, 42, 44, 45, 92, 113, 116, 127
Edburga 16
Egbert 169
Ellington, Ramsgate 98, 153, 171
Elmwood Avenue, Broadstairs 120
English Channel 28, 29, 31, 44, 45, 52, 55, 57, 141, 167
Eorcenberht 169
Eormenred 169
Evans, J. 14

Fairholme, G. 32-33
Fausett, Rev. B.G. 15
Fisher, T. 12
fisheries 9, 93, 107, 116, 170, 174
flintwork
   Bronze Age 97-8
   Lower Palaeolithic 54
   Mesolithic 59-60
   Neolithic 59-60, 70
Fordwich, nr Canterbury 142
forest 28, 55, 57-8, 59, 63, 69, 93, 118, *see also* woodland
Fort Hill, Margate 123, 124, 129, 131
Frankish Kingdom 164, 166
   trade with 167

Gateway Island, The 24
Gaul 132, 139, 156, 154, 167
Genlade 36
geology
   central ridge 26
   clay-with-flints 53, 54
   Coombe rock, *see* solifluction deposits
   cover sands and loess 27
   dendritic valley systems 29
   drainage 30
   Eocene sands 26
   patterned ground 27
   solifluction deposits 27, 53
   tectonic folding 26
   Thanet Beds 26
   Upper Chalk 26
   water erosion in chalk 26
Goodwin Sands 142
Gore End, Birchington 98
Grace, R. 21

Great Stonar 43, 92, 139
Great Stour (Stour) 30, 42, 43, 45, 49, 52, 142
grey literature 175
Grimes, W.F. 22

Hackemdown Banks 12, 96
Haine 172
Half Mile Ride, Margate 163
Ham Fen, nr Finglesham 59
handaxes
    lower Palaeolithic 54
Hartsdown 121, 124, 136, 150
Hasted, E. 12, 13
    History of the County of Kent 12
Hawkes, C.F.C. 20, 22
Hawkes, Mrs K. 21
Hawkes, S.C. 23
Hawley Square, Margate 16
henge
    Ringlemere farm, Woodnesborough 76
Hengest (and Horsa) 158, 160
hengiform enclosures 72-6
    Bradstow School, Broadstairs 74
    cropmarks of 74
    Lord-of-the-Manor, Ramsgate 73
    Mill Lane, Margate 74
    North Foreland 76
    social function of 75-6
    structure, internal 73
Henneburg 36
Heopwines floet 39
herding
    Bronze Age 93
    Iron Age 116, 118, 120, 121
    Mesolithic 63
    Neolithic 61, 63-4
    Roman 145
Hereson 171
Hicks, R. 18
Hills, W. 18
Hogarth, A.C. 23
Holland, Lord, H. 12
Hollicondane 108
Holocene 28
    ecology 54
    reconstruction of early landscape 29
Hurd, H. 19-20, 21, 22
    Valletta House, Broadstairs, excavations at 19

Iron Age
    aerial photography 134
    bridle bits 129
    burials 124, 136
    clearance for agriculture 118
    cremations 136
    decorated pottery 131
    hollow ways 120
    landscape 116
    Late Iron Age enclosures 134, 135
    post built structures 127-31
    pottery with continental associations 131
    quarries 136
    settlement 118-22
    social conditions in 118
    storage pits 123
    textile production 135
    timber resources 118
    trade with Gaul 132
iron working
    bloomery 152
    waste pits 152

Joss Bay 93, 116, 120, 138, 148, 155
Joss Farm, North Foreland 16
Jutes 160
Jutland 164

Kent Archaeological Rescue Group 23
Kent Archaeological Rescue Unit (KARU) 23
Kent Archaeological Research Group 22
Kent Archaeological Society 14-17, 18, 24
    Abbey Farm villa, excavation 24
    Charles Museum 14
    Sarre Anglo-Saxon cemetery, excavation 14
King Edward Avenue, Broadstairs 101
Kingdom of Kent 167
Kingsgate 68, 93, 116

La Tène style pottery 131
Lane Fox A.H., *see* Pitt Rivers
Langdale, Cumbria 70
Larking, L.B. 14
Laundry Hill, Minster 82
Lewis, Rev. J. 9-12, 13, 34
    Isle of Thanet, History and Antiquities of 9-12
Little Brooksend Farm 68
Little Stour 52
Little Woodbury, Wiltshire 124

London, City of 36
Lord of the Manor 24, 73, 75, 95, 97, 99, 147, 152
Lydden Valley, Deal 92
Lyminge, Kent 30, 169

Maiden Castle, Dorset 118
malt kiln 155-56
Manpower Services Commission, Community Programme 24
Manston 79, 82, 84, 85, 97, 99, 101, 120, 134, 152, 170, 171
Manston Airfield 22, 60, 99, 152
Margate 9, 12, 13, 16, 19, 20, 23, 59, 60, 68, 69, 70, 75, 93, 98, 99, 101, 116, 117, 121, 122, 131, 136, 138, 141, 147, 150, 171
Margate and Broadstairs Urban Waste Water Treatment Scheme excavations 25
Margate Bay 60, 116, 120, 124
Margate Charity School 13
Margate Museum 21, 147
Martin, K.B. 13, 33
Medway Valley 64
Merewahl 169
Mesolithic
    environment 57-8
    flintwork 59-60
    landscape 55-57
    settlement 61
    woodland 57
Mill Lane, Margate 74
Millmead Estate, Margate 24
Minnis Bay 21, 22, 60, 101, 111, 122, 141
Minster 9, 16, 24, 26, 36, 43, 60, 69, 116, 136, 140, 142, 143, 145, 149, 169-70, 174
Minster Abbey 169, 174
Minster Court (Minster Abbey) 16
Minster Mills 152
Monastery
    Lyminge, Kent 169
    Minster (Thanet) 36, 163, 169-70, 173, 174
    Sheppey, Kent 169
Monkton 36, 45, 72, 73, 82, 84, 116, 120, 140, 150, 151, 171, 174
Monkton Court Farm 109, 117
Monkton experimental Barrow reconstruction 97
Motherwicks 10, 12
    bronze hoard at 10, 12-13
Mount Pleasant, Minster 163
Mucking, Essex 170

Index

Nailbourne 30
Nash Court, Margate 16
Neolithic
   burials 69
   causewayed enclosures 64-9
   cursus monuments 71
   decorated pottery 70-1
   deforestation 69
   distribution of settlement 64, 69
   Hengiform enclosures 72-8
   landscape 63
   long barrows 64
   polished axes 70
   pottery 70, 73
Nethercourt, Ramsgate 22, 69
Newington 171
Norman invasion 174
North Downs 26, 29, 30, 141
North Foreland 16, 18, 54, 70, 76, 85, 93, 96, 116, 117, 118, 123, 127, 131, 132, 133, 134, 141, 142, 147, 150
North Foreland Avenue 84, 87, 88
North Foreland Lighthouse 16
North Germany 158
North Minster 169
North Stream 30
Northdown Estate 12
Northdown, Margate 12, 98
Northmouth 37
Northwood 172

Ozengell 13, 15, 18, 24

painted plaster, Roman 150
Palaeolithic
   hand axes 54
   landscape 53
Pas de Calais, France 131
Payne, G. 18
Pegwell Bay 27, 42, 45, 49, 59, 73, 75, 92, 99
Pegwell, Ramsgate 26, 45, 57, 59, 64, 69, 76, 93
Perkins, D.R.J. 24
Pevensey, Sussex 174
Pitt Rivers, A.H.L.F., General 16
pottery
   beakers 79
   Belgic 132
   Deverel-Rimbury 101
   Early Neolithic 69
   food vessel 87, 98
   Grooved Ware 73
   haematite-coated 131
   kiln at Tivoli, Margate 135
   La Tène style decoration 131
   Late Iron Age production 135
   Marnian type 124
   Middle Bronze Age ring-stamped 101
   Neolithic 70
   painted Iron Age 131
   perforated cup 98
   Peterborough Ware 69, 71
   Trevisker Urn 107
Poulders Farm, Sandwich 59
Powell-Cotton Museum 22
Powell-Cotton, A. 21, 22
Powell-Cotton, P.H.G. 19
Ptolemy (Claudius Ptolemaeus) 35

Quex Museum, *see* Powell-Cotton Museum
Quex Park, Birchington 14, 19, 60, 127

Railway construction 13
Ramsgate 9, 13, 16, 18, 19, 20, 21, 23, 29, 40, 45, 48, 53, 54, 68, 69, 70, 93, 97, 101, 108, 116, 120, 136, 138, 141, 152, 153, 171
   growth of town 13
   harbour 13, 18
   Ozengell cemetery 14
   Roman coin hoard 23
   Romesgate (Rome's Gat) 12, 13, 171
Reading Street 134, 171
Reculver 16, 30, 36, 39, 44, 141, 145, 153, 154
   Regulbi/Regulbio 35
Reculver Excavation Group 23
Regional Archaeological Surveys 23
RESCUE 23
Rescue excavation in Kent 23
Regulbi/Regulbio 35
Rhine 28
Richborough 30, 35, 37, 39, 40, 41, 42, 44, 45, 48, 116, 145, 156, 158
   Claudian invasion 139-41
   Late Roman period 159
   Roman fort 13
   Rutupiae 35
   Saxon-Shore fort 153-54, 159
Ringlemere Farm, Woodensborough 59, 76
Roach Smith, Charles, *see* Smith, C.R.
Robins, Rev. S. 14
Rolfe, W. 13, 14

Roman artefacts
   Abbey Farm Villa 149
   copper-alloy athlete's head 150
   leaf-shaped pendants 149
   personal objects 149
Roman buildings 142
   Boxlees Hill 149
   cellared industrial buildings at Monkton 151
   Cottington Hill 147
   Dumpton Gap 147
   Malting kiln 155
   North Foreland 147
   Sunken Gardens, Westbrook 148
Roman
   burials 149, 152-3
   chalk quarries 152
   Claudian invasion 139, 141
   departure of troops 158
   governance of Britain 142
   grain processing 145
   herding 145
   Iron working sites 152
   land market 142
   landscape 139-41
   later settlement 159-60
   location of Claudian invasion 139-42
   ports 142
   roads and tracks 150-2
   transport routes 142
   urban economy 157, 159
   wharf at Ramsgate 152
round barrows 93-7
   association with hengiform enclosures 94
   classification by cropmark dimensions 95
   cropmarks of 94
   excavated on Thanet 95
   experimental reconstruction 97
   location of 93-4
   multiple inhumations South Dumpton Down 87
   social function of 97
   truncation by ploughing 97
Rowe, Dr A. 20
Rutupiae 35

Salmestone Grange, Margate 16
Salmestone, Margate 16, 171
Sandown, Deal 49
Sandwich 13, 36, 40, 41, 42, 48, 49, 59, 92, 116, 139, 140
Sandwich Bay 41, 48

Sandwich Bay Spit 49
  formation of 49
  Roman finds on 49
Sandwich Haven 37
Sarre 26, 36, 37, 45, 52, 58, 92, 93, 120, 134, 140, 141, 142, 148, 149, 159, 161, 162, 163, 164, 169, 171
  ferry crossing at 37, 116, 138
  tidal effects at 48
  windmill 14, 15
Sarre Penn 30
Scandinavia 158, 160, 163, 164, 172
  late Roman trade with 159-60
  pirates from 160
Scott Robertson, Rev. 17, 37
sea-level 29, 33, 35, 41-2, 44, 48, 55, 61, 63
  rise in Early Mesolithic 28
Sea View estate, *see* Chessboard estate
sea-craft 107, 177
Seven Stones Estate 23
Sheppey, Isle of 32, 169, 172
ship tolls 169
Smith, C.R. 13, 14
  Collectanea Antiqua 14
Somner, J. 37
South Dumpton Down, Broadstairs 25, 87-88, 95, 99, 108, 118, 120, 123, 124, 129, 131
Southwood, Ramsgate 19, 172
Sowell Street 171
SRTM (Shuttle Radar Terrain Mission) 49
St Augustine's Abbey, Canterbury 36, 37, 174
St Lawrence College, Ramsgate 20
St Augustine, *see* Augustine
St Giles, Sarre Church of 174
St John's, Margate Church of 16, 17
St Mary's, Minster in Thanet, Church of 170
St Mildred, monastery of 36
St Mildred's Bay 10, 54, 101, 122, 148, 170
St Nicholas at Wade 16, 17, 99, 101, 116, 170
St Peter's, Church of 14, 19, 162
St Peters, village of 16, 161
Starr Carr 59

Stebbing, W.P.D. 22
Stonar 40, 41, 42, 43, 45, 49, 116
  Roman finds at 43
Stonar Bank 40, 42, 43
  formation of 40, 42, 44-48, 49, 92
Stonar House 43
Stonar military port 43, 49
Stone Bay 18, 60, 116, 128, 131, 143, 148
Stone Gap 22, 23, 93, 145, 147, 150, 154
Stone House Archaeology Group 23
Stone House School 23
Stone Road, Broadstairs 147, 154
Stour, *see* Great Stour
Stourmouth 30, 37, 172
Street, Westgate 171
Stukeley W. 10
sunken-featured buildings 170
Sunken Gardens, Westbrook 148

Tenterden 37
Thames 26, 28-31, 36, 39, 44, 45, 49, 52, 55, 57, 59, 82, 142
Thanet Archaeological Society, Isle of 24
Thanet Archaeological Unit, Isle of 24
Thanet District Council 24
Thanet Excavation Group 22, 23
Thanet Sites and Monuments Register 24
Thanet, Isle of 9
Thomas of Elmham 37
Tivoli Brook 121, 135
Tivoli Villa, Margate 20, 147, 150
Tivoli, Margate 131
traveller's guides 12
Trinity Square, Margate 124, 124
Trust for Thanet Archaeology 24-5
Twyne, J. 37

Uantsumu 35
Upton, Broadstairs 120, 147, 150, 152, 171

Valletta House, Broadstairs, *see* Bradstow School
Vikings 172

villas
  Abbey Farm Villa, Minster in Thanet 143
  distribution of 156
  final occupation 154, 156
  St Mildreds Bay 148
  Stone Gap 145
  Tivoli Villa, Margate 147
Villette, J. 23
Vortigern 39, 158, 160

Wall End 37
Wantsum Channel 35, 48-52, 61, 69, 76, 92, 107, 109, 116, 123, 137-138, 142, 143, 145, 149, 154, 156, 159, 160, 169-170, 172, 174
  Bede's description of 35
  Claudian invasion fleet 139-141
  embankment of 36
  formation of 39-45, 92
  silting of 37
  tidal flows in 36, 48
  Uantsumu use of name by Bede 35
Wantsum Marshes 59-60
Weatherlees 36, 57, 59, 118
Weatherlees Hill 26, 37, 42, 43, 45
Wessex Archaeology 25
West Cliff, Ramsgate 18, 20, 69, 97, 108, 153
Westbrook 141
Westgate 10, 20, 32, 54, 173
Westwood, Broadstairs 54, 60, 99, 136, 172
White Ness 116
Wight, Isle of 32
William of Normandy 174
Woodchurch, Birchington 116, 134, 172
woodland
  Anglo-Saxon period 171
  Mesolithic 57
Woodnesborough, Ash 160
Woodruff, C. 18-19
Worsfold, F.H. 22
Wright, T. 14
Wypeddes floet 39

Yenlade, *see* Genlade
Yorkshire Wolds 16, 97, 122
Ypwines floet 39